Zen
and the Art of
Mixing

Mixerman

Hal Leonard Books
An Imprint of Hal Leonard Corporation

Published in 2010 by Hal Leonard Books
An Imprint of Hal Leonard Corporation
7777 West Bluemound Road
Milwaukee, WI 53213

Trade Book Division Editorial Offices
33 Plymouth Street, Suite 302, Montclair, NJ 07042

Cover design by Jeff Mutschler
Book design by UB Communications

Printed in the United States of America

Library of Congress Cataloging-in-Publication Data

Mixerman.
 Zen and the art of mixing / Mixerman.
    p. cm.
 Includes bibliographical references.
 ISBN 978-1-4234-9150-7
 1. Mixerman. 2. Sound engineers—United States. 3. Popular music—Production and direction. 4. Sound—Recording and reproducing.
 5. Sound studios. I. Title.

ML429.M57A5 2010
781.49—dc22

                            2010034833

www.halleonard.com

Acknowledgments

Special thanks to:

Jeff Mutschler

David Wozmak

John Dooher

Hal Leonard

John Cerullo and his entire team

Rusty Cutchin

Carolyn Keating

Jeffery Lesser

David Collins

Bridget Gardiner

Peter Bunetta

Bob Olhsson

Slipperman

Aardvark

The Womb Forums and all of my friends who run the place with me

A posthumous thank-you to Dave Hill of Dimension Sound Studios for everything he taught me

Contents

Chapter Five
Dealing with Clients

Chapter Six
Mastering

Introduction

*Mixing, done properly, and much like anything
else worth doing, is an art.*

So you want to mix. Let me guess—you've done more than one
mix in your life, probably several, maybe a hundred, and every
time you make a new mix you're sure you've done a great job, only
to realize later that your mix is terrible. That sounds vaguely familiar
to me.

The good news is you're not delusional. You're not listening to
your god-awful mixes thinking, "Man, I should be getting *paid*!"
That's a good first step.

Great mixers are few and far between. You can just look at the
successful mixer's pay scale to understand that the supply of great
mixers is considerably less than the demand. Granted, the major
labels have taken this view to the point of almost irrational super-
stition, but there's no doubt that a mix can make or break the
success of a production, so on some level you can understand their
position. The problem is that the labels have lost sight of what
makes a mix great and have ultimately settled for nothing more
than homogenized mediocrity, what with sending their productions

to veritable mixing and mastering factories. There is no art in a factory. Not even in an art factory.

The importance of music in our lives can't be overstated. We connect with each other through music. Whether we're singing "Auld Lang Syne," "Happy Birthday," a national anthem, a school fight song, or even "We Will Rock You," music brings us together, both young and old. We don't need an orchestra or a band to sing. We don't need an arrangement, and we most certainly don't need a mix. We just need ourselves, and in the spirit of sociability, our friends and acquaintances.

Our memory where music is concerned can be nearly flawless. We can have an entire orchestra in our heads playing the "1812 Overture" in a flash. We can lose ourselves in music without the presence of any outward sound, although admittedly even the most reserved of us will probably be blowing off air cannons. For some reason visual memory pales in comparison to auditory memory. Sure, we can recall a picture that we're familiar with, but the details are lost and are nowhere near as clear as our recall of a familiar song.

Even if you were to disagree with this assessment, at the very least we can agree that a visual memory is far less transferable than an auditory one. I can scribble down some resemblance of a picture, but it probably won't mean very much to anyone else. But a song? A song I can sing, and more importantly, I can get *you* to sing it with me.

I took a day job one summer between college semesters. For the most part I was a shipping clerk, but at the end of each day it was my job to vacuum the sales office. This was in the late '80s, just a few years after *The Breakfast Club* came out. There's a memorable scene in that movie where one of the troubled teens begins to aimlessly whistle the "Colonel Bogey March," a universally familiar song. Within moments the entire gang of teens joins in.

There was something about the camaraderie of that scene that I adored. I wanted to experience that for myself. So one day, as I made my way through the office with my vacuum, I started whistling the song, and you know what? The entire office joined in. And they didn't just whistle, they moved as they whistled. They swayed, bounced, and nodded enthusiastically. Every day I'd whistle, and every day, the entire office staff would join in. No one ever talked about it. No one ever acknowledged it other than to participate. Here I was, a 20-year-old student, and I could get an entire office of 30-something salespeople to whistle and move their bodies to a simple song each and every day.

Think about that. That's powerful. Sure, I had a good relationship with all the salespeople in the office, but I wasn't their leader by any stretch of the imagination. I was just the office support kid who would be gone once the summer ended, and they all knew that. Yet with something as simple as a song, I could lead them. At first I'm sure it was just entertaining, but after a few days of it, I'm certain my whistle began to represent the end of a long workday. They were all too willing to celebrate that fact with anyone who would sound the call. Simply put, music is a celebration.

All too often in this business of recording and mixing music we lose sight of the music itself. If you go on the Internet you can find thousands of debates comparing converters, compressors, mic pre's, DAWs, etc. These arguments always relate specifically to sound—in particular good sound versus bad—but sound is just a means to an end. I was whistling over the noise of a vacuum cleaner and not one person ever asked me to stop vacuuming just so they could enjoy the sound of the whistling. Of course, you've never heard my whistling. Just the same, I can assure you it's the music that's important, not the sound. Our job, whether we're the artist, producer, recordist, or mixer, is to deliver that music in a way that causes an emotional reaction. Whether that's glee, sadness, love, anger—you name it, this is what music brings to our lives.

Oddly enough, the arguments on the Internet are always about specs and electronic measurements of distortion, jitter, frequency response, blah, blah, blah. Of course, there are usually a few participants who will pipe in with the argument that one has to measure how the gear affects emotional impact—myself included—but this sort of argument always gets dismissed as voodoo or magic, as if it's irrelevant somehow. The problem is that there's really only one way to personally measure emotional impact, and that's with your ears and brain. Further confusing the issue is how a song's impact will differ from person to person. How a song affects any given individual is beyond our control. It's how a song affects overall human consciousness that offers *prima facie* evidence regarding its overall effectiveness. It's through purposeful intent and some tried-and-true composition techniques that one can accomplish the lofty goal of a highly effective song.

Certainly we all know plenty of great songs that didn't reach the overall human consciousness, so that can't possibly be the bar for determining the effectiveness of a song. It does, however, offer us some context for what goes into a great song. At some point, if you can separate yourself from your own personal likes and dislikes, you can begin to understand when you're working on a song that is on par with the great ones—it manipulates our emotions.

Composers use all sorts of techniques to manipulate us. We know that major chords make us feel happy and minor chords make us feel sad. We learned that in grade school. We know that a diminished chord brings on a feeling of mystery. A suspended fourth leaves us in anticipation until that fourth is finally resolved to the third of the chord. We know that ending a song on a suspended fourth is purposely used to rob the listener of a feeling of completion. It's understood that higher notes relative to the overall melody increase the excitement of the music—a technique often reserved for the chorus. Certain tempos are better than others for making us move in certain ways.

How we combine frequencies matters too. For instance, the enormous frequency gap between an isolated low drone in conjunction with the high pitch of a violin in its upper register will make the listener feel uncomfortable. Every thriller movie uses this particular technique. An instrumentation that contains little high-end frequency information will seem dark and make us feel sad. Dissonance will add suspense.

The use of dynamics also elicits an emotional response. Whether that dynamic is achieved by speeding up and slowing down the tempo (which has been all but eradicated from modern music) or through changes in volume, this is a highly effective tool available to the composer. Of course, frequency and dynamics in volume also happen to be in the purview of the mixer. Our arrangement choices alone supply us with these particular tools, and although dynamics have been greatly reduced in modern music, we can use contrast to create the illusion of dynamics. Make no mistake; the mixer has a tangible role in how a song and its production affect people.

Pulling emotional impact out of a track is accomplished through concrete techniques, so you can actually learn how to do this. Once you begin to recognize all that goes into a great song and arrangement, which in turn should promote an inspired performance (knock on wood), you'll start to work on a different level from everyone else. Manipulating sound as it relates purely to sound is irrelevant to music. It's your ability to manipulate emotional impact as it relates to sound that will make you a great artist, producer, or mixer.

This doesn't mean there aren't real-world consequences to the gear we choose. Gear surely matters, and we'll be discussing exactly what gear matters and why. But if you haven't developed your ears enough to readily identify the differences you're hearing and how they actually affect sound, then what does it really matter? As you get better at mixing, as you become more adept at hearing and more sensitive to emotional impact, you'll naturally become more sensitive to what you want out of your gear. You could have the greatest, most accurate mixing setup in the world, but until you have some years under your belt you're not going to hear even half the things that I do. The good news is that your hearing and mixing will improve concurrently with your gear. Even the most modest mixing setup should be good enough for now, and certainly won't preclude you from this book. I'll bet you're glad to read that!

It was really no different for me. I first started mixing at the now defunct Dimension Sound Studios in Jamaica Plain, a suburb of Boston. This was where George Thorogood had recorded several of his early best-selling albums, including his most well-known single, "Bad to the Bone." I arrived on the scene in the late '80s, and the perception of technological advances had left many studios in the dust. At the time, the studio was hanging on for dear life, and as a consequence I had plenty of time to practice recording and mixing. Although Dimension was a professional-grade 24-track recording facility with plenty of positive attributes, it was also lacking in many ways. In hindsight, however, it was a great learning environment.

At the time, I always felt like I was on an island trying to learn how to mix. I remember actually thinking that. There were no "big time" engineers or mixers in Boston to learn from. George and Rounder Records had long moved on and no longer recorded there. There really wasn't a recording community like there is here in LA, and I didn't have access to the Internet back then, although that might be just as well, given the stunning amount of misinformation one can find online.

I'll never forget the overwhelming frustration of learning how to mix on my own. I had *some* mentoring, sure, but the only way I ever seemed to learn anything useful toward becoming a better mixer was by trying and failing on my own—over and over and over again. I can remember saying to myself, "I've finally got it!" after just about every mix between 1987 and 1990. Of course, I'd soon realize I didn't actually have anything of the sort. In fact, I still sucked—just not as badly as before. Perhaps it was that incremental improvement that kept me from giving up—that and an almost compulsive belief that there should be nothing in music that I couldn't do. Thank Buddha for ego! Without it, who knows what I'd be writing about right now.

It would be difficult to blame my early mixing struggles on a lack of musical aptitude. It wasn't as if I came from a long line of roadies and I just happened to wake up one day and decide it was time to stop moving equipment and start moving faders. I was already a musician who had been involved in a number of rock bands. By the time I was 20 I'd studied classical piano for 14 years, played the trumpet for 12 years in various school wind ensembles and jazz bands, and even had several years of songwriting under my belt.

You certainly couldn't claim that I wasn't dedicated enough to the craft. I literally lived at the studio, in an apartment right above it. During the day I was learning about arranging and songwriting at Berklee College of Music. At night I was recording and mixing everything I could get my hands on. I'd bring in bands from Berklee. I was writing and recording with friends. I lived and breathed music. Even with that kind of discipline, it *still* took me well over three years before my mixes actually competed on some level with the "real pros" of the time. Once they did, I moved to LA.

I suppose I could have just moved to LA the moment I realized I belonged in the studio. Perhaps if I'd mentored with a big LA mixer at the time I'd have flattened the learning curve a bit. I can't say for sure. Not that it matters; I didn't want to learn how someone else did things. I wanted to learn how *I* did things. Besides, mentors can only take you so far.

Since moving to Los Angeles, I've mixed hundreds upon hundreds of songs, in just about every genre you can name: hip-hop, rock, funk, roots, folk, country, indie rock, hard rock, blues, pop, jazz, Latin, even adult contemporary. I've spent the better part of my recording career mixing, and there were several years when I did nothing but mix, day in and day out.

In all honesty, I never actually intended to become a mixer *per se.* I only wanted to become a good mixer because I thought it was important to becoming a great producer. I thought the producer had to know how to do everything. I didn't realize I could just order people around and let those who knew better make me look good. Not that I regret the path I took. Mixing was a coveted skill in LA. It was specialized, and if you were good at mixing, you could work. And I did work, almost right out of the gate. In fact, the skill I had unwittingly developed in the pressure-free environment of Boston allowed me to make a lightning-quick transition from studio assistant to bona-fide mixer.

There's no doubt in my mind that mixing on a daily basis made me both a better recordist and producer. Mixing successful projects not only illuminated the production and recording mistakes of others, it taught me about the end game. I mean, the mix *is* the end game. It's the culmination of the entire recording process. Once I was able to picture in my mind exactly what I wanted to achieve on a recording, it became far easier to set myself up for the final product, and right from the beginning of the process. This is often referred to in the business as having "vision." Even if you have no intention of ever becoming a mixer, the more you understand the end game, the more developed your vision, the better you'll become at making music. It really doesn't matter whether you're making your own music or other people's music; learning about mixing is a worthy pursuit.

Which brings us to the obvious question: Who is this book for? Why it's for you, of course. Go to the checkout counter and purchase it immediately!

Not buying it? Okay. I suppose I've written this book for anyone who makes music in any capacity. Whether you're a hobbyist with a desire to make music for a living one day, or a songwriter who wants to put together more effective demos, or an artist who wants to understand how to improve your productions, or an aspiring producer who wants to improve your vision, you should develop your understanding of what goes into a successful end game. I can help you with this. Although, before you can acquire a clear vision of the end game, we have to start from the beginning. First we must address how you *think* about mixing.

The process of mixing requires intense focus and openness. If you're not in the right mind-set to mix, you're done before you've even begun. End game, schmend game! If we don't correct how you think about mixing, there won't *be* an end game—just you and an empty studio.

Pressure

While there's no doubt that *what* you think about while mixing is critical to making good decisions, it's what you *avoid* thinking about that can ultimately determine your success on any given mix. As a professional major label mixer, before I even put up a track, I face all kinds of external pressures: some that I may be aware of right from the start, some that I might become aware of as I proceed, and some that are directly contradictory to one another.

There's the inherent pressure from the label to provide them with a salable product, coupled with the pressure from the artist to release an album that gives them that coveted respect. There's the pressure from each of the band members to keep their favorite useless parts, or somehow make their parts louder than everyone else's—never mind the impossibility of making each and every member of the band louder than the other. There's the pressure to perform a rough mix that everyone loves, even though they don't want the final mix to be anything like it ("make it just like the rough, only good!"). There's the pressure of every great record ever made, and the inevitable comparisons to them, despite the remarkable lack of relevance of such comparisons (I'm sorry, but no, you're not the next Beatles). There's the pressure to finish the project in a timely manner because I have another project lined up, or because I foolishly agreed to cover any extra studio days out of my end. There are the external personal pressures—those that likely have absolutely nothing to do with the project I'm working on—pressures that serve as nothing more than a distraction. Then there's the greatest pressure of them all: The pressure to win the trust of everyone in the room—a pressure ignored at the peril of being fired from the job.

Forgive me for what seems to be an obvious follow-up statement: That's a *lot* of pressure! And those are just some of the pressures that one faces as a professional mixer each and every day. Of course, underlying pressure exists in all phases of a recording project and at all levels. It's just that the finality of mixing serves to amplify the load. Your clients can defer decisions endlessly while they're recording. Not once you're mixing. All those deferred decisions, which populate your session like little anvils waiting to crush you, now fall upon you as the mixer. And as if that's not bad enough, every choice you make needs to be backed up by a logical explanation; if not for your clients, then for yourself. While the discovery of any given mix solution can be completely random, the same cannot be said regarding your decisions. There can be no arbitrary decisions in a mix.

Even if you're not a professional mixer, even if you're a musician trying to mix your own work, or if you're a studio owner in a smaller market, you have your own set of pressures that you have to deal with while you're mixing—pressures that will affect your decisions, often to the detriment of the mix. Regardless of what those pressures are, it's important to identify and recognize them, if for no other reason than so you can learn to completely ignore them.

That's right, I'm telling you that in general, you need to ignore all external pressure. But how?

That's where the Zen comes in.

Zen asserts that the universal nature of inherent wisdom is nothing other than the nature of the mind itself. In simple terms, God comes from within, and enlightenment is attained through meditation. Meditation is concentration, and concentration is the active rejection of all distracting information.

When I think back to my best mixes—regardless of their commercial success—in each and every case, I can only describe the experience as one in which I was working from deep within, outside of any external forces. I wasn't thinking; I was doing. I wasn't scared of what anyone would think. I wasn't scared of failure. All my decisions were made with confidence, and once a judgment was made, I didn't second guess myself. I allowed the music to guide me, and I based all of my mix decisions on nothing more than one simple criterion: Are the song and production doing what they're supposed to be doing?

If I kick ass on a mix—or for that matter, if *you* kick ass on a mix—two things have occurred. We were given stellar material to start with, and we were able to operate "in the zone." The material you're given before you mix is beyond your control. Operating "in the zone" is nothing more than a modern interpretation of Zen.

Just like in sports, the concept of working in the zone indicates an ability to remove all outside pressures from your thoughts. That said, unlike professional sports, there is no true opposition, and the parameters within which we must work are provided purely by our own team. In other words, it's considerably easier to get in the zone when you're not dealing with a bad song, a limp performance, an amateur production, or any combination of the three.

Comprehension

Of course, ignoring external pressures doesn't mean ignoring your clients. That would not only be foolish, seeing as they're the ones paying you for your services, but also remarkably obtuse. Regardless of how much or what kind of communication you have with your clients, they will most assuredly divulge their intentions to you directly through the production. That's right: All the information you're ever going to need will be contained prominently in the track itself. Frankly, the moment you bring up a track it should speak to you. There's a story contained in every track, and as you become more adept at mixing you'll become equally adept at reading the story contained within.

In the most simplistic terms, the individual tracks should immediately tell you the kind of song you're dealing with. If it's a dance song, the track will have an infectious beat, which is certainly a good indicator of that beat's importance in the song. As such the drums should probably be mixed prominently. I mean, if the first thing you pull up is a kik drum playing four to the floor, followed up by the disco "shoop" of a hi-hat, you really shouldn't need your client to explicitly tell you that you're mixing a dance song, right? They've told you that in the track.

If your client is looking for an aggressive treatment, you're pretty much going to know it based on all those cymbal crashes and huge, distorted guitars. This will be plain regardless of whether your client directly mentions their intentions. If the track derives its overall rhythm from the acoustic guitars, and if the drums are quite simple in their part, the acoustic guitars are most assuredly designed to play a prominent role in the mix. You don't have to be an exceptionally intuitive person to extract this sort of information from a track, but you must also learn to read between the lines.

If you mix for any length of time at all, there will be occasions when you will pull up parts that don't seem to belong. These sorts of parts are generally an indicator that something went awry during the recording process. In most cases, either your clients got confused somewhere along the way, or they had a disagreement of some kind. I can assure you, any part you find confusing, your clients likely find equally as confusing. If they didn't, they're the ones that should be able to explain it to you, preferably in the form of a rough mix. The more likely scenario is that they just didn't want to be the ones to kill the idea. That's your job as the mixer, and they're relying on you to be the faithful executioner. Off with its head!

If, on the other hand, you discover kik and snare drum samples that line up perfectly with the kik and snare from the recorded kit, you can safely surmise that your client feels that the timbre of those particular drum hits is inconsistent and of poor tone. Or your client desires a prominent kik and snare in the mix. Of course, their provided solution to this underlying problem may or may not be the right one. You may be able to use compression and EQ to deal with the inconsistency and tone issues in a much more effective manner for the mix. It doesn't really matter whether you agree with what your clients are telling you. What matters is that you read and comprehend what you're essentially being told in any given track.

That said, if you wish to mix effectively and in a manner that not only pleases your clients but brings the track you've been provided to its fullest potential, then there has to be some inherent willingness to work within the confines of the artist's intentions. At least you need to give those intentions their due consideration before deciding otherwise. On those occasions when you do choose to break away from what your client is telling you in the track, you should be able to explain your decision-making process. Mark my words, if you don't make your mix decisions in a deliberate manner, you'll be caught flat-footed come mix notes time. This will not please your clients.

Steps to Enlightenment

Half the art of mixing is in how you deal with your clients. In fact, that's one of the pillars of my article, "Mixerman's 10 Steps to Better Mixing," which I wrote in 1999, the same year I began posting as Mixerman. The article first appeared on Usenet's pro audio group, rec.audio.pro, and has found its way onto nearly every recording forum since that time. I've actually had people print it out and send it to me, which, when you think about it, is pretty funny, although very much appreciated.

I wrote this particular article in response to another post containing a wholly different list of 10 steps. The original list was nothing more than a clinical step-by-step cookbook approach to mixing. I can't think of anything more useless. Anyone can push up a fader, turn a pan pot, and boost an EQ. This wasn't useful information—least of all for people looking to learn how to actually mix. Learning about mixing isn't like learning about signal flow. Mixing is neither a linear process nor a technical one. It's a musical process, and as such, a mix is something that one performs—like an artist.

Frankly, I was incensed when I read this particular post about mixing. I know that sounds silly, but it used to drive me crazy to read all the appalling misinformation on the Internet about recording. As was often the case, perhaps too often in those early years, I was compelled to correct the record. I could barely type fast enough as I came up with my own steps. They poured out of me so quickly I was done in less than five minutes. Remarkably, since writing that article, I've been unable to improve upon it in any significant way.

Don't be thrown off by the age of the article. I can assure you where mixing philosophy is concerned that there have been no great technological advances in the last 30 years, let alone the last 10. It makes no difference if you're mixing on a DAW or using an analog machine through a Neve 8068 console—the *art* of mixing remains the same.

Mixerman's 10 Steps to Better Mixing

1 Mixing is an attitude.

2 If the song sucks, the mix is irrelevant.

3 Working the room, keeping people happy and relaxed, is half of mixing successfully.

4 Putting everything proportional in a mix is going to make for a shitty mix.

5 Gear used on a mix are tools that will make your life either easier or more difficult; they are not what makes a mix good or bad.

6 A mix can be great and not have great sound.

7 If the mix doesn't somehow, and in some way, annoy someone in the room, the mix likely isn't done.

8 Mixing cannot be taught; it can only be learned.

9 The overall vibe of the track is much more important than any individual part.

10 Just because a part was recorded doesn't mean it needs to be in the mix.

11 Be aggressive! (Oops, that's 11!)

I know what you're thinking. That's not a list of steps at all! This is true, but as I've already pointed out to you, mixing isn't a linear process, and as such there really aren't any steps to actually tell you about. That's one of the major points of the article. I'm also fairly certain that number eight on the list caught your eye. I know it would have caught mine were I in the market for a book on the subject of mixing.

Mixing cannot be taught; it can only be learned.

Isn't that just great? A book about mixing in which the author admits he can't teach you how to mix. Hopefully you've already bought this book, but just in case you're still in the bookstore right now, worry not. Remember, I'm going to teach you how to *think* about mixing, not *how* to mix. The learning how to mix part is on you. If you change how you *think* about mixing, you'll be well on your way to learning *how* to mix.

Now, I'm presenting these steps to you here in the Introduction because we're going to discuss them in detail throughout the course of this book. I don't offer you these steps as some sort of outline—it's far too limiting a list to be that. It's just that everything in a mix is interdependent, and this book is much like mixing in that regard. I spent an inordinate amount of time figuring out the best and most logical way to present the art of mixing to you, and I've determined that there isn't one, so I guess you're in for a wild ride.

Communication and Compromise

Seeing as half of mixing successfully has to do with people skills, I'm going to devote an entire chapter to the subject. Even if your work is wholly self-contained, dealing with others in the creation of art is a critical skill to develop. Furthermore, the information contained here regarding bedside manner can be just as useful for dealing with clients as for becoming a good client yourself. Whether or not you intend to become a professional mixer, your interpersonal skills are a vital part of any creative process. It doesn't really matter what your role is in the creation of a recording; disagreements will come up, compromises will be made, and negotiations will ensue. Hell, when I'm mixing, I spend half my time negotiating with myself. Such is to be expected for an activity so tied to the art of compromise.

Anyone who's spent any amount of time attempting to make a kik drum work effectively with the bass understands compromise as it relates to mixing. Still, the real art of mixing lies not in negotiating with oneself (I'm thinking you're always going to win that one), but rather in negotiating with those who have hired you in the first place.

I really can't overemphasize just how critical communication is on a mix session. As the mixer, you must be able to explain relatively complex concepts in easily understandable terms. These can't be meandering speeches that lack focus. You need to be concise and to the point. Your arguments must be demonstrable. Even when the producer is in the room, you're the leader of the mixing process, and as such you should be clear in how you express yourself. Conversely, you have a responsibility to guide your clients toward good communication habits themselves.

I can't tell you how often I come across a client's debilitating inability to state with alacrity a specific problem with the mix— particularly when we're in the home stretch of the process. There is a point in the mix where most solutions involve nothing more than half a dB change in level. Still, it seems there's always the one client who prefers to offer absurdly complex solutions to simple problems. It's at this point in a mix that I interrupt pointless meandering with an almost militant command:

"Instrument. Section. Up or down."

While this may seem somewhat abrasive on the surface, I can assure you it serves a very useful purpose. You don't really need to hear your client's reasons why she might want "the piano, on the third chorus, louder." For starters, you can't judge the merits of any particular mix note until you listen to it. The detailed philosophical reasons as to why the piano, in the third chorus, should be louder is useless information until you've determined whether you agree with the note. If everyone agrees (and in particular if you agree), there is no debate. Besides, you could very well bring the level of that piano up and have your client instantly declare herself wrong. If you allow your client to argue endlessly all her reasons for a simple mix note before it's actually implemented and evaluated by everyone, your client unwittingly puts herself in the position of having to defend her note regardless of the results. By steering your clients toward clear, concise communication, you allow yourself the opportunity to avoid a total breakdown of it.

Once you hone your ability to communicate effectively, you'll have an edge in negotiating through the varying needs of the A&R rep, the band, the artist, the manager, the producer, the manager's girlfriend, etc. Believe me, each and every one of those people will have an opinion and an agenda, all of which will have to be dealt with appropriately. Even if it's your own music, and none of those people are involved in your project, or even if you're a young mixer in a small city working with self-funded local bands, you're going to have to deal with multiple, and often unwanted, opinions. Feedback is generally a good thing, but when the manager's girlfriend is complaining that you axed her favorite part—a part that was long abandoned or forgotten about and for whatever reason was never deleted from the session—this kind of feedback is not helpful to the process.

A large part of communicating effectively requires respect. It's always somewhat awkward when a band girlfriend gets in your face because she doesn't get why your opinions are deemed more important than hers. Believe me, I know. Been there, done that. While it's certainly not necessary to get the girlfriend's respect, the same cannot be said about your clients. If you don't have their trust and respect, you need to gain it somehow, or you'll find yourself unable to perform your job effectively.

Making a record under the best of circumstances is an emotional process. Metaphorically speaking, you're dealing with someone's baby. That's how personal art can be to its creator. If you treat that art with respect, you'll have a much easier time acquiring respect yourself. Of course, there is one simple way to gain everyone's respect: Deliver a great mix. But therein lies the rub.

Caveats and Definitions

Anything and everything that has to do with mixing has to do with perspective. How the listener hears the relative vocal balance within a track is perspective. How loud your particular track sounds compared with someone else's track in iTunes is perspective. This we'll talk about, but as we do, you should also take into account my perspectives as a professional, particularly as they relate to your own.

I've been a freelance mixer and producer for nearly 20 years. The sum total of my experiences as a freelance mixer won't correspond perfectly with someone who owns a full-blown recording studio and must deal with the realities of a massive monthly overhead, nor will they correlate exactly with the professional songwriter looking to improve his or her own mixes. Since I must assume that the overwhelming majority of those reading this book are not currently, and may never become, professional mixers, you will surely come across some information in this book that has no direct relevance to your circumstance. That doesn't mean this information won't have relevance in the future, and it most certainly doesn't mean the information contained within these pages won't prove useful in the broader context of creating music.

If you understand the thinking that goes into a successful mix, and if you understand your ultimate goal with a song or a production, you understand how to set yourself up to succeed in making music regardless of your role in that process. It would be impossible for me to discuss mixing without also discussing songwriting, arrangement, performance, and recording. Everything that happens before a mix affects the mix itself. Therefore, understanding what goes into effective mixing will only serve to make you better at everything that comes before the mix itself.

Just so there's no misunderstanding, this book was not written solely for those who wish to become professional freelance mixers. I can assure you, I wouldn't bother writing a book for such a miniscule audience. *Zen and the Art of Mixing* is for people who want to understand the kind of thinking that goes into high-level mixing. If you're involved in music in any way, there's plenty in this book to help you improve your craft.

For reasons that will soon become obvious, I will spend much of our time together hammering on the importance of the vocal. Certainly there will be occasions when there is no vocal in a mix. For ease of writing and reading, you can consider the melody instrument to be equivalent to the vocal. For the most part, they serve the same role.

As you've probably surmised, I've spent most of my career mixing on an analog console. While I'm most comfortable mixing in this manner, there will be far more of you who use DAWs and plug-ins exclusively than who work in fully analog studios or even in hybrid situations. Let's face it—if you know how to use a console, you know how to use a DAW. The same can't necessarily be said for the reverse. Given this, anything that translates to either medium will generally be discussed from the perspective of the DAW.

I will often use the term "clients" in a rather global manner. This basically refers to anyone in the process who has veto power. This can be the artist, the producer, the A&R rep, the band, the manager, the investor, etc. If they have a say in the product, then you have a responsibility to make them happy.

The term "parts" refers to instrumentation. There are drum parts, guitar parts, keyboard parts, percussion parts, etc. This is just an easy way for me to describe the instruments that are contained within an arrangement.

Lastly, and most importantly, the concepts involved in music and mixing can be remarkably complex. Any general rule I might provide you regarding music or mixing will likely have more than one exception. This book would be 10 times longer and impossible to get through were I to go through every exception to every rule—not that I could actually think of them all. For this reason, from the long view of your overall career, you can treat any rule that I present to you as a tool. Use the tools where they're warranted, abandon them where they're not, and understand that the more tools you use and the better you implement those tools, the more effective your mixes will be.

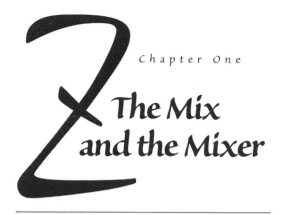

Chapter One

The Mix and the Mixer

The Great Mix

It seems almost ridiculous to define a mix in a book about mixing. Would you really have gotten this far if you didn't even know what a mix was? Just the same, I would probably be nothing short of negligent were I to forgo such a definition. Besides, this way, I get to define it.

A mix is the final 2-track (left and right) presentation of a production (which contains the performance of an arrangement of a song).

Let's expand on that a bit.

Once the recording process is complete, the production is ready for the mix. Our job is to take the many individual recorded parts, anywhere from two to 100 or more, and combine and order these parts to create a stereo track playable by the consumer.

Given such a broad definition, it's fair to say that anyone can make a mix. But few can make a *great* mix, which is probably the more relevant definition for the purposes of this book.

A *great* mix is one that brings a production of a great song to its *fullest potential* by effectively manipulating the listener's emotions and focus, thereby forcing an appropriate and desired physical reaction while simultaneously causing the listener to sing.

That's a mouthful, I know! But that's what's involved in a great mix, and I'll break it all down for you. First, you'll notice I slipped in the phrase "great song" in that definition. There's a very good reason for that.

If the song sucks, the mix is irrelevant.

As I've already pointed out, the subjectivity involved in evaluating a song has no bearing on its quality. There are billions of people on this earth from diverse cultures that hear music in different ways. There's no such thing as a song that works for everyone. In fact, any song that you and I might agree is great (even an internationally successful one) would probably have more detractors than fans were we to poll every person on the planet.

Any individual can hate any song, even one that is adored by millions of people. If someone hates a song, regardless of how popular that song may be, then the mix has no relevance to them. They hate the song; what the hell do they care about the mix? As far as they're concerned, everything about it is terrible. Therefore, it's the listener that determines whether your mix has relevance, and thus, we as mixers must try hard regardless of the circumstance. Our goal remains the same: to bring a production of a song to its fullest potential. Whether the song is deemed great or not is out of our hands.

Now if the listener likes the song, then the mix can make a huge difference where its impact is concerned. For example, if you bury the vocal in such a way that the lyrics are all but inaudible and the melody is given no importance whatsoever, you've ruined any possibility of pulling emotional impact from the listener. At that point it really doesn't matter how great the song is. The good news (for the songwriter anyway) is that your bad mix with the buried vocal doesn't render the song irrelevant. The song can be recorded and mixed by someone else in the future. A mix can only render a particular production of a song ineffective.

This is an important distinction. There are probably a thousand different productions of a song such as "White Christmas." Does a single bad mix or production render that song irrelevant? Absolutely not. The song remains adored by millions.

If you personally don't like a song, are you really going to evaluate the mix? This might be the case for some audiophiles, but come on! Most audiophiles have completely lost the plot, and I'm convinced they don't even listen to music—they listen to *sound*. We must reject this particular crowd as nothing more than an anomaly. For the majority of us the only thing that matters is the music itself. If that music elicits an emotional response, then we'll appreciate it; if it doesn't, we won't. The mix and production can only enhance the emotional response caused by a song. We're mixing *music* here; we're not mixing mixes. The mix doesn't even exist without a song, a production, and a performance.

Song, Production, and Performance

Unlike visual art, music elapses over time. I can look at a painting, and appreciate it nearly instantly. Granted, I might want to take some time to digest all the details, but the entire painting presents itself the instant I look at it. A song reveals itself over the course of several minutes, and a great song must push the listener forward through time. Whereas a painting fills space, music fills time.

As we've already discussed, a familiar song remains in your mind. If you wish to recall a painting you love, you can do so, but the impact of that painting is lost. Not so with a song. You can hum a familiar song, and before you know it you'll have an entire orchestra in your head. Try it. Think of your favorite song, and play it in your head. You can probably recall the whole production. Now think of the *Mona Lisa*. It's nowhere near as effective, is it? Sure, you can imagine the *Mona Lisa*, but you can't get the impact that you would if you went to the Louvre. Yet the song that plays in your head can invoke an emotional response in a matter of moments. If you're imagining a familiar production, you can clearly "hear" all the parts. The song can make you dance, and make you sing. You'll sing countermelodies and drum parts, you'll conduct if it's classical, you'll play air guitar if it's rock. You can engage in everything that you enjoy about the music right from your head.

As strong as our sense of sight is, and as much as we rely on sight more than any other sense, for whatever reason our brain has a far keener memory for what we hear than what we see. Our auditory memory is crystal clear. We can recall multiple simultaneous parts of an arrangement as if we're hearing them rather than merely imagining them.

I can actually sing a familiar song and others can join me. I don't need any sheet music, I don't need a track, I don't need a production, I don't need a mix, I don't even need a piano or guitar. I can just start singing the song, and everyone around me can join in as long as they know the song. If we sing a happy song, we're probably going to feel happiness. We'll feel a consistent corresponding emotion from any effective song, whether it's a sad song, a love song, or even an angry song. Sometimes we find ourselves inspired to sing a song because of how we feel at the moment; sometimes singing that song makes us feel a particular way. Either way, the song evokes emotion.

Further increasing the impact of music is the way it's tied to memory. A familiar song can bring us back to a particular place and time, even if it was decades earlier. Songs act like markers in our lives, which complicates (and perhaps enhances) the emotions we feel when we hear or even imagine a song. In essence, a song is interactive.

Music also has a physical effect on us. Scientists like Carol Krumhansl at Cornell University have demonstrated scientifically that songs elicit emotion, which correlates directly to how our bodies react physically. Songs with an upbeat tempo written in a major key can cause our heart and breathing rate to increase. Sad songs can cause our pulse to slow and blood pressure to increase. We *react* physically to music, because music generates an emotional response. It's no coincidence that we describe a song that has had some success as one that's garnered a "reaction." That's always the goal with a song—to cause people to react.

Don't confuse a song's inherent quality and overall effectiveness with the subjectivity involved in how you personally view it. If you don't like a song, then it either doesn't touch you, or it touches you in such a negative way that you reject it. Either way, the subjectivity lies within you as an individual. The song is still either effective or ineffective at causing an overall reaction beyond your own personal feelings about it. There have been countless songs proclaimed "hits" based on the reaction (and high hopes) of the few, only to fall well short of that mark when subjected to the collective scrutiny of the many. Even if an effective song irritates you, it's still causing a reaction, and it's probably even causing the physical reaction it was designed to elicit. You just don't happen to like how that song makes you feel. That just makes the song ineffective to you as an individual.

While an effective song can remain undiscovered, an ineffective song will rarely break through to human consciousness. We can only measure the effectiveness of a song by the overall reaction to it, and there is no single person who can stake a claim as the arbiter of all great and effective music—not even Clive Davis. Sure, he can market the shit out of a song, and he can make sure enough people hear it to cause a spark. But he can't *cause* a reaction just because he puts marketing money behind a track. He can, however, give a great song an even better shot at reaching overall human consciousness if he matches the song with the right combination of producer and performer.

There is an inherent separation between a song and its production. The melody and lyric (if there is a lyric) are their own entity, completely removed from any kind of production or mix. Before technology, a song could be handed down through generations without ever having a production or an arrangement. If all recording and playback devices ceased to exist today, the great songs of our time would survive purely through our ability to pass them down through performance. Which brings us to the definition of a production.

A production is the performance of an arrangement of a song. It's the vehicle a performer uses to deliver an *interpretation* of a song. The first recording of a song (aside from the demo) is the original interpretation. If the song is great, and it manages to reach mainstream consciousness, it will be interpreted by other artists many times in the future. Each new recording will provide us with yet another interpretation of the song, but the song remains the same. Other than a parody version (which is a derivative version), that song can be sung or hummed any time, by anyone, with anyone, for anyone.

The production doesn't dictate the quality of a song, just the interpretation of it. The less effective a song is at inspiring emotion, the more important the production becomes by default—although a production, no matter how well executed, fails miserably as a substitute for a great song. Sometimes the best production for a song is nothing more than an acoustic guitar and a vocal. Frankly, a song that can't be sung effectively by one person with one instrument can't possibly be considered a great song.

It's crucial that you recognize a song as a separate entity from the presentation of it. Regardless of whether you're the producer, artist, or mixer, you're attempting to give a song the most effective presentation possible. If you accept that the song is of supreme importance, that the production is nothing more than a delivery vehicle for the song, and that the performers (particularly the singer) deliver that song *to* us, then you recognize that the production is subservient to the song. Once you acknowledge this you quickly realize that your job as the producer or mixer is simple: follow the song.

Just because the production is subordinate to the song in no way detracts from the artistry involved in the production itself. It's just that a song is made up out of whole cloth, and the production is designed based on how the song makes us feel. Yes, I realize that there are only 12 notes, and that most modern songs are somewhat derivative in nature, but my point is that the song is the creation here. Done properly, the production provides the foundation necessary for a singer to deliver a compelling performance. The performance provides the power of the song. Therefore, the production should be subservient to the performance. If the production gets in the way of the performance, the listener will never connect with the singer, which means that they won't connect with the song.

This is not to say that the production can't be built before the song, or for that matter, the performance. Many songs have been written based around a track, and many performances have had tracks built around them. But in the end, the effectiveness of the track will still depend on the song itself. It's the melody that will be hummed and the lyric that will be sung—not the track.

Even an instrumental song, like Jan Hammer's "*Miami Vice* Theme," has a melody, and if you know the song, that melody is probably going through your head right now. Of course, relaying that song to the person next to you requires you to sing the melody. When the melody stops, you'll probably sing the rhythmic response parts, since that's the compelling feature of the production that occurs between the melodic synth lines. While those rhythmic breaks between melodic phrases push us forward through the song (which is supremely important from a production standpoint), the melody is still the song.

Given that the production is the performance of an arrangement, it would follow that a weak performance makes for a weak production. As the mixer, you have no bearing on the actual quality of the performance. You will, however, have an *influence* over how that performance affects the listener, particularly where the arrangement is concerned.

What happens in the arrangement directly affects how the listener focuses on a performance. For instance, if the track is littered with guitar licks and horn stabs that occur simultaneously with the vocal, the listener will surely be distracted and unable to focus on the singer's performance. The greatest vocal performance of all time can be rendered uninspiring if it's lost amid the other parts in an arrangement. If on the other hand those guitar licks and horn stabs are placed between the phrases of a prominently placed vocal, not only will the listener focus intently on the vocal, but those other parts will work to push the listener forward through the song. There are some exceptions to this. New Orleans–style music will often feature a busy arrangement in which multiple instruments are soloing at the same time as the vocal. This music works because it's designed to be a frenetic celebration. I can promise you, the vocal will have to be extremely loud for anyone to be able to make out the words.

Clearly we can't control free will with our mix or production. The listener can focus on the hi-hat if they concentrate hard enough (and they might, if they smoke a little weed beforehand). Our job as mixers is to determine and provide a clear *intent* for the listener.

You don't want the listener thinking; you want them reacting. You manipulate how the listener reacts by how you mix the production. Choosing to make the vocal nice and loud tells the listener in no uncertain terms that your intent is for them to listen to that vocal. In most cases, the listener will gladly follow your intent. Believe me, the listener doesn't *want* to have to think or concentrate. They just want to sing.

Sing It Loud!

If you can make the listener sing, you've got them right where you want them. That's the ultimate sign of enjoyment! This is why I've made it part of the definition of a great mix. One thing I've noticed after all these years of mixing is if I can't stop myself from singing a song, I'm on to something with my mix.

Clearly, you're not going to get the listener to sing the song the first time they hear it. They don't know the words, and they don't know where the song is going. It's unfolding for them for the very first time. If the listener doesn't like the song, they'll skip to the next one before it reaches the second verse (if not sooner). If the listener likes the song, it gets a second and third listen, and it's not going to be long before they're attempting to sing along.

Causing people to sing the song is the ultimate goal. This is what we strive for.

Now, if you're going to be manipulating emotions, you'd better be causing the listener to do more than just sing. No matter what the song, a good production is designed to cause a physical reaction, and how you mix the production will have a part in this. It doesn't matter whether you cause the listener to dance, jump, bounce, bang their head, pump their fist, tap their toe, sway, cry, laugh, run, play air guitar, air drums, or even get goose bumps—if you can cause them to do *something*, the production and the mix are doing their jobs.

Fullest Potential

By now, you've probably come to the horrifying conclusion that we as mixers are completely at the mercy of the material we're given. That's fucked up, I know. We can improve the production and the arrangement with our decisions; we can improve the technical aspects of a performance, like pitch and timing; we can even improve the overall emotional impact of a relatively unin-spiring song, but the maximum improvement possible will only bring the production of a song to its fullest potential, whatever that happens to be. If its fullest potential is "not much," well, there you go.

I'm aware that this whole "fullest potential" description could be a bit slippery for some of you reading this. I wish I could give you something a bit more concrete. I mean, really, how is anyone supposed to know whether they brought the production of a song to its fullest potential? It's not like you get to evaluate 20 different mixes to determine which one reached that particular apex. Even if you could evaluate that many mixes, it wouldn't be long before you were completely desensitized to them, regardless of how much experience you have in this regard. And while combining the best attributes of each mix might seem like a decent idea in theory, in practice it won't work in a million years. I've been involved in this sort of lunacy on more than one occasion. To date, it has yet to turn out well.

Really, only the people involved would be familiar enough with the recording to understand whether you brought a mix to its fullest potential. Your clients are the arbiters of a song's fullest potential. If you blow your clients away with the mix, there will never be any doubt that you accomplished this goal.

The Production and the Mixer

As the mixer, you don't deal with the song. You deal with the production of the song, which contains the performances. When you're done with the mix and ready for notes from the client, the producer and the artist are going to evaluate your mix based on how it makes them feel about the song. If it's more than they hoped for, the mix notes will be nothing more than minor grievances. If it's less than they hoped for, then the producer is going to have to explain where you've missed the mark, and then you need to determine whether that mark is even attainable.

Your best mixes are going to come from the best productions, and the best productions from the best songs. Even if your clients become completely lost in the process, even if they have no earthly idea what they have any more and they believe the song is going to be dropped from the album (and this happens), if what you need to make that track great exists in your session, then you should be able to deliver a great mix. The definition of "fullest potential" has nothing to do with your client's warm feelings about their recording. Either you're given what you need to make a great mix or you're not. It's up to you as the mixer to figure out the best, most effective way to present a production and offer it up in the form of a mix.

Given that you deal directly with the arrangement as a mixer, and since the performance of an arrangement *is* a production, we are by default involved in the production. As the mixer, we are basically an extension of the producer, and as such there is certainly some blurring of the lines between roles. But make no mistake about it—in all but the rarest of cases, the producer retains veto power over the mixer. So don't get a big head.

There are some mixers who have no problems editing and sample-replacing drums or even tuning vocals. There are times when this sort of ultra-aggressive treatment is necessary and fair game. Just understand that when you do this, you're going well beyond your capacity as the mixer. Once you start altering the tracks, you're engaging in production. If production work is what your client wants from you, and if you're comfortable doing that kind of work for nothing more than mix credit, be my guest. But that's producing first, and then mixing. You're still attempting to bring a production to its fullest potential; it's just that now you're changing the production in order to achieve your mix goals.

Don't get me wrong here. I'm not in any way arguing that there aren't times when you can do some production work as a mixer. You can get into a mix and find a snare hit out of time, a vocal note out of tune, a bass note out of the pocket, or any number of problems that would do well with some form of touch-up. Oftentimes these kinds of small details are far more obvious within the context of a highly focused mix than they might have been during the recording phase. So it's quite possible that your clients never noticed a particular problem. Don't go crazy with this, though.

Some tuning and timing problems have a charm to them. You perform a disservice to the music by eradicating all human moments. Of course, if a performance issue seems to pull you out of the mix each and every time it occurs, then you should alter the part. There is surely no charm in being pulled out of the mix, and it's well within your job description to fix these sorts of jolting problems.

Occasionally, you'll come across an arrangement that's in desperate need of an additional part. This could be just about anything from a synth pad in the lower midrange register to a tambourine in the chorus. It's not, by any stretch of the imagination, out of line for you as the mixer to diplomatically suggest the addition of a part, particularly if you don't do it too often. On the other hand, if you're personally adding multiple parts to the production, you're totally out of line. As the mixer for hire, it would be outrageous to take it upon yourself to start adding parts. Frankly, it's risky to even *offer* to add a part to anyone other than an established client. If there's an arrangement problem that directly affects your ability to mix, then tell your client, suggest a few solutions, and let them implement the solutions.

While indiscriminately adding parts to an arrangement would be completely out of bounds for the mixer for hire, the removal of superfluous parts is an entirely different matter. It is completely within reason for you as the mixer to manipulate the arrangement based on what you've been provided—this includes muting parts. Arrangement affects every aspect of a mix, and discarding parts is an essential part of your job.

How far you can go with production decisions on a mix really depends on a number of factors, including the personality of the producer (if there is a producer), your relationship with the clients, and your own personal desire to actually get involved in the production aspects. The line of inappropriateness is unclear at best, and while you most certainly will want to be careful not to cross that particular line, there's absolutely nothing wrong with walking right up to it.

Mixing is an attitude.

If you walk into a mix trying to make everyone happy, you're going to make no one happy. There is no way to please everyone, no matter what you're doing. So why try? You're the mixer. You're the one being hired for your expertise. If the producer could mix the song, he would. If the label could mix it, they would. If the artist could mix the song, she would. They can't! They hired you to mix the record. Use that leverage to your advantage and take a little pressure off yourself. As long as you follow the song and the production and make the best decisions possible based on what you're given, you're going to deliver the best mix possible.

By the time you come in as the mixer, everyone else on the project is considering things that have no bearing on the final product. If you start out a mix by compromising with all the external forces that exist beyond the mix, you're never going to be able to make the necessary compromises within the mix itself. Make the mix first. Please yourself first, then deal with compromises to accommodate some other external factor. At least then you have a good starting point. It's what you ignore that makes you dangerous as a mixer. That's why it's so important for you to view mixing as an attitude.

Let's say you get to the end of the mix, and you think it's kicking ass, and your client hates the mix. Are you going to beat yourself up over this? Are you going to view yourself as a failure because the client doesn't like a mix? Are you going to let them make you believe that you didn't deliver the best mix possible? The answer to all of these questions should be "of course not!" Besides, your client could be wrong, which is why you should always print your mix before you start making sweeping alterations.

Even if you're working in a DAW you should print the mix before you start overhauling it for the client. Saving the mix isn't enough. You need a stereo print for later reference, and you want to make sure your clients know you're reserving your version of the mix. This allows you to pull it out later, without seeming underhanded about it.

You don't want to be rude about this. That's not what I mean by "attitude." But you can't spend hours on a mix, learn every nuance of the track, evaluate how the parts affect you, and immediately accept that your mix is somehow totally wrong for the song. The track tells you the story. If you're good at reading the track and you're good at following the song, it's actually hard to completely miss. That said, your clients could be absolutely right. You might work out a new mix in short order that makes everyone happy, including yourself.

The difference between a client hating a mix and loving it can be as little as three tiny little changes. Hell, one time I had a client ask me to put a gate on his vocal, only to proclaim the mix done once it was inserted in the chain (and yes, it was bypassed). Don't ask me how one goes from hating a mix to loving it like this, but hey, if my clients want to conflate their role in the mix, as long as they don't give themselves half credit in the liner notes, what the hell do I care?

Of course, you and your clients could very well be pulling your hair out two hours later as you go around in circles on a mix you've already personally spent eight hours going around in circles on. In those scenarios, you'll come out looking like a genius when you pull the ultimate solution out of your back pocket—that mix you printed earlier (*please let it be great, please let it be great*). Maybe check it out in private first.

Then there are those times when your client is convinced they've improved the mix that you're sure they've destroyed. This is when you put your earlier mix onto your client's reference CD, right next to the new mix. This way, they get to compare the mixes themselves, and in a comfortable environment. You're the professional mixer, and there's absolutely nothing wrong with proving it to your clients when warranted.

Confidence Is an Attitude, Too

Mixing is a game of confidence. If you're confident, you'll mix great. If you're not, you won't. Confidence in mixing is critical. I mean, if you don't believe you're the most qualified person in the room to be mixing, then why should your clients? Of course, if you're reading this book, I have to assume you're probably lacking confidence when it comes to mixing. So let's put all this into some sort of perspective. The good news is if you make a bad mix, you're not going to kill someone.

Perhaps that's little consolation during those times when you want to gouge your ears out with a sharp utensil because the mix you were certain was nothing short of fantastic last week clearly sucks this week. This is part of the process. You can throw away your early mixes. They're not going to be worth a damn. Whether your "early" mixes constitute the first 10 or the first 100 cannot be accurately predicted. Hopefully this book will bring the number of those embarrassing mixes down considerably.

Don't let yourself get bogged down by this depressing statistic. Just because your early mixes suck doesn't mean you should give up. Don't let your confidence take a beating over this. Mixing is hard. You *will* improve. Each mix will be better than the last, and your improvement will have nothing to do with gear or any cookie-cutter process you read about on the Internet.

Regardless of your current skill level, you need to walk into each and every mix with the confidence that you're going to kill the mix ("killing" a mix is a good thing). If you don't *think* you can kill the mix, then you will have no chance of doing so. At some point you're going to deliver a high-quality, professional-grade mix that does everything it should. Since you have no idea when you'll reach that point, it would be best to assume that this glorious accomplishment will occur on your very next mix.

I've been recording and mixing for just over 20 years, and to this day I *still* get myself pumped up for each and every mix. I assure you, I'm not the kind of person who sits in front of the mirror giving myself affirmations like the Stuart Smalley character from *Saturday Night Live*. I shudder at the thought. Even so, I actually tell myself I'm going to kill the mix as I drive to the studio each day. Believe it or not, this simple routine actually makes an enormous difference in getting into the right mind-set before I walk into the room.

Don't confuse this attitude toward mixing with having the attitude of a prick. Your clients will most assuredly replace you with a nicer mixer—like myself, for instance. Mixing attitude has nothing to do with how you act as a person, but rather your overall mind-set regarding a mix. Your attitude allows you to approach decisions with confidence and lock out external forces from affecting otherwise good decisions. I'll give you a personal example of this.

In 1995, I mixed Ben Harper's second album, *Fight for Your Mind*, which was produced by J.P. Plunier. If you're unfamiliar with Ben Harper, his main axe is an acoustic lap steel called the

Weisenborn, which was manufactured in the early part of the 20th century. Ben is undoubtedly one of the best Weisenborn players in the world, and through the application of custom-designed pick-ups, he's able to use it as both a beautiful acoustic instrument and a fiercely aggressive electric one. This has given him a one-of-a-kind sound. Combine this with inspiringly raw and emotional vocals on top of good songwriting, and you have a combination that would make just about any producer or mixer happy.

On this particular album, J.P. and Ben actually gave me the choice between the comped vocals (vocal performances recorded as overdubs and then compiled onto one track) and the scratch vocals, which he cut live with the band. I picked the scratch on each and every song. Let me tell you, regardless of the swirly and phasey artifacts from Ben's aggressive mic technique in close proximity to his acoustic guitar mic, it wasn't even a close contest. The scratch vocals were far too raw, emotional, and engaging to abandon for pure sonic considerations.

By the time I'd come to the song "By My Side," I already had Ben and J.P.'s trust, and I could be as aggressive as I wanted. The arrangement on tape included bass, drums, percussion, Hammond B3, and Ben, who played acoustic guitar on this particular arrangement. The entire track was built around Ben, as they all were, but this one was different from the others. This production didn't feature Ben's guitar. In fact, Ben wasn't really doing anything of note on the acoustic. It was the Hammond B3 that was playing the most compelling part in the arrangement.

Now, in the context of the album, the B3 was a unique texture. In the context of the song, it was the only instrument, aside from the vocal, doing anything exceptionally interesting. So I mixed it louder than anything else in the track. In fact, I mixed it super loud. Mind you, I didn't think about this consciously. I didn't say to myself, "aside from the vocal, that B3 needs to be the loudest instrument in the song." I just mixed it that way.

I'll never forget playing that mix for Ben and J.P. Here I thought I kicked ass, and I don't think either of them moved a muscle as the song played down. This always makes me maddeningly uncomfortable, given my definition of a great mix. As if that wasn't bad enough, when the song finished, they remained motionless and didn't say anything whatsoever, even after a minute of silence. Well, I was fairly certain they hated the mix, and they just didn't know where to start. So I broke the ice.

"That bad, huh?"

"I never imagined the organ that loud," J.P. replied immediately, as if we were already in the midst of a conversation.

"Me neither," Ben agreed.

As much as I don't really give a shit about what anyone else wants *while* I'm mixing, I'm more than willing to accept notes from the client. There's usually some middle ground that can be found for any difference in opinion, and if I completely disagree, I have an opportunity to make my case. Besides, by the time I'm playing a mix for the client, I *want* feedback.

"I can bring the organ down . . ."

Ben and J.P. recoiled at the suggestion, and took an almost defensive posture. They didn't want me to touch the mix. They wanted me to play it for them again, which I did. After the second playback, they asked to hear it again. I swear to you, I played that mix for them five times before J.P. finally offered an opinion.

"I think it's perfect."

Ben agreed.

I can't tell you how many people have commented on the boldness of the organ in that song. Ben isn't an organ player. The B3 was played by a sideman, and to have an organ as the main focus of a song could be argued as being counterintuitive in the context of his album, but then that would be an example of an external consideration, one that has nothing to do with the song and arrangement as they were given to me. This is exactly why we don't want to compromise with external considerations before we've even begun the mix. J.P. and Ben were the producers of this album, and they were the ones who made these calculations. They were the ones who left loads of room for the organ player in the arrangement, and the B3 player took what they gave. Even though Ben and J.P. never actually considered placing the organ that loud in the mix, it made perfect sense to them when it was delivered in that manner. The B3 is without a doubt the instrument that makes this particular production special. They just didn't realize it until I mixed it for them.

Let's set aside the mix benefits of a bold balance decision, the importance of which I'll discuss with you later. Had I mixed this particular song based on the preconceptions of the artist and producer, I would have come up short where the mix's fullest potential is concerned. Surely it's possible that we would have ultimately come to a similar conclusion had I attempted to balance all the instruments in a more conventional manner. This would be impossible to say. The point is, I didn't.

If you constrain yourself to a passive role in this process, you are most assuredly going to miss great opportunities.

Be aggressive!

These days there doesn't seem to be much distinction between "attitude" and "aggressiveness." They're often used interchangeably, but I might point out that there are such things as good attitudes. While aggressiveness is counterproductive in occupations such as anthropology and brain surgery, there are many jobs in which aggressiveness is a requirement. Mixing is one of them.

Aggressiveness, where mixing is concerned, is often equated with how one processes the mix, particularly in regard to compression. While this is certainly part of mixing aggressively, it's not really the defining point. Surely, you need to keep your mix in control. Compressors and limiters are great tools for harnessing your mix. But aggression where compression is concerned typically refers to artifacts caused by both overcompression and true analog tape compression. These artifacts include heavy breathing, lopped transients, and strident frequencies. This sort of effect can be heard on many Radiohead recordings, and it's a sound often used as a production tool by the recordist, producer, or mixer. Overcompression should not be considered a default way of using a compressor, unless that's somehow your personal "sound," and I always advise against having a "sound." For starters, it makes you boring and one-dimensional from a creative standpoint, and it only serves to make you more important than the artist.

While overcompression is indeed aggressive, you can use compression aggressively without obvious artifacts. Frankly, my overall definition of aggressiveness has far more to do with speed and decisiveness than anything else. Compression and limiting have a role in speeding up the process of mixing, and as such they are a part of mixing aggressively, but they also need to be used appropriately for the song, production, and genre.

The actual sonic shape you create with your compressors is far less critical than how you stick to your decisions in that regard. The process of mixing entails a long series of interdependent decisions. As it is, mixing is an exercise in chasing your tail. If you can't make decisions and stick with them, you're never going to finish a mix. Since all your mix choices are predicated on earlier ones, if you change your mind on an early decision, you risk completely dismantling your mix. This is particularly true if you go against decisions that affect the overall foundation of the track.

If you second-guess your earliest decisions late in the mix, I promise that you'll find yourself nearly starting over. If, for instance, you decide at the six-hour mark that you don't like the low-end relationship between your kik and bass—a relationship that affects the very foundation of your mix—you could very well lose several hours of work. While it's certainly important to work quickly and decisively, it's equally important to make good choices—ones that will stand up over the course of the mixing process.

That said, many early decisions in a mix are made with a limited amount of information. The mix is in a constant state of flux in the early stages, and until you have all of your parts placed in the mix, decisions won't necessarily be permanent. So it's okay to internally debate a decision, and it's normal to take several unfruitful paths in your mix, particularly when you're working out the best overall course. But once that course is determined, you need to stick with your decision in all but the rarest of circumstances.

The beginning of a mix is front-loaded with broad decisions, which act as a foundation for all the many detail-oriented decisions you'll make over the course of the mix. If you second-guess those early broad decisions, and you start to change them late in the mix, you're essentially tearing your mix down to its core. While there are occasions when this can't be helped, in general you'd be best to trust your early instincts. There's a good reason to trust yourself where early decisions are concerned—your foundation is laid with a clear head, while your desire to change that foundation is made in an intellectual fog. The back third of a mix is not a good time to go up against the good judgments of the first third.

Mixing fast is aggressive mixing, and it's always a good way to ensure you're mixing well. If you don't mix fast you risk losing sight of the big picture, and you could very well find yourself mired in details and unable to function properly as a mixer. I don't think I'm going out on a limb by telling you that this is not a desirable place to be while mixing. The aggressive act of mixing quickly virtually forces you to trust your instincts. If you can trust your instincts and thereby trust your decisions, you can avoid constantly second-guessing yourself. If you're constantly second-guessing your decisions, you can forget about finishing the mix, and you can kiss a good night's sleep goodbye, since you'll be worrying about your mix all night long. You might even find yourself mixing in your dreams—a nightmare if there ever was one, since nobody ever finishes a mix while they're sleeping.

Of course, if you get to hour 10 on a mix, and you realize your mix is completely fucked, you really have no option but to go back and start over. You won't be the first mixer this has happened to, and you won't be the last. The problem is you could very well be wrong. You're in a fog! Resist the temptation to make major changes in this state of mind. You're far better off leaving the mix and coming back to it later than to start fucking with its very foundation. If coming back isn't an option, take a long break, but changing early decisions must be left as a last resort.

Before the advent of DAWs, changing your mind on an early and critical decision (this would include anything having to do with the bottom end of your mix) meant coming back and spending a second consecutive day on the mix. On a DAW you don't have to operate within these kinds of constraints. You can come back to a mix any time you like, particularly if you're working on an entire album. While you're still going to have to spend a second day on the mix, it doesn't necessarily have to be the next day, and the passage of time allows you to come back fresh—days later if you want. Of course, if this is the first mix with a new client, you could very well have a problem, as finishing a mix is how you gain their trust.

If you're mixing on an analog console, you pretty much need to take a break and forge ahead. Skipping a mix on an analog console is not a particularly efficient way to work. Such a decision would require writing down the position of every knob on the console and outboard gear. Even if you have total recall available, it will take two to three hours to bring the mix back to its current state. Just from the standpoint of perception, tearing down an analog mix is a crushing defeat. In fact, it's such a poor option, I can't recall ever having chosen it.

On the surface it may seem like the ability to put away your DAW mix for another day is a huge advantage. On occasion it may be, but overall, it's actually a disadvantage. Tearing down a mix is an aggressive and definitive act lost to the perfect recall of a DAW. A mix on an analog console is dismantled once the mix has been printed. Getting back to that mix is relatively time-consuming, and there is no true exactness to the recall. Sure, you can get close enough, but recalling a mix in order to bring up an incidental part two-tenths of a dB isn't an option, and frankly, it shouldn't be. Not so on a DAW. The mix on a DAW is never really done, even if you proclaim it is. You can come back to your DAW mix over and over again until you've managed to suck every bit of life from it. Believe me, not only is that an undesirable effect, it's easy to do.

Since your mix on a DAW is always preserved in the computer, you are at all times just one last change from a completed mix. While that may sound like a good thing to many of you, there is a point where you can actually go past the mix. Printing the mix and moving on was always a great safeguard against your client bringing you past the mix. Surely a well-timed file save amounts to a similar safeguard, but you're far better off preventing the client from passing the mix in the first place. You don't want to risk getting into the comparison game between two relatively similar mixes. That's only going to confuse the shit out of everyone, including you. The perfect recall technology of a DAW works inherently toward allowing you and your clients to *avoid* finality. Avoiding finality is counter to aggressive mixing. If you work in an aggressive manner, then you work fast and furiously toward completing the mix.

When I'm mixing on an analog console, I start to get very nervous when the client wants to continue to make tiny little changes to a mix that's doing everything it's supposed to from a big-picture perspective. The line between details that improve a mix and details that destroy a mix is razor thin. Part of the aggressiveness on your part is protecting that line. Work hard and fast toward the end of the mix, and when you get there, protect it like it's your child.

Obviously, one final change of half a dB on the shaker isn't going to put you over that line. It's the unintended compounding of these tiny little changes over the course of time that is the inherent danger, especially once you've determined that the mix is done. It's incumbent upon you as the mixer to prevent your clients from going past the mix. Since you know there will be a point when you'll put a stop to your client's destructive ways, you may as well stop them the moment you know the mix is right. In other words, don't let your clients fuck up a good mix.

There's another inherent problem that results from the DAW mix that's never truly done: the mix never ages. I noticed early on in my career that the playback of mixes sounded completely different the moment the mix had been torn down from the console. The listening experience of a mix that's still alterable is considerably different from that of a 2-track playback of a mix that's not. I can't tell you for certain why this is, but it seems to me that when you can no longer make changes, your brain no longer seeks problems. We spend the lion's share of a mix listening for things that need to be fixed. Once we're forced to accept that changes can no longer be made, we get to listen to the overall impact of the mix.

Most of you who work on a DAW won't ever get the opportunity to hear this difference, at least not until the CD is pressed. This is too bad, because listening to a mix that can't be changed is actually the best way to know for sure it's great. It's always best to determine this before the first pressing.

Still, we must adapt to the advantages and disadvantages of any situation, and since the mix is never done, there could be a very good argument for working in a manner that leaves the finishing of mixes to the last day. At least that would allow you to work in an aggressive manner toward the completion of the mixes.

> *Just because a part was recorded doesn't mean it*
> *needs to be in the mix.*

I met with a producer once who played me his rough mixes before hiring me. I'll never forget the one song he played me with a string arrangement, which was completely fucking up the song. Even he acknowledged a certain distaste for the strings, and I suggested that we mute them come mix time. His response? "I spent $25,000 on those strings, and I'll be damned if they don't make the mix."

Rather than facing legitimate questions from the artist, manager, and label over the squandering of $25,000, this particular producer made the decision to keep parts that didn't manage to improve his song. Oh, I'm not criticizing his decision. He was stuck. What's he going to do—admit he really didn't test out his string arrangement sufficiently before committing to a string section of triple-scale players? Unfortunately, the strings did indeed stay, and the production and mix were weakened to the point that the track would never recover that $25,000 in the first place.

Then there's the whole "guest star" problem. More often than not, a guest performer of some notoriety somehow manages to record tracks that are nothing short of disappointing and useless. Coaxing the artist to recognize the failure of the guest appearance isn't the difficult part. It's convincing them to mute the failure that proves challenging. Artists are loath to cut guest performances for fear of insulting them. I might point out that the good feelings of a guest star have nothing do with what's best for a song or production.

Guest performers on albums are rarely brought in to serve the music, but rather to serve as some sort of gimmick. That may seem a bit harsh, but unless the guest is being brought in because they're essential to the production, it's a marketing ploy, and that's a gimmick any way you slice it. I'm not saying promotional considerations aren't valid. I want a song to sell as much as the next guy, particularly when I'm profit sharing on the success of that production. But the music is more important than the marketing ploy. Unfortunately, by the time a gimmick goes awry, the discipline needed to abandon it is often too great to overcome.

As the mixer, your first job is the ruthless removal of all that is bad for the mix and consequently for the song. If a part doesn't help the production it's not a part you should use. Unfortunately, if the producer insists that you keep a part in the mix regardless of your opinion, you don't have a choice. Ultimately it's not your decision. The artist, producer, and the label all have the power of veto. Really, all of your aggressive arrangement decisions could very well be put under the microscope and eventually vetoed. Your best defense against this is a great mix. The better the mix, the less likely those discarded parts will be missed.

There are occasions when you might actually inquire about the thinking behind a part. This strategy is particularly useful if your instincts tell you there will be resistance to the removal of that part from the arrangement. Interviewing your client is a good way to determine the exact standing of a questionable part, and you'll often discover a point of contention within the creative team.

Parts that are both featured and terrible can be particularly problematic to you as the mixer. At least if there's some internal disagreement among your clients, you can put your thumb on the scale. But if everyone other than you seems to be on the same page, then all you can do is state your opinion, and hope that the seed of doubt will take hold. If you decide to offer your opinion, you'll usually want to do so diplomatically, although there are times when coming right out and saying "it's terrible" is just the jolt everyone needs. Understand there are inherent risks to proclaiming your disdain for a part that everyone else adores. A veto of your opinion will cause the artist and producer to question whether you like your own mix. Nobody wants to feel as though the mixer hates her own mix. Of course, that can also be a good leveraging tool under the right circumstances.

In order to prevent problems, particularly before you begin the first mix, you should take some time to explain to your clients that you'll likely be muting parts. Follow this with the assurance that you can easily put a missing part back in if they happen to disagree with your decisions. Your clients will rarely have a problem with this, and if they do, you just saved yourself an awkward situation. Of course, if you build a highly focused kick-ass mix, you'll likely render many of those discarded parts useless in the context of your mix. And so it's somewhat of a self-fulfilling prophecy, but we'll keep that our little secret.

Even if your client insists that you use everything you were given in the arrangement, there are still muting decisions that need to be made. It's quite common to get two mics on one guitar cabinet. These are usually intended by the recordist to be used together, but you're in no way obligated to keep both mics in the mix, nor are you beholden to the recordist's blending of those two mics (should you receive the actual session files with balances). If the recordist bussed the two mics together, then he tied your hands, and there's nothing you can do. That's the tone you have to work with. If he recorded both mics onto different tracks, he's left the decision to you as the mixer. Make the decision.

It's also not uncommon to have tracks delivered with stereo guitars, pianos, keyboards, etc. You are not committed to any stereo recording treatment. Filling the mix with stereo parts only serves to create a mess of instruments coming from no particular place. Stereo pianos, for instance, often gobble up space when placed stereo in a mix. Now if the piano is the dominant instrument in the production with little competition, that's a fine treatment. Otherwise, piano is often better placed within the stereo field as a mono source. Furthermore, if you're supplied with any kind of "*faux* stereo" part, whether created by a mono source that's been copied and delayed, or by two mics on a single source, you should consider abandoning the stereo treatment. This kind of faux stereo doesn't break down properly to mono, and as much as we mix for stereo, you still need to be concerned about what happens to your mix in mono. FM radio often modulates to mono, and many consumer-grade computer speakers are daisy-chained and don't offer the full breadth of the stereo field, so how your mix breaks down to mono is still a concern.

Some instruments have a definitive stereo characteristic to them, and these are often best left in stereo. The spinning of a

Leslie miked from each side for instance, or the auto-panning tremolo from a Rhodes suitcase require stereo placement in order for the listener to properly perceive those effects. This doesn't mean you have to keep them in stereo, but they're certainly designed to be stereo, and this should be taken into consideration.

The overall vibe of the track is much more important than any individual part.

The overall vibe of a track is basically the big picture. There's no doubt that your attention to detail in a mix will separate a good mix from a great one. But those details must serve the big picture of how the song affects the listener. It's very easy to lose sight of the whole while you're mixing. How you make the listener move and sing, and how you focus their attention is based on how you use your arrangement. While individual parts have some bearing on the overall track, it's how the parts work in context with each other that makes a track effective.

We're going to go into great detail about this later, but everything in a mix is relative, not only from the immediate standpoint of what we're hearing at any given moment, but also from the perspective of how the mix unfolds over time. Every section sets up the next section in the song, and you need to evaluate how the arrangement carries the listener through time. The individual parts when combined properly make the mix, and that mix should be heard as a single 2-track entity.

Your Musical Brain

Mixing is half analytical, half big picture, and is therefore an activity that requires the use of both halves of your brain. The right hemisphere of the brain is responsible for viewing the whole. It's the big-picture hemisphere, and is considered the more creative side of your brain. The left hemisphere is the analytical side of your brain, and is responsible for the minutiae. While this is an exceptionally simplistic explanation of the brain, one that would horrify any decent neuroscientist, it should suffice for the purposes of this book.

As the mixer, you must be able to focus on detail to an exceptional degree while never losing sight of the big picture. Most people tend to use one side of their brain more than the other, although there are naturally middle-brained people. I'm one of them, but that's not automatically an advantage. It still takes vigilance to actually switch from detail to big-picture thinking.

We all think and use our brains differently. If you take a test on the Internet and discover that you're left-brain dominant, that doesn't mean you can't become a great mixer. It means you're going to have to put some conscious effort into viewing the big-picture aspect of a mix. Conversely, if you lean toward right-brain activity, you probably tend to have less patience dealing with the details, which means you'll need to put in some effort in this regard. From my experience, musicians tend to be right-brained, and as such they also tend to be the best raw mixers.

I suppose anyone who has acquired some modicum of proficiency on a musical instrument has a distinct advantage in mixing since they tend to think along the lines of arrangement. The lion's share of mixing is based on arrangement decisions, and this fact alone gives someone familiar with music and arrangement a head start. Further, given that musicians naturally lean toward right-brained thinking, they also tend to view the big picture far more readily than left-brained thinkers. This bodes well for creating a mix that does what it's supposed to overall, but it doesn't finish the job. Attention to detail in a mix is of equal importance to the big picture—they go hand in hand.

Of course, left-brain dominance is equally problematic. The job of a recordist is a left-brain-dominant activity, especially when there's a producer there to deal with the big-picture aspects of the performances. If you apply the kind of thinking that goes into recording to mixing, you're missing half the thinking that goes into a great mix.

While I can give you no real evidence that a musician would have a leg up on a non-musician in becoming a world-class mixer, it certainly can't hurt to know and understand music. Frankly, if you want to learn to mix, I think you need to learn about music as well, and this should not be discouraging news. It's all part of the learning process, and if you're serious about mixing (you bought this book, so I'm guessing you are), then you should probably pick up an instrument too. It really doesn't matter what instrument, so long as you start making and playing music. This will provide you with a sensibility that you can't possibly have without musical experience. Even a rudimentary understanding of music is better than none at all. So take some lessons, practice, learn a bit about music theory, and jam with a friend at your studio. Until you add music to your arsenal, you'll always be at a disadvantage.

Third-Party Mixers

In general, it's far easier to be aggressive when you're being hired as a third-party mixer than it is when you've been involved with the project as a recordist. Far be it from me to suggest that the recordist should never mix a project he's recorded, but there are certain advantages to being a mixer for hire. The specialization offers you the perception of authority, which can be important when dealing with major labels. Even as a seasoned mixer, it was rare for me to get the mix on projects where I was the recordist. The perception issue in the major label arena is often too great to overcome.

Many engineers have become adept at working the entire project. There are shops that are veritable production houses, and supply both the facilities and the entire scope of personnel necessary to produce the project. My good friend Slipperman, who co-hosts the Mixerman Radio Show with me, owns one of these shops. He overcomes perception issues by establishing himself as the patriarch of a project early on. If you own a shop, I would recommend this methodology.

I suppose the biggest problem with mixing what you've recorded is how insanely difficult it can be to go back to big-picture thinking, particularly when you've spent the better part of a month predominantly using your left brain for recording. It's not so much that it's difficult to go back and forth between the two brains—we do this all the time—it's that your job throughout the recording process has been almost purely analytical in nature. Done right, the producer is camping out on the right side of his brain, while the recordist is predominantly using her left. The recordist has spent the better part of the process trained to *avoid* the big picture. That's the producer's job. This makes the transition from recordist to mixer a mind fuck of epic proportions. The exception to this is when you're the producer *and* recordist. In that case you've spent your time on the project evaluating the music from both a right- and left-brain perspective.

Then there's the issue of aggressiveness. If you become an aggressive mixer, you'll likely become an aggressive recordist, and this can cause problems come mix time. An aggressive recordist will print the tracks exactly as they expect them to be mixed. This means all processing is performed as if the track is actually being mixed. I call this technique "tying the hands" of the mixer, and if you *are* the mixer, you just tied your own hands. I'm not arguing against this methodology; I'm all for it. But if you record in this manner, you have no option but to capitulate to your recording decisions come mix time. You will not be able to manhandle your tracks again. If you're used to mixing aggressively, you could very well find yourself out of your usual element. This can be overcome, but there's definitely a learning curve.

Personally, I can't stand recording in a non-aggressive manner. As a producer, I like tying my hands, as I trust my early instincts. But this means I've had to adapt to mixing less aggressively on projects that I've recorded and produced. Both methodologies are valid—you just have to choose which works best for you.

Forty years ago, it was unheard of to bring in a third-party mixer. But mixing at that time was a community event. Everyone had their hands on the faders and mutes, everyone was a part of the decision-making process. Records had a much shorter recording phase, so getting lost in the weeds was less of a concern. Limited tracks made it nearly impossible to postpone arrangement decisions or to engage in overproduction. Tape was considerably more forgiving, and engineers had to go through a methodical mentoring system. By the time you were actually recording, you were qualified to record. Today, the only qualification is that you own some gear.

I'm assuming you own some gear, so by today's standards you're qualified. I'm sure you've figured out by now that learning how to use the gear is the easy part. It's learning how to use the gear to maximize the impact of the music that's the challenge. Worry not! We've already gotten over the first major hurdle. Not only do you now understand what a great mix is, you have the mind-set necessary for creating a great mix in the first place. Good on ya!

Chapter Two

Arrangement and Focus

Function

Placing the vocal prominently in a mix establishes its importance. This is the primary method of harnessing the listener's focus. While the vocal carries the all-important melody and lyrics, it's still only one part of the total production. There are other parts in a track, and not only do those other parts have important functions, but our brains can actually decode them all at once. There are five basic functions in any given arrangement: melody, harmony, rhythm, response, and countermelody.

The melody, which is usually carried by the vocal, has the most important function of the arrangement and song. Clearly, we want the listener to focus mainly on the melody. The best way to accomplish this is to place the melody right in the center of the stereo field and as the loudest part in the mix. Just don't make it so loud that it takes away the listener's ability to decode the other parts of the arrangement. There *is* a track after all.

Harmony is basically the chord changes. Any instruments or combination of parts that are providing the harmony are giving chordal support (i.e., harmonic support) to the melody. Whether that support is provided by polyphonic instruments like guitar or keys, or by a group of monophonic instruments as in a jazz ensemble, if the role of a part is to support the melody with the chord changes, it's part of the overall harmony.

The rhythm of a track is what makes us move, particularly internal rhythm. While the drums and percussion often supply much of the rhythm on any given modern track, just about any other instrument can perform a rhythmic function in the arrangement. The bass, for example, often offers a profoundly rhythmic foundation in conjunction with the drums.

How you mix the rhythmic parts within the track depends on how important they are to the overall production. In modern pop and rock the rhythm tends to play a prominent role—particularly the backbeat (the two and the four). In hip-hop the rhythm is even more important—particularly the downbeat (the one and the three). In any given arrangement there are also internal rhythms. Within a drum pattern the internal rhythm is typically provided by the hi-hat and ride, but internal rhythm can come from other places as well. Percussion, guitar, and keyboards, for example, can all provide internal rhythm in a track.

Response refers to "call and response," which is found all over Western music. Traditionally, the term *call and response* refers to those situations where the singer offers the call and the chorus the response. The Who's "My Generation" is a great example of this technique. Roger Daltrey sounds the call: "People try to put me down," and the band sings the response: "Talkin' 'bout my generation."

Response can also be instrumental in nature. If guitar licks occur between vocal phrases, those parts act as a response to the vocal. This kind of musical response is designed to momentarily grab the listener's focus and pass it right back to the vocal, and while there can be some minor overlap, for the most part a response part rarely steps on the vocal. When it does, it's not a bad idea to ride the response level down at the point of overlap.

The countermelody is a separate melody that plays in conjunction with the vocal (or primary melody). It's commonly subordinate to the melody, and often operates within contrasting rhythmic phrasing and melodic motion (going down while the primary melody goes up). Put in more simplistic terms, when the melody moves, the counter typically holds, and when the melody holds the counter usually moves. If the countermelody doesn't weave its way around the vocal, then there is an inherent risk that the countermelody will compete for the listener's focus. When you come across this problem there are really only three options—cut the counter-melody, bring the countermelody down, or bring the vocal up. Frankly, the last option is the worst of the three. If you're forced to place the vocal too prominently in your mix because of a competing part, you risk weakening the track significantly. The more effective a countermelody is, the louder you'll be able to place it in a mix without pulling the listener's focus from the vocal.

Any given part can play more than one role in an arrangement. A guitar playing a countermelody or harmony could also offer rhythmic support, depending on the part. Even a tom beat can function as both rhythm and countermelody. The Genesis song "Mama" is a good example of a tom beat playing a countermelodic role in conjunction with its rhythmic function within the track.

If you view a mix from the perspective of these five functions, you simplify mixing considerably. A drum kit and percussion can easily occupy 20 tracks in a rather large mix, yet they all serve a rhythmic function in the arrangement. You can break those 20 tracks down to a stereo pair. Many mixers naturally create stereo subgroups in order to manipulate them as a whole—myself included.

Arrangement isn't just about what parts come in when—arrangement is also about how loud a part is within the context of a track. The relative balances of the parts will have a profound effect on how the listener hears the performance. As we've already established, a good arrangement is designed to cause a physical reaction. If importance is placed on the rhythmic instruments in a track, in both their quantity and prominence in the mix, the track is clearly designed to cause the listener to dance. Much of our modern music is designed around the principle of causing the listener not only to sing, but to dance as well.

Couple a heavy beat with a vocalist singing trite lyrics about moving *to* the beat, and it would be nothing short of ridiculous to bury the drums in the mix. You're mixing a dance song. Given the relative unimportance of the lyric and the abundance of rhythmic parts, it should be clear that the beat is designed to have a more prominent role than the vocal. This doesn't mean you're going to bury the vocalist, particularly if she's a kick-ass singer. But you certainly don't want to place her in such a way that she weakens the driving force of the song. The parts themselves provide you with the information you need to mix the song. In this case the singer is literally *telling* you how to mix the song. There's a word for this: prosody.

Prosody

Prosody is the consistency between lyrics and music. For the songwriter, prosody is an important tool. A song in a minor key with a sad melody is going to have a sad lyric. If it didn't, it'd be a bit weird. A song like "Wind Beneath My Wings" by design has a melody and a lyric that are both meant to be inspirational in nature (to someone other than myself, I'm sure). The emotional impact of the music is generally going to match the lyric, and this is the most basic form of prosody. Most good songwriters use basic prosody naturally and without even thinking about it, but there are also more literal examples of prosody.

In the song "Stop in the Name of Love," the melody actually stops on the word "stop." The melody does precisely what the lyric says. The word "stop" is sung, and the melody stops on that word. That's prosody. A melody moving up on the word "up" or down on the word "down" is another great example of prosody in songwriting.

Good prosody isn't always quite so obvious. In Johnny Cash's song "Ring of Fire," the melody in the chorus actually moves up as he sings the word "down" three times. He sings: "I went down, down, down, and the flames went higher." While at first blush, the lyric seems to literally contradict the melody, in reality Johnny is exposing the inherent contradiction between *falling* in love as opposed to love being an *uplifting* experience. This idea is represented brilliantly by the imagery of the lyric and specifically how it works counter to the melody, thereby illustrating musically the contradiction. There's no doubt that this was a conscious decision by a great songwriter.

I bring up prosody here because as mixers we need to be aware of not only how the lyric interacts with the melody, but also how the melody and lyric interact with the production. Steven Stills's famous '60s song "For What It's Worth," which was first recorded by Buffalo Springfield, is an excellent example of how prosody was enhanced by the production. If the song doesn't immediately come to mind, you'll probably recognize the chorus lyric, "Stop children, what's that sound, everybody look what's going down." In the last chorus of that song, the entire production comes to a halt on the word "stop." Now, that was probably done in the recording process, not the mixing process, but these sorts of opportunities are often overlooked, and if you watch out for them, you can take advantage.

Another example of prosody from a production standpoint would be the Genesis song "Just a Job to Do," in which Phil Collins sings "bang, bang, bang" in quick succession followed by two reverberant snare hits and the lyric "down they go." In this case, the snare hits act as gunshots within the production. This is not only effective, it's smart.

Don't go nuts with this. If you add reverb to the snare every time you hear a word like "shoot," or "bang," you risk turning a good tool into an overused joke. The literal translation of a lyric into a production technique is good when used sparingly, particularly if the prosody accentuates something important within the context of the song. Furthermore, don't use prosody to accentuate your role as the mixer, unless the song happens to be about the mixer (which occurs sometimes in hip-hop). If you turn up the vocal when you hear the word "up," you're viewing prosody from the context of a mix move. We don't ever want the listener to notice the mix, and that wouldn't fall within the spirit of prosody as it relates to the production.

Mixing Is an Illusion

Much like a painter uses angles and shadowing to create the illusion of a three-dimensional image on a two-dimensional canvas, we create the illusion of three-dimensional space from two speakers. When you add time into the equation—given that a production unfolds over the course of time—we're actually operating within four dimensions.

In the greater context of the animal kingdom, hearing is not our most powerful sense. Even relative to our own senses, sight is what we rely on most heavily for processing external information about our surroundings. Given the awful choice between losing our eyesight or our hearing, the majority of us would most certainly choose to keep our eyesight. Perhaps some of you would choose hearing, but that would probably have something to do with your interest in making music.

Our senses are our way of processing information. While we get unique information from each sense, it all breaks down to *information*. Whereas we as humans use our eyes to move about our surroundings and avoid running into obstacles, a bat uses its remarkable ability to process sound reflections for the same purpose. Dogs can "see" with their intense sense of smell, which is so exceptional that they can actually see backward in time.

Our brains are constantly and simultaneously processing external information, and each of our senses influences the others. If, for example, you hear an unfamiliar child screaming, you will likely choose to investigate further. Seeing this child smiling and laughing as she screams will change how you interpret the screams. Food that smells delicious but looks unappetizing will reduce your desire to eat it.

I always find it fascinating to hear TV theme songs on the radio. How our brains process music that's normally tied directly to video can be quite a surprise the first time the two mediums are separated. I had this experience when I heard the original theme from *Star Trek* on the radio. Without the video, the mix sounded completely different to me. It was so odd to hear it in this manner that I actually had to internally debate whether it was indeed the *Star Trek* theme song, despite having heard it hundreds upon hundreds of times. The absence of visual context allowed me to hear things in the music that I'd never actually noticed before.

Visual stimulation will affect how you hear. So much so that when I get toward the end of a mix, I turn down all the lights and shut off the computer monitor. If you don't do this, try it. Believe me, you'll hear your mix completely differently when you're not being influenced by what's on the screen. Reducing the amount of visual stimulation makes your hearing more acute—there's no doubt about this.

Obviously, you can't work the entire day with the lights down low. There are certain procedures that must be implemented using our eyes, particularly with DAWs. The analytical, left-brained attention to detail in mixing can only be attended to if we can see what we're doing. It's the right-brained, big-picture thinking that's most effectively performed with minimal visual stimulation.

When you get really good at mixing and producing music, your hearing becomes so acute that you actually will be just as comfortable with that sense as you are with sight. Hearing becomes nearly the same as seeing when you develop the sense to a certain level. Fortunately, you don't need to wait for years to see what you're hearing. If you go to your control room and place yourself directly in the middle of the stereo field, you can experience this for yourself right now.

Turn off your computer monitor and lower the lights in your control room. Don't make it pitch black. That can be just as distracting. Play a song that you consider to be a stellar mix. As you listen to the song, try and actually "visualize" where everything is coming from in the mix. Close your eyes if it helps. If you're truly placed within the stereo image, you'll notice instruments that are coming at you from the left, and some that are coming at you from the right. Some parts will sound louder than others, and those parts should literally appear more forward and bigger than everything else. If the vocal is placed properly in the mix, you can actually picture it in your mind like a big head floating in the middle of the mix. Your low end will appear to come from below the speakers, rather than directly from them. Your top end will appear to come from the top portion of your speakers (level with the tweeters). If there's a part with reverb and delay on it, that part will appear farther away. Parts that are completely dry will appear close to you, particularly if the part is louder relative to other parts in the mix.

When you conduct this experiment, your brain is translating what you hear into what you see. This is a powerful and important tool for mixing, particularly when you understand how to manipulate this visual representation from within the virtual dimensions of your mix.

Planes of Space

In a stereo image there are planes of space that we use to create a four-dimensional image (the fourth dimension being time). All in all, I've determined that there are five basic planes of space replicated by two speakers: panning—left to right; frequency—up to down; balance—front to back; reflectivity—far to near; and contrast (dynamics)—sparse to dense.

Panning—Left to Right

It never ceases to amaze me how many people get wigged out by wide mixes. This is especially so in relation to their own music and despite an overabundant precedent to the contrary. There's only so much space available to us in our mixing palette. Using the full spectrum of left and right is just as important as using the full spectrum of the frequency range. As far as I'm concerned, anyone who would consider using less than the full width of panning available to them might as well also consider using filters to cut off the very top and bottom frequencies of the mix.

Equally befuddling to me are those who believe that we should all be mixing in surround sound. The large preponderance of music is listened to in stereo, and until that changes dramatically I'm not mixing for four speakers (okay, five and a subwoofer) any time soon. For starters, I can't tell you how often I walk into a store and end up switching wires on one of the speakers in order to put them in phase. Most people can't get two speakers wired in phase. What then is the likelihood of your average punter successfully wiring four speakers in phase? At least with stereo they have a 50/50 shot at getting their speakers wired properly. With four speakers, they have a 50/50 shot times two, which means that if left to chance there's a high likelihood that one of the four speakers will be wired out of phase. Besides, it's difficult enough to find a household with an actual established center position in a proper stereo field—we're going to erect four speakers in perfect symmetry how?

Let's face it: Most people don't sit down in a listening room to play their favorite music. They do, however, given the preponderance of boom boxes, computer speakers, earbuds, and cars, often find themselves in some reasonable vicinity of the stereo field. Therefore, there's not much argument for using anything less than the entire field.

Panning is the most underutilized plane of space in a mix, particularly by neophyte mixers. It's a mistake to not use the entire width of the stereo field, because you're abandoning valuable space. For many professional mixers, myself included, the pan knobs are rarely anywhere but left, center, or right, and there's even a name for mixing like this—it's called LCR mixing (which stands for left/center/right—go figure). This isn't to say that there aren't times to soft-pan parts, but in my experience, this should be a rare occurrence in most modern music mixing. Wide mixes are considerably more exciting since you're using the entire width of your palette.

My recommendation is this: When in doubt, pan hard or don't pan at all. Over time, you'll figure out when to use internal panning positions. Background vocals are often a good candidate for this. Soft-panning a mono Rhodes in a predominantly guitar-driven mix can be a reasonable solution, particularly if the guitars are panned hard (as they should be). A single acoustic guitar is certainly best soft-panned in a guitar/vocal production. So there are certainly times to soft pan; it's just that overall, hard panning is usually the better option.

Now, you might be thinking of several modern rock tracks that clearly don't make use of the entire stereo field. This kind of mixing was en vogue for a period of time, but there's really only one reason a professional mixer might choose to use less than the full stereo field, and that's the perception of increased loudness.

Basically, loudness has to do with the amount of dynamic range that's being used in a mix. The less dynamic range, the more the audio information is pressed up against digital zero, and the louder the mix will sound compared with other mixes at an identical monitoring volume. Anyone with a diverse library of music in their iTunes library or CD tray has noticed that some productions are inherently louder in comparison with others. When you find a mix that isn't using the stereo field to the fullest, odds are that this was done purely for the purposes of loudness.

So let's think about this for a second. In the case of the ultra-loud (and mono) modern rock track, not only has the mixer managed to avoid using the entire stereo field, but he's also reduced his dynamic range down to nearly nothing. We only have so many tools for making an exciting mix. In this case, two of them have been removed right from the get-go. That better be one hell of a vocal and song.

Frequency—Up and Down

Just like we have width in a mix, we also have height, and this is an illusion that's created by frequency.

Frequency is somewhat technical in nature, given that it's basically explained with physics. I don't really want to get bogged down too heavily in the science, but we need to touch on some basic information, particularly since EQ is the most used and abused tool of a mixer. Besides, if you're going to think in terms of frequency, you need to have a basic understanding of it.

The human range of hearing, and I'm being exceptionably charitable here, extends from 20 Hz to 20 kHz. In my experience, most people can't hear above 18 kHz, and even if they can, that ability will drop considerably over time. Anything below 20 Hz is nothing more than rumble and anything above 20 kHz tends to be nothing more than noise (hiss or spitting, take your pick). That doesn't mean there isn't useful information extending well above 20 kHz (many of us believe there is); we just can't actually hear it directly, and so we can't properly manipulate frequencies this high. The rumble caused by 20 Hz only serves to shake our woofers violently, which I can assure you isn't great for their overall longevity.

High-frequency soundwaves require less space to fully develop than long, drawn-out low-frequency soundwaves. Consequently, higher frequencies are far more directional in nature. Consider a garden hose for a moment. When set to "jet," the spray from the hose is focused and highly directional in nature. Very little spray goes to the left or the right. When the jet stream hits a hard object, it immediately reflects. When it hits a soft object (like a towel), it's absorbed. This is precisely how high-frequency waves react.

When we adjust our hose to a gentler, wider setting, the spray goes everywhere. It's not directional in nature, and it doesn't reflect much, as it generally gets everything in the area wet. This is precisely how low-frequency soundwaves react. This is why you can put a subwoofer just about anywhere in the room. The low end goes everywhere, traveling easily along (and through) walls and floors. High-frequency waves are directional in nature, and you have to actually be in the line of fire of the tweeters or horns to get their full brilliance.

Frequency also relates directly to music. All musical notes correspond to a fundamental frequency. For instance, the open E string on a bass has a fundamental frequency of 41 Hz. This is the loudest frequency that can be heard from a plucked E string. The tones we deal with from musical instruments are caused by vibration, which produces both a fundamental tone and overtones (or harmonics). The first overtone (which is the second harmonic) is always an octave higher than the fundamental. If the fundamental is 41 Hz, then the octave above it is double that, in this case 82 Hz. All harmonic octaves extending up are doubled in frequency. The next harmonic is a fifth higher than the first octave, and the next a fourth higher than that (which together equals an octave, and thus the third overtone on that low E is 164 Hz). The harmonics continue infinitely, and they can be mapped out in what we call the Harmonic Series. Since the fundamental is the loudest frequency on any given note, our brain perceives this as the actual note, but the harmonics are what provide us with the timbre of an instrument. Without the interaction of harmonics in sound, a piano would sound just like a guitar which would sound just like a sine wave.

Great skill is required for a musician to properly make an instrument sing. Everything from how the string is plucked, hit, or blown will affect amplitude (loudness), which also affects timbre (tone), which affects how we hear the harmonics, which affects how we perceive the note. Further complicating matters are the acoustics of the room in which the player is performing and how we perceive the reflections of sound from any given location.

Then of course, there's recording technique, although if the player is generating beautiful sound in a great acoustic space, technique is greatly reduced as a factor. Put simply, the better the player's technique is, the less important the recordist's technique needs to be. A great player performing in a great-sounding room will be recorded easily and with little need for processing (barring some desired effect). A lousy player will tend to lack evenness in tone and balance, and will therefore require more processing in both the recording and the mix.

Equalizers (a.k.a. EQs)

As mixers and recordists we use EQ as our main tool for manipulating frequency; that is, as long as the frequency we're seeking to manipulate actually exists. For instance, barring some proximity effect, there is little to no low-end information on a violin played in its uppermost register. Conversely, there is minimal high-frequency information on the low B from a five-string bass. Boosting 40 Hz on that ultra-high violin is going to give you nothing more than unwanted low-end ambience from the room. Boosting 16 kHz on the bass guitar is generally going to bring up unwanted line and string noise.

Much like the fundamental of a note, parametric EQs (digital or analog) deal in a fundamental frequency. There are two types of EQ adjustments on a parametric EQ—bell curve and shelf. On a bell curve EQ, the selected frequency is the center frequency within a specified range. The width of this bell curve is called the

Q, and the wider the Q, the more frequencies will be affected by either a cut or boost.

Shelving EQ, of which there are only two—high shelf and low shelf—also affects a range of frequencies, but the selected frequency is the starting point, not the middle point. For example, a high-frequency shelf set to 10 kHz will affect all frequencies from 10 kHz up, regardless of whether you're applying a cut or boost. Conversely, a low-frequency shelf set to 100 Hz will affect all frequencies from 100 Hz down. Most analog EQs will have a high and low shelf (usually also selectable as a bell) with one or two midrange bell curves. Many plug-ins, aside from those that supposedly emulate an analog piece of gear, will include a low and high shelf with four or five bell curve EQs.

Along with shelving EQ, we have filters at our disposal. There are two kinds of EQ filters: the high-pass filter (HPF), which allows the high frequencies to pass unabated, and the low-pass filter (LPF), which allows the low frequencies to pass unabated. An HPF set to 100 Hz will filter out all frequencies from 100 Hz down. An LPF set to 10 kHz will filter out all frequencies from 10 kHz up. I've seen some engineers, particularly outside of the United States, put HPFs on all channels as a matter of course. I would recommend against this unless there's some low-end artifact from the room that you need to remove. Until you have the entire arrangement at your disposal, you generally shouldn't be making a decision as to how far you want the bottom end to extend unless you're absolutely sure you're filtering out totally unwanted information.

Since any given note includes the harmonics above the fundamental, and since any given instrument will sound within a range of notes determined by the physical characteristics of the instrument—and the physical abilities of the player—an EQ will affect far more than a given note or even a range of notes. You can actually locate and boost particular harmonics on any given part.

DAW EQs usually provide the mixer with a visual representation of the frequency manipulation. This visual representation also represents how wide your Q is, and you can actually see the range of frequencies you're affecting. While the visual modeling is useless for making your EQ decisions (those are made purely by ear), it's quite useful in accelerating your understanding of EQ in general.

While every instrument has a range, and while a good arranger will select instruments that fit in certain ranges to achieve a certain frequency balance, it's not so important for you as the mixer to have these ranges memorized. You don't actually have to know what the top note of a cello is, as you can only deal with what's provided to you. It's pretty easy to tell that a cello fundamentally occupies low-end space while simultaneously offering the high-frequency grind of the bow against the string. Your EQ decisions will be made based on how a part works within the track, particularly where frequency is concerned.

For our purposes in mixing, we can break down frequency into four basic ranges: low end, lower midrange, upper midrange, and high end. I've compiled a list of some basic frequencies, how we hear them, and how they might affect your mix.

Low End

20–30 Hz: This is mostly rumble and/or subs. These are not frequencies you want to be actively adjusting unless there's a problem that you wish to actually filter out, like air conditioner rumble. In general this is not a good range for applying an EQ boost.

30–60 Hz: These frequencies are quite low and "boomy" in nature, and will not replicate in most small speakers. This range should be considered when compromising between types of playback systems (i.e., a boom box or full-blown stereo system with subs). While this frequency range is particularly useful in making a mix sound big, it can easily overpower the mix in general if too abundant.

100 Hz: This frequency is low but punchy and is easily replicated in a six-inch speaker. It's a far more focused low frequency than the subs, although it's still not high enough to be considered directional in nature.

Lower Midrange

250 Hz: This is the start of the lower midrange. It can be described as "woofy," as it's not a very clean low end. Too much 250 Hz can cause a mix to sound thick, dark, and muddy. Too little of this frequency and your mix will sound scooped out and lacking in power. This frequency replicates well in a two- to four-inch speaker, and can be quite useful for making the bass audible in boom boxes.

500 Hz: This frequency is the middle of the lower midrange. It is often accused of sounding "boxy," and for good reason—it sounds boxy!

750 Hz: This is getting toward the upper end of the lower midrange. This frequency is also boxy in tone and tends to reduce clarity in a mix; however, it can also add presence to a part in the right situation. If you find yourself cutting or boosting this frequency often, you either have a monitoring problem or your console has a natural buildup in this range.

Upper Midrange

1 kHz: This is the beginning of the upper midrange. It's an exceptionally "present" frequency as it's getting close to the peak of our hearing. This can be a very handy frequency for bringing out presence, but can also sound boxy if used too liberally.

2 kHz: This happens to be the basic frequency of a crying baby, which might explain why it's our most easily heard frequency as humans. Too much of this frequency and "harsh" will be an adjective you'll often hear when someone describes your mix. This frequency is at the upper end of the presence frequencies.

3–4 kHz: This frequency range, much like 2 kHz, is helpful in adding or removing bite from a recording.

6–9 kHz: This is the tail end of the upper midrange. This is where we exit the "bite" range and enter into dentist drill territory. This range of frequencies can give you a nasty headache, and quick.

High End

10–12 kHz: This is the lower end of the high-end frequencies (say that three times fast). The addition of this frequency range can be helpful in opening up a sound and/or offsetting the coloration of a microphone, or processing.

16 kHz: This is extreme high end. It will often add artifacts as quickly as it will open up a sound, but it can still be quite useful, depending on the overall quality of the EQ.

18–20 kHz: This range is beyond most of our actual hearing, and while there is definitely information that extends far beyond our hearing, bringing this range up with EQ tends to add audible spitting and noise. Even if you can hear frequencies this high, you don't want to aggressively boost this information.

Since different instruments occupy particular ranges of notes, by default, they also occupy a particular range of frequencies. For instance, a bass covers the low to lower midrange. Yes, we can boost 5 kHz on a bass and bring out some upper harmonics and string noise, allowing the note to cut more, but when playing in its normal register, the bass doesn't fundamentally occupy the upper midrange space. Kik drums also cover the low to lower midrange, and although we've all heard plenty of clicky kik drums, those particular upper frequencies are transitory in nature.

Note duration has much to do with how much frequency space an instrument occupies. Since attacks on the bass and kik have a short duration, that momentary burst of high-frequency information occupies very little space in your mix. Of course, if you have a hundred double kick drums per minute, like on some death metal tracks, then the aggregate of that attack will take up quite a bit of space in your mix.

We are really dealing with only about eight octaves in music and mixing. Some instruments, like violins, have a limited range within those eight octaves. Other instruments, like piano, guitar, or Hammond B3 organ, work within that full range. As a result, pianos and organs can take up an enormous amount of frequency space within a mix. While full-spectrum instruments like keyboards tend to excel at filling in a mix, they also tend to eat up space. Some rock mixers actually choose to mute keyboard parts on a guitar-driven track as a matter of course. As I've said before, and will say again, I don't recommend doing anything as a matter of course.

I always find it handy when explaining frequency and how it relates to a mix to discuss Beethoven. Clearly, Beethoven didn't have a console. If he wanted more low end in his mix, he had to either write more low-end parts and/or direct the instrumentalists within that range to play louder. Beethoven used instrumentation and direction to give himself more bass. Like Beethoven, we also have instruments that fit within certain octave ranges at our disposal; we just control their balances electronically.

As important as it is to think along frequency lines in a mix, that's only one consideration. If you feel your mix needs more high-frequency information, but the rhythm of the tambourine is clashing with that of the picking guitar, one of them has to go. Believe me, you often have to make choices like this in a mix. When you come across a part that's causing you problems from both a frequency and performance perspective, the mute button just might be your best option.

The more buildup there is in a certain frequency range, the more difficult your job is as a mixer. For instance, if a production has a Farfisa organ, multiple guitars, and piano all playing in the same narrow middle range, you're going to have a considerably harder time fitting them all into that space than if they're spread out across the full spectrum. If there are two basses, a djun-djun, a low tom beat, and a cello, you're going to have a hell of a time carving out enough space in the low end to avoid a muddy, undefined mess in the bottom of your mix. And if there's too much high-frequency information in the mix, the mixer and subsequently the listener are going to find themselves exhausted in short order.

The power that frequency has over the listener should not be underestimated. How you use frequency information in a mix can have a direct bearing on how that mix makes the listener feel. How your parts fill the frequency spectrum in an arrangement can be just as important as how they fill their role musically. Keep this in mind as you mix.

Contrast—Sparse to Dense and Bright to Dark

Contrast relates not to what is happening at any given moment, but to how the mix works over the course of time—the fourth dimension of your mix plane. Whereas we can listen to a mix and immediately hear frequency, panning, and balance decisions, we discover contrast decisions over the course of the mix.

Contrast is used to create the illusion of dynamics in modern music. By definition, dynamics is a variation in force or intensity, especially in musical sound. Unfortunately, dynamics in music has been greatly reduced over the years. Generally speaking, we've completely eradicated tempo fluctuations from modern music, and these days we don't use much more than about 4 dB of dynamic range from the loudest to the quietest parts of a mix. In fact, the loudest mixes don't even use *that much* range. While 4 dB may seem small, if you wish to hear the softer parts of your mix in the car, or while the dishwasher or vacuum is running in the next room, you're not going to get away with using much more range than that. This means that we need to create the *illusion* of dynamic range, and we accomplish that with contrast.

When I mixed Ben Harper's "Roses for My Friends" (from his third album, *Will to Live*), I originally sculpted an enormous dynamic range for the mix. The chorus was incredibly exciting because it was so much louder than the verses. Unfortunately, once I got the mix into my car, I found myself just tuning out until the chorus kicked in. What was an exceptionally effective payoff in the sound-isolated studio became a completely nonexistent payoff in the real-world environment of a car. Given this problem, we brought the verses up 2 dB in level during the mastering phase.

Now while we had to reduce the actual dynamic range of the mix in order for it to work in a real-world environment, the mix wasn't by any means ruined. On this particular track, the dynamic range is naturally enhanced by the contrast in overall density between the two sections. The verse is sparse and sweet, while the chorus is dense and aggressive, so we get the illusion of more dynamic range than actually exists. That's a good example of contrast providing the illusion of greater dynamics.

There are other ways to produce contrast. Suppose you have a single electric guitar panned hard left on the verse with no other harmonic part to balance it out on the right. Given this panning treatment, your mix during that verse will be wholly asymmetrical in nature. If a second guitar comes in on the right at the chorus, at that point the mix will have symmetry. The contrast between the asymmetrical panning in the verse and the symmetrical landscape in the chorus will accentuate the payoff and produce dynamics. Whereas the panning in the verse provides us with an unbalanced stereo image, the panning in the chorus provides us with a contrasting balanced image. But there's more in play here than just contrast in symmetry. There's also contrast in density. Implemented properly, density can make a bigger and louder chorus with more power and an intensified payoff.

To continue with our previous example, if we add a Rhodes in its lower register and place it in the verse opposite the guitar, we will now have stereo symmetry in the verse. This will greatly minimize the symmetrical contrast we had earlier—but where we've lost we've also gained. There is now a contrast in frequency that occurs between the dark Rhodes in the verse and the (presumably) bright, gritty electric guitars that take over in the chorus. It doesn't matter where the contrast comes from, as long as it exists.

There will be times when you will need to manufacture contrast. Certain genres require the mixer to create the dynamics throughout the whole song. I've mixed many hip-hop tracks in which every part and sample played from the top to the bottom of the track, and I was completely responsible for creating an arrangement, contrast and all.

That said, contrast, while a definitive plane of space, is nothing more than a tool. Just as you can mix a song in mono, and thereby reject all that great stereo width, you and the producer can choose to use little to no contrast. How blatantly or obviously you use contrast depends on the track. Sometimes the contrast will come from the song itself. The more powerfully the song pushes you forward as a listener, the less the producer and mixer need to worry about contrast.

Reflectivity or Reflection—Far to Near

Reflectivity is the illusion of space. Whereas we accomplish the three-dimensional illusion of width, height, and depth through panning, frequency, and balance, respectively, we accomplish the illusion of reflectivity within all three dimensions plus the fourth—time.

Sound exists within the context of its surroundings. We don't just hear a direct sound source (unless the source happens to be right next to our ear); we hear sound within a certain space. A drum struck in a small room sounds completely different from the same drum struck in a hall, which sounds completely different from a drum struck at the precipice of a giant cavern. We perceive the sound and space by how the soundwave travels, and its reflections over time. The amount of time it takes for a sound to fully dissipate in any given space is called decay time. We all know that a large hall will have a much longer decay time than a small room, but in either case those reflections occur over time.

The decay time of any given room is determined by its overall size and shape, as well as the nature of the materials contained within the space. An empty large hall will have a considerably longer decay time than when it's filled with people. That's because people absorb sound, and the more absorptive materials there are within a space, the shorter the decay time will be. The more reflective surfaces there are in a space, the more the sound will bounce around.

Just as the contrast plane relates to time, so too does reflectivity. In fact, how we perceive reflectivity is defined mostly by decay time. For instance, the smack from a snare hit will travel through a room and reverberate. Depending on how big the room is, that reverberation will be perceived to occur some quantifiable amount of time after the snare is actually struck. We usually measure that time in milliseconds, since many reflections fully decay in under a second. There are 1,000 milliseconds in one second.

Reflections will appear to us as reverb in enclosed spaces, and as delay (with the possibility of some reverberation) in open spaces, particularly where there are obstacles nearby. While reverberation is the quick, successive bouncing of a soundwave throughout a space, delay is a singular reverberation caused by a sound traveling for a significant distance, hitting an object, and returning back to us. We've all experienced this kind of delay in real life; whether we are yodeling across a ravine (who among us can resist this?), or calling out to a friend near a large building, we perceive a one-time direct reflection from a distant object as delay.

We perceive space and distance based on both the quality and length of the decay. We also perceive our relative distance from a particular source based on frequency response and the ratio of direct source to reverberation. The more reverberation in the ratio, the farther away a sound source will appear to us, although one must also consider the context of the mix.

You can't create the illusion of distance within a mix purely by drenching a sound in reverb. Internal balances determine the depth plane of a mix, and the relative balance of a sound must appear low in the mix in conjunction with the reverberation. Furthermore, since high end is so directional in nature, it will typically reflect and dissipate if anything gets in its way, so we can further enhance the illusion of distance by rolling off high-end frequencies from the sound source.

If you want to create the illusion of a dog barking way in the distance within a mix (don't ask me why a dog is barking in your mix, just go with it), you would have to place it low in the mix, roll off the high end, and add plenty of reverberation. Putting the barking dog low in the mix places it back in the sound field, but the reverberation provides the illusion of distance, and the attenuated high-frequency response assists with the illusion.

Sometimes reflectivity is contained within a recording, as would be the case if you put a room mic on the drums. Sometimes reflectivity is added into the mix after the fact to create the illusion of a space that didn't exist during the actual recording. Unfortunately, our control of reflectivity in a mix only works well in one direction. Whereas reflectivity can easily be added, it really can't be taken away. Sure, we can use gates and mutes to cut off the decay at the moment a part goes tacit, but we can't take away the audible room reflectivity while the part is actually sounding. This is why so many recordists use close-miking techniques when recording. When you consider the possible ramifications come mix time, it's better to err on the side of too little space than too much. The best way to do this is to control how much reflectivity gets into the mic in the first place.

Personally, when I'm looking for the sound of "big" rock drums, I record them in a large space built with reflective materials (like concrete or wood, depending on how live I want the sound). In general, I prefer not to put off overall reflectivity decisions, as I'm not particularly fond of digital reverb. I'd rather have the real thing, if possible. Of course, that doesn't mean I don't take steps to give myself some control later.

Even close mics will pick up reflectivity from a large concrete room. Well-placed baffles and other deadening materials in somewhat close proximity to the kit can offer immense control over how much reflectivity is picked up by the close mics. In an especially live room, this can be a necessity if you want to have any control over the illusion of space. The room mics—which in this case would be far outside the baffle zone—are responsible for capturing the excitement and reflectivity of the room. This technique offers considerably more control in regard to how much (or how little) reflective information I can put on the drums come mix time. In this particular scenario the room mics act much like a reverb return (or a chamber), since they're picking up the aggregate of the room reflection rather than the aggregate of the direct source.

As you can imagine, if you were to place the entire band in a large concrete room, things would get pretty messy rather quickly. Even if you were to record each instrument separately, one at a time in that large room, the reflectivity would be captured on every instrument mic. You would have no way of reducing that reflectivity later once it was recorded. This would tend to smear the overall sound to such a degree that the listener would have great difficulty making out the nuances of the performance.

If you're provided tracks covered with room reflectivity, your hands are pretty much tied. There's not a whole lot you can do about the number of spatial artifacts present in your mix. You're resigned to deliver nothing more than a reverberant mess. To make matters worse, the moment you add a compressor to any part, you'll merely bring up the reverberation of the room within the context of the source. Fortunately, most recordists and mixers realize the danger of this fairly early on in their careers, so you're far more likely to get close-miked instruments without overbearing amounts of reflective information.

Recordings in which reflectivity has been harnessed are far easier for mixers to deal with than the opposite scenario. We have all sorts of digital reverbs and delays at our disposal to create the illusion of a space in the context of any given part. How much or how little reflection you choose to add to your mix depends on the song and production.

It's not uncommon to mix and match acoustic spaces in a mix. For example, it's rare to find crunch guitar or bass tracks recorded in a large room with an overt amount of room reflection. This is true even on tracks where a large room is used for the drum treatment. The listener is rarely offended by the reasonable use of mixed spaces, even though they couldn't possibly encounter such a scenario in real life. The drums can sound like they're in a large, reflective space, and the guitars can sound like they're in an anechoic chamber, with no ill effect on the listener. This is really the only way we can create the illusion of a rock band in a large room without the resulting product sounding like nothing more than a smeary mess.

Still, you have to be careful about how you mix and match acoustic spaces within a mix. You don't want to create a combination that is so foreign to the listener that it pulls them out of the mix. If, for instance, the entire band is recorded in a bone-dry, carpeted room, with little to no reflective information, and the singer sounds like he's in an indoor basketball stadium, this could be a bit disconcerting for the listener. Flaunting your power to break the bounds of physics where acoustic space is concerned can serve to distract the listener and make them notice the mix. Remember, if the listener notices the mix, then it's not a good mix. In the case of roomy drums and dry guitars, you're creating a spatial illusion—one that listeners have bought into for a great many years. Therefore, it's important to evaluate exactly what you're trying to achieve when you address the spatial landscape of a mix.

If the singer is performing a song where the desired illusion is intimacy, then you're certainly not going to drown her in a large hall. You probably don't want any space whatsoever in that scenario. Intimacy is personal, and a personal performance would be done in either a living room or a bedroom (wah, wah, wah, wah!). If you want the singer to sound like they're singing softly in your ear, then you should probably avoid any kind of reflection in your mix.

If, on the other hand, the singer is performing a dramatic ballad, then you'll probably want the benefit of a soaring reverb and/or delay on the vocal, among other parts. This treatment not only provides the illusion of a large space (which makes the listener feel as if the song is being sung in front of the entire world), but the long reverb tail also accentuates the drama of the song.

In general, drums and percussion react well to reflective treatment, since short, percussive bursts don't lose much clarity from the acoustic slap of a reflective space. Electric crunch guitars, on the other hand, lose all clarity within an overly reflective space. Sometimes that's the desired effect, but usually not. Spring reverbs, plates, and delays are far more appropriate for electric guitars, and if they're part of the amp signal, the player will adjust how she plays based on how the effect reacts. Violins become far less aggressive sounding in a large space, so this is a great way to soften the overall tone of the instrument. If the violin is supposed to be aggressive, then you don't want a reflective treatment. If, on the other hand, the violin is meant to be soothing, then reverb is probably the best call. Singers are also good candidates for reflective treatment, although it's important to consider the overall feeling of the track when choosing the size and decay time of the reflection.

In general, long reverbs tend to soften sound. If the music you're mixing is aggressive in any way, then dramatic reflectivity can counter the desired effect. When you put a long, sweet reverb on a hard-rock vocal, you instantly soften both the vocal and the production. Yes, hair-metal bands from the '80s often used reverb, but hair bands don't generally perform hard rock; they perform pop rock in the guise of hard rock. The whole point of using reverb on a hair band is to soften the tone to appeal to a wider audience. That's not to say you can't use reverb in hard rock (particularly if it's nice and ratty), but you should consider exactly how that reflectivity affects the overall tone of the production.

How you deal with the spatial reflectivity in a mix can completely make or break a production. Too often mixers use reverb as a reflex rather than as a tool for manipulating the listener. Think of reflectivity as creating an illusion appropriate to the production. If the production works great with no additional space, then leave it as it is. If the production is in need of spatial illusion, add it.

Balance—Front to Back, Large to Small

Balance is a game of relativity and is the holy grail of the five spatial planes. I've left balance for last since it affects everything in a mix.

Fundamentally, the balance of an instrument has to do with how loud it is in comparison with all the other parts that are playing at a given moment. A loud vocal doesn't exist in a vacuum. We deem it's loud because it's loud in comparison to everything else in the mix. All internal balances are merely an exercise in relative comparison. Balance is our most effective tool for directing the listener's attention. If we make the vocal loud, the listener will tend to focus on it.

Every physical adjustment that we make in a mix is nothing more than a balance adjustment. A pan knob is a balance knob between speakers. Turn the pan knob to the left, and you're turning up the level of a part in the left speaker and down in the right. Boosting or cutting a particular frequency is literally altering the balance of that frequency within the context of the part you're processing.

> *Putting everything proportional in a mix will make for a shitty mix.*

An overly balanced mix reduces contrast, neglects to offer the listener a clear focal point, and therefore reduces forward motion. Given this, a perfectly proportional mix does a poor job of manipulating the listener's emotions. In other words, an overly balanced mix would be the exact opposite of a great mix, and this is without doubt a common mistake in mixing. It's like a disease.

I've actually been thanked on more than one occasion for my "unbalanced mixes." I don't know for certain, but I think that would insult most mixers. I can assure you it's meant as a compliment and taken as such. Frankly, there's nothing more boring than a perfectly balanced mix.

Balance isn't just about the relative levels within a mix. Balance also exists within the other planes of a mix. The louder a part is within the context of the mix, the bigger and more up front that part will appear. A loud, robust vocal placed smack in the middle of the stereo field (really, where else are we going to put it?) will not only appear more forward than any other part in terms of planes, but it will also take up the most space in the mix. Not only is it louder than the other parts, but it fills up the entire stereo field, and occupies a large frequency range.

The lower a part is placed within the mix, the smaller it will appear. While high-end frequencies have the energy to cut through the other parts, low-end frequencies need volume in order to generate energy. Therefore, a part placed back in a mix has an inherently reduced low-end push, particularly compared with the more forward parts in the mix. Low end and level are what make a part sound big. Reduce both of those relative to everything else in the mix, and that part will sound small.

Forward Motion

Good songwriters, whether unconsciously or consciously, use a variety of tools to force the listener forward in a song, and these can get pretty deep into harmonic theory. We're not going to go there, but I'll give you some specific examples of tools that can be used to push a listener forward through the craft of songwriting.

Reserving the highest melody note in the song for the chorus is an effective way of boosting the payoff, since a higher melody line in the chorus relative to the verse tends to generate more excitement. Reserving a particular rhyme for the chorus is also effective. If the verses and the pre-chorus use "ee" and "ay" vowels in the rhyme structure, and an "oh" rhyme is reserved for the chorus, this can serve to increase the payoff. Accelerating the rate at which the chords change is an exceptionally strong technique. If, for instance, the chord changes in the verse occur at a rate of once per measure, as compared to two changes per measure in the pre-chorus, this will have the effect of pushing the listener toward the chorus.

Then there's accelerating the melodic structure, particularly in conjunction with the rhyme structure. If the verse rhyme structure is ABAB, and the pre-chorus rhyme structure switches to AABB, particularly with shorter and more frequent melodic phrases, this will effectively hurl the listener into the chorus.

Good songwriters understand that the tonic (which is the root note of the key) essentially ends forward motion. We learned in grade school that the tonic was "home." Avoiding the use of that particular melody note until the chorus serves to enhance the payoff. Certain chords produce forward motion, like sus chords (or suspended chords), where the third of the chord is replaced with the fourth note in the scale. Our brains naturally want the fourth note in a sus chord to resolve. If I played you a sus chord, and asked you to sing the next note, you would naturally sing the third of the chord. This was a common technique used by both Genesis and Phil Collins, although it's certainly not unique to them.

While this isn't a book on the craft of songwriting, it's important to understand that a good songwriter employs specific tools for the purpose of pushing the listener forward. I've only named a few of these tools. Not every tool is used for every song, and just because a particular tool isn't used doesn't mean the song is weak. Furthermore, the songwriter may or may not use these tools consciously. When I was actively songwriting, I used many of these tools unconsciously, and didn't even recognize them as tools until they were defined for me in college. Frankly, those definitions helped me more as a producer than as a songwriter.

Now, these sorts of tools alone are not what make a song great. If the melody and lyric are less than compelling, the listener has a very effective tool of their own for forward motion—it's called the skip button. So, good content trumps forward push. In other words, a songwriter can employ every tool in her arsenal, but if she writes a lousy melody and stupid lyrics, it doesn't really matter; the song is irrelevant, and so is forward push.

You can go as deep under the songwriting hood as you like, and I encourage you to do so, but the important concept to grasp here is the principle of forward motion. While you can't control what tools the songwriter used, you have tools of your own. You as the mixer have an active role in promoting and accentuating that motion.

A good producer is going to supply you with everything you need to push the listener forward and accentuate the payoff. That doesn't mean you can't fuck it up with your mix if you don't pay attention. Arrangement as it relates to balance is a crucial part of good mixing. Not only will the parts themselves dictate forward motion, but how you place them in the mix will too. Much of the excitement in a mix is created by the constant forward push toward the chorus. The chorus is often referred to as the "payoff" for precisely this reason. A mixer can use balance, not only to assist with forward thrust, but also to enhance the payoff. This is achieved through relativity.

Relativity

Every balance decision that you make affects the mix in an equal and opposite manner, particularly as it relates to what comes next in the song.

You should always think of balance in purely relative terms. Setting aside the complicating factors of the stereo bus compressor, if you bring up the drums, you've also essentially brought down all the other parts. If you bring up every part but the vocals, you've pretty much brought down the vocal.

Relativity also exists between sections. Whatever is currently happening in a mix serves to set up what happens next. The push and pull of balance is the fulcrum you use to manipulate the listener forward. If you bring the entire verse up 1 dB in overall level, the listener only perceives that level change relative to the sections before and after it. If you bring up a simple snare fill before a chorus, you've effectively added an exciting push forward for the listener. But if you bring that snare drum up too much, you can actually weaken the entrance of the chorus by making it seem small in comparison.

You should give as much weight to how a balance decision affects the current section as you do to how it affects the next one. Two electric guitars blaring from the top to the bottom of a mix do little to enhance contrast. Bringing down the relative level of the guitars in the verse would be a reasonable solution to the problem. While the timbre of the instruments won't change, the level difference will provide you with some contrast. Muting one of the guitars might prove even more useful for promoting forward motion and payoff. Or you could let the mix just be static, but if that's your decision, the song better have plenty of forward motion on its own. Otherwise your mix is going to fall short. Just because the songwriter and the producer ignored the benefit of a good payoff doesn't mean you should. Someone needs to stop the insanity—it might as well be you.

Suppose we have an egg shaker on a rock production that plays relentlessly in the verses. An egg shaker can wreak havoc on the payoff of the chorus, particularly if it stops once the verse ends. It doesn't really matter how great the egg shaker works in the context of the verse if it ultimately destroys the chorus payoff. This is far too great a price to pay. I use this example because shakers, particularly egg shakers, which contain mostly high-frequency information, can be difficult to bring in and out of rock mixes, as they often have the undesirable effect of causing the guitars to sound dull when they go tacit.

These are extremely broad generalizations, and I'm a bit reticent to provide more. Not every shaker will dull every track, as that's frequency-dependent on both the overall program material and the shaker itself. You can make an egg shaker far louder on a sparse R&B track than you can on a rock track. That's because the basic sonic landscape of an R&B track tends to make less use of the midrange than your basic rock track. Shakers don't cause the low end to sound dull in contrast. Shakers dull parts that exist in the upper midrange—like guitars. Not so with tambourines. You can bring those up as loud as you like.

Relativity affects everything in a mix. If you bring up the low end on the bass, you risk making the kik sound too small. If you place a big, beautiful acoustic guitar on top of a gritty rock band, you could very well dwarf the drums. If you pack a mix with parts in the upper midrange, you'll probably be forced to place the vocal exceptionally forward in the mix, as all those midrange parts will compete directly with the vocal.

Each and every balance decision causes an equal and opposite balance reaction, both in real time and in what lies ahead.

I could go on for hours with rhetorical examples of balance decisions that can potentially affect other balance decisions, but the specifics aren't going to be of much help. From a pure process perspective, balance decisions are the lion's share of mixing. These sorts of interdependent decisions are made constantly throughout a mix. But if you start to think about your balance decisions based on how they affect what comes next, you'll have a far easier time achieving an effective mix in terms of the big picture.

Visualizing Space

If you can visualize your mix and use all five planes fully and in a well-thought-out manner, you bring yourself a long way toward creating a mix that does what it should. This is especially true if you can start to work relativity to your advantage. It's not enough to think about how a part sounds in the mix; you have to think about how the part *affects* the mix, both in terms of the moment and in terms of what comes next.

To review: We have five planes of space that fit neatly within the four dimensions of width, height, depth, and time. Panning uses balance across the speakers to provide us the illusion of width; frequency uses balance across the spectrum to supply us with the illusion of height. Contrast is balance relative to the next event in time, which provides us with both real dynamics and the illusion of dynamics. Reflectivity creates the perception of space based on how it's balanced within all four dimensions of the mix. And balance in conjunction with the other four planes provides us with the perception of depth, making balance the driving force behind all five planes.

Easy. Now let's make a mix.

Chapter Three

The Mechanics

There's a stunning lack of linearity involved in the process of mixing. While the beginning and end of a mix are relatively defined processes, it's that massive middle chunk where you are seemingly always fucking up the mix. This remarkable lack of linearity can be ascribed to the utter interdependence of everything in a mix. It's a complicated puzzle, in which blind luck can be just as useful in finding a given solution as considered evaluation.

The mixing process is front-loaded with broad decisions in an unfocused mix, and back-loaded with minute adjustments in a highly focused mix. Whereas an internal balance change of 1 dB is nothing short of miniscule at the beginning of a mix, it's a stunningly enormous adjustment toward the end. The more focused and refined your mix becomes, the more minute your adjustments will tend to be, to the point that any change to the mix is a detrimental one.

Clearly, if you've never heard the song you're going to mix, it's going to take you some time to completely familiarize yourself with it. You're going to notice relative strengths and weaknesses in the tracks. In general, you'll want to maximize the strengths, and minimize the weaknesses, although admittedly that's not always the case. You're also going to find a whole series of problems, all of which need solutions. As you delve further into your mix, some of those problems may very well be self-inflicted. This book can't save you from self-inflicted mix problems. I'd have to be able to save myself from them first. Tail chasing just goes with the territory of mixing. Welcome to the club.

Discovery and Framing

Discovery is the process in which you gather information about your new track. Before you can start making decisions regarding the mix, you need to learn the song, the parts, the recording, the performances, and how they all work together. If the track is simple, the discovery process will be a relatively short one. If the track is bloated with the seemingly infinite remains of deferred arrangement decisions, you could find yourself in the discovery process for many long hours.

The parts you choose will directly affect how you mix the song. If you accept this premise (and you should), then you really can't start mixing until you know exactly what's in your arrangement. There's just one tiny little problem. You can't possibly determine the overall purpose of a part unless you actually listen to it within the context of the track itself. Given this, you have to actually build a mix as you go through your discovery. I call this *framing*.

Framing is the "broad strokes" process of building your mix. It's an important counterpart to the discovery process. One cannot be accomplished without the other. As you build your frame, you'll make discoveries; as you discover, you'll build your frame.

Since you're going to have a great number of decisions to make over the course of the mix, the early stages are a good time to identify problems within the track and determine the relative strengths and weaknesses of the production. A track with a mediocre drummer in the middle of an otherwise solid band will require a different mix approach from the same track propelled by a solid drummer in the middle of an average band. Typically, you're not going to go out of your way to showcase the worst player in the band. These value judgments will drive your decision-making process in the mix.

As you derive more information from the track, and as you prepare more parts for the frame, you'll surely change your mind about a great many things—especially early on in the mix. This is a normal part of the process. Your initial mix judgments are inherently flawed, given your complete lack of information. The good news is that no one will die from your first best guess, and the label representative isn't waiting in the back of the room to rush your mix to the pressing plant.

The discovery and framing processes are mostly investigative in nature. The completion of your frame is what forms the foundation of your mix. Until your foundation is set, all decisions are temporary. As such, you should be open to all possibilities. This is the time to experiment with any ideas that come to mind. It's through experimentation that you'll make your greatest discoveries.

Your value judgments regarding the song's strengths and weaknesses will have a direct bearing on how you approach your frame. Suppose the drum part on a track is nothing particularly special, and the bass part is not only compelling, but provides a solid groove for the track. Given this circumstance, you should probably lead with the bass. If you treat the bass with the importance it deserves, no one will ever notice the drums. Besides, a great bass part can be just as effective—if not more effective—than a drum part where rhythm is concerned.

Take Michael Jackson's "Billy Jean," for example. Obviously, the drums aren't weak in this song, but they certainly are simple. The kik hits the one and three; the snare hits the two and four. That's it. And although the kik and snare are the most forward parts in the mix, it's the bass part that makes us move. Yes, there are internal rhythms driven by the shaker and the hat, and they're important in how the track makes us move, but the bass is the unmistakable driving force of that bed. Frankly, I feel the bass part is mixed too low for the track. But that has *everything* to do with the mixing and production trends of the time as compared to now, and should not be taken as a criticism of either Quincy Jones or Bruce Swedien's mix judgments. I think there's way too much reverb on Michael's vocal, too, but that's how songs were mixed in the '80s. (I realize I've just offered mix notes on the most successful album of all time, but I have to provide *something* juicy for the kids on the Internet audio forums to talk about.)

Ultimately, you'll probably program automation on your mix. How much automation you'll need depends on a number of factors, including the relative aggressiveness of the recordist and producer, the overall scope and size of the arrangement, and your own personal level of compulsiveness. Don't let the word "compulsiveness" throw you. It's gotten a bad rap over the years given its clinical definition. While compulsiveness might be a somewhat negative trait for your spouse to exhibit, it's a wholly necessary one as a mixer. Still, there are specific times to be compulsive, and the early stages of a mix don't qualify. So before you exhibit that beautiful compulsive nature of yours (don't let anyone tell you otherwise), you need to operate in broad strokes. Your goal at this stage of the game is to create a reasonably solid static mix, one in which the large majority of your part decisions have been made.

While there will certainly be arrangements that are in desperate need of some heavy-handed pruning, it's a reasonably safe bet that you'll be using most of the parts in the session. Given this, you might as well dig right in and start mixing the beast. Since you need context to make arrangement decisions, there's no reason to fuck around. Start with the meat of the track, and no, that's not the vocal.

Surely, the vocal is the primary focus of the track, but it's the track itself that forms the foundation of your mix. If the track doesn't kick ass, the vocal will be ineffective. In particular, the bottom of the track acts as the overall foundation, and in most modern music, that's going to be the bass and drums. Since bass alone offers no useful context, you should start with the drums.

Phase Coherency

The multiple microphones that surround a live drum kit provide more context at the beginning of a mix than any other single instrument. Although you'll occasionally find drum kits recorded with only one or two mics, the usual fare is more in the order of eight to 12 mics, all recorded to their own discrete tracks. Given the abundance of microphones, drums are the first instrument that we can actually process, balance, and for that matter, mix.

Multiple microphones contained within a 6 × 6-foot swath of real estate can be nothing short of problematic. Microphones in close proximity to one another can cause phase coherency issues, and it's best to discover and fix phase coherency problems early in the mix, particularly when there's nothing else to distract you. This is yet another argument for starting with the drums.

Microphones have distinct pickup patterns, and when those pickup patterns intersect, they interact. This can cause wacky things to happen, including the total eradication of certain frequencies and the odd skewing of center information within a stereo image. When either of these symptoms occurs, you have a phase coherency issue.

The general rule of thumb is, the better the drummer, the less mics the recordist needs. A great drummer has such control over her own balances and is so consistent in tone and timbre that nothing more than a well-placed pair of microphones is needed. Of course, that doesn't necessarily prevent a given recordist from putting 20 mics on a world-class drummer. It also doesn't prevent you from muting some of those mics, particularly if you discover phase coherency problems.

The most egregious example of a phase coherency issue is reverse polarization, and this phenomenon can be easily demonstrated. All you need to do is reverse the polarization on one side of a stereo track. This can be done physically by switching the two input wires on the back of one passive monitor (active monitors have XLR inputs), or electronically by inserting a plug-in with a phase reverse engaged on one side of the stereo track. A polarity reversal button (virtual or otherwise) will have the following symbol on it: $\varnothing$

If you work on a DAW, you will be quite familiar with the visual representation of a soundwave. Any portion of the wave that is above the null point (the center line) is positive, and any portion of the wave that dips below the null point is negative. In the most simplistic terms, the positive part of the soundwave pushes the speaker out, and the negative part pulls the speaker in. If you reverse the polarity, you are literally reversing the soundwave so that the positive becomes negative, and the negative becomes positive. By reversing the polarity on one side, you will in effect cause one cone to push out while the other pulls in.

If you've never heard what reversed polarity on one side of a stereo track sounds like, you need to. Experiment with this using your favorite professionally mixed reference track to be sure you have some identifiable center information to evaluate. Played normally, the vocal will seem to come from the very center of your two monitors. Played with one side reversed, your center will become so skewed and evasive within the stereo image that you'll feel as though the music is actually surrounding your head rather than emanating from the speakers before you. As if that's not weird enough, you'll also lose a considerable amount of low end. This polarity reversal is often referred to as "180 degrees out of phase," which is the maximum that two signals can be out of phase with one another. If you haven't done so already, I highly suggest you learn what this sounds like, memorize it, and become allergic to it.

On paper there is no worse phase coherency issue than two signals 180 degrees out of phase with one another. In practicality, there's no more desirable phase coherency issue to have, since it's so easy to fix—simply depress the phase reverse button on one of the two sources and *bam*—everything's great! It's the gradations of phase coherency that are far more problematic. In reality, a phase coherency issue of 90 degrees is the worst problem to have, since reversing polarity will only serve to make the tracks equally and oppositely out of phase. I can't even begin to tell you how to get two mics to be precisely 90 degrees out of phase with each other, but you'll know it when you come across it—your phase reversal button will be rendered mostly irrelevant.

Phase coherency will also negatively affect two combined mono signals. If you point two microphones directly toward each other, for all intents and purposes, they will be 180 degrees out of phase with one another. While there's no stereo image to skew between the two mics, there will most certainly be a significant loss of low-end information. Many recordists like to mic both the top and bottom of a snare drum: the top mic essentially faces the bottom mic, with the snare drum between them. If these two mics have been combined on one track, there's nothing you can do about it other than to hope and pray the recordist knew what she was doing. I can promise you, if the recordist didn't reverse polarity on the bottom mic, you're going to be adding a whole shitload of low-end EQ onto that snare track. If the recordist gave you both the top and bottom mics separately, then you'll have full control over their relative polarity.

Whenever you get a top and bottom miked snare, you should select a plug-in that has phase reverse as an option and flip the polarity of the bottom mic while listening to the two mics combined. If you're working on an analog console, you'll probably have a polarity reversal button on every module. Be sure to get the blend of the two mics reasonably close to how you imagine them. Balances between combined mics in close proximity will greatly affect how they interact. Once you reverse the polarity of the bottom snare channel, you'll either lose significant low end, or you'll gain it. If you gain low end, the mics were out of phase with one another; if you lose low end, the polarity was right. Even if you somehow prefer the snare with the bottom mic 180 degrees out of phase, you should still get your phase coherency right. There are way too many other mics that will interact with the bottom snare mic for you to leave it like that. You should get your coherency right, and use your EQ and compression to shape the tones.

Some problems aren't nearly as simple as two snare mics facing one another. For instance, in relation to the overheads, you could find that the kik drum gets considerably deeper when you reverse the polarity on it, but this tonality change can occur at the expense of a punchier, sockier low end. Which tone is better really depends on the track, but you would be hard-pressed to change the recorded tonality of the kik in this manner unless you find it to be plainly better for the track as a whole. In this particular example, there probably wasn't an issue of phase coherency between the overheads and the kik—not one that needed to be addressed, anyway.

You should also check the phase coherency between any and all stereo pairs of microphones. Frankly, it would be quite an accomplishment for you to spend weeks working on a track with two overheads 180 degrees out of phase, so this is an unlikely event. But check anyway, at least until you're completely allergic to stereo phase issues.

Now, if one overhead is indeed reversed, then you'll want to figure out whether it's the left or the right one that's the problem. If reversing the left overhead (over the snare) negatively affects the low-end information on the snare, then you'll want to reverse the polarity on the right overhead. Conversely, if reversing the right overhead eradicates the low end on the floor tom, you'll want to reverse the left overhead. If reversing the left kills the snare low end and reversing the right kills the tom low end, then you're going to have to reverse one of the overheads *and* the corresponding mic below it. Fun, huh?

It's not uncommon for a stereo pair of overhead mics to be 180 degrees out of phase with all the close mics. This usually happens when an XY pair was set up facing the kit behind the drummer. Your recordist should have dealt with this, but we're not trying to lay blame here. Your only concern is getting the mics to work in the best way possible. There's little benefit to mentioning phase reversal issues to clients unless you really have it out for the recordist. Bagging on the recording team is usually not recommended, as it can surely backfire.

By the time I get to mix as a producer, I'm usually pretty familiar with any phase coherency issues. But shit happens. Microphones occasionally get bumped just moments before that perfect take, and then moved back without a word. So phase coherency issues can happen to anyone, even the most compulsive recordists and producers. Even if you're familiar with the track, allow yourself the time to go through the full discovery process on the drums, experiment with phase reversal, and make sure you didn't miss some coherency issue during the recording process.

Keep in mind that any microphones that are in close proximity to one another can have phase coherency issues. You need to check the coherency on double-miked guitar cabinets, double-miked acoustic guitars, and stereo-miked B3s, piano, percussion, etc. For the record, while there are occasions when two mics on one mono source works out well, I find it's usually one mic too many.

Drums

As you frame your initial drum mix, you will only have the context of the drums themselves, but this should tell you plenty right off the bat. For instance, the size of the room the drums were recorded in will be quite apparent as you bring up your mics. If the drums were recorded in a large, reflective room with little baffling, the close mics will surely contain some room information. This will tend to tie your hands a bit as a mixer, as you can't eradicate the reflectivity captured by those mics. If, on the other hand, the close mics are relatively dry in nature, you've been given considerably more control over how much reflectivity you can use on your drums.

As we discussed earlier, the reflective information from a large room, which then folds back into the close mics, is difficult to change. Your two options are to gate the close-miked drums (either with a noise gate or by editing between the drum hits), or to sample-replace the drums. I abhor both options, as they sound highly unnatural, but regardless of my opinion on this, there will be times when such treatment is appropriate. You would think the producer would provide the sampled drum tracks if she was interested in such a distinctly unnatural sound. Regardless, if you believe you can improve the overall continuity of the drums within the track by gating, sample-boosting, or sample-replacing them, then by all means you should do it.

Gating toms is a common technique for reducing their sympathetic ring, although completely eradicating that tone is noticeably unnatural in a live kit. If you find the ring to be too overbearing in the overall drum mix, and you'd rather not have to automate every single tom hit, you can always make a duplicate copy of each tom track, leave one wide open (as recorded), gate or edit the copy, and combine to taste. As long as the two tracks are in the exact same time-stamp locations (and we're talking to the sample), you'll have no issues with phasing. This technique will offer you control over just how much ring there is without completely negating the gluing effect that the tom ring provides a drum kit.

For my money, noise gates are a relatively archaic piece of gear, particularly since you can easily program mutes on an automated console, or quickly edit out the junk with your DAW. I'd much rather edit the track than have to deal with the inevitable misfires of a gate. The principles are the same, so the methodology is purely a matter of preference.

Some mixers like to combine an overall compressed signal on the drums with the uncompressed individual drum channels. This is called parallel compression, and it can be an effective technique. Parallel compression applied to a drum kit is sometimes referred to as New York compression, reportedly because it was a popular and fashionable technique in that region. While there is no single effect that parallel compression offers, as it depends largely on how you blend the compressed and uncompressed signals and how heavily you compress the drums, it's certainly a technique you should explore.

Parallel compression can also be quite useful on individual drums. For instance, if your kik drum is a little woofy, blending an overcompressed kik signal with the uncompressed one will give you more attack without diminishing the low-end push. Go ahead and pin the input meter on the compressor if you like, and adjust the blend to taste. You won't need very much of that compressed signal to get the desired benefit of a hard attack. This is an especially useful technique for hip-hop, since it's so important to get that massive low end from your kik without completely sacrificing its punch. Drum loops are also good candidates for this technique. Frankly, parallel compression works best with analog compressors, particularly fast-acting ones, like any of the dbx 160 series compressors.

While a full live drum kit is the most common setup for a rock mix, hip-hop, R&B, and pop music often use drum loops and/or programmed drums. There's not a whole lot I can tell you about mixing programmed drums, other than to balance EQ and move on. Compression isn't typically necessary on a sample, unless perhaps the producer went a little overboard with the velocity programming. Drum samples rarely sound natural, and usually aren't meant to, so they're not particularly challenging to deal with. The same cannot be said about drum loops.

Drum loops are nothing more exotic than pre-mixed drums. Loops are sometimes stereo, sometimes mono. Bringing up a drum loop can give you instant satisfaction as a mixer. *Bam!* Drum mix done. Well, maybe not. If all you have on your drum palette is a loop or two, you'll probably need to manipulate those loops to maximize the effectiveness of your mix. EQ processing can be slightly problematic, as it will affect the entire drum mix uniformly. If you add low end in the hopes of pushing more air with the kik, your snare drum tone could become overbearingly beefy. Likewise, if you add more crack to your snare with a 2 kHz boost, you could make the transient on the kik unbearable. Such is the nature of loops.

Working with loops is the ultimate exercise in compromise given the limited control you have. In most cases, you won't have to perform surgery. I mean, the producer and artist have been listening to the track with that loop for a while now, so unless they're clueless, the loop is probably going to work. However, there are occasions when extreme measures are necessary, and if duplicating a loop and chopping it up for boosting purposes helps the overall impact of the mix, by all means do it. You can even use phase reversal techniques on a radically EQ'ed copy of the loop in order to cancel out certain frequencies. Multiband compression is a useful tool as well. Be as aggressive as you need to be with a loop, but only as aggressive as you have to be.

Regardless of whether you're mixing live, programmed, or looped drums, your context in the early stages of framing is limited to the drums themselves. As telling as this can be, you won't have a firm understanding of the big picture until you have considerably more parts. For all you know, those awesomely huge room mics could be completely wrong for the track. Conversely, those wickedly dry drums, which sound as though they were recorded in an anechoic chamber, could be in desperate need of some reflective treatment once you bring up the other parts. You can't make your full treatment decisions until you have a reasonable understanding of the overall production. Given this, it would be pointless to spend an inordinate amount of time trying to overhaul drums that could very well work perfectly with the track. Until you discover otherwise, work quickly, process the individual drums, make them work together, and move on to the bass.

Bass

The bass can be the most difficult part to get right in your mix. It's the part that I slave over, since a strong bass and a solid bottom are critical to an effective mix. The best way to make a mix appear big is with bottom end. Unfortunately, an overbearing low end can also swallow the mix whole, so there's good reason to pay special attention to this area. Without a solid foundation, your mix will crumble, and I promise you, the bass is an integral part of that foundation.

There are two main issues in dealing with the bass. The first is how you approach the overall marriage and interaction of the bass and kik. The second is how you provide strong low end without washing out the overall musical movement of the part. There's nothing more disappointing in a mix than a bass that is merely taking up low-end space and making no real musical contribution. This could very well be your only available option if the bass player is weak or uninventive in his part. If, on the other hand, the bass player is strong and creative, it's incumbent upon you to make sure his part is prominent in the mix without letting it steal the show.

How mixers deal with the low end in their mixes is what separates the men from the boys in this business, and I consider myself quite manly in this regard. I spend an inordinate amount of time making sure my low end is exactly right. Solid low end is what makes a mix sing (which we'll talk about in a moment). Frankly, I'd rather have a weak drummer than a weak bass player. Absent a strong bass part and performance, a mix falls apart like a house built directly on a swamp.

Your only context for the bass at this early stage will be the drums; the kik drum in particular. The bass, unlike the kik drum, is a harmonic instrument. While the fundamental frequency the bass produces is wholly dependent upon the note that's being played, the bass will generally take up an overall low-frequency space. Likewise, the kik takes up an overall low-frequency space. The trick lies in providing a clear separation between your kik low end and your bass low end. The way to do this is to allow one to go above or below the other.

As we discussed earlier, lower frequencies appear lower within the sound field. The bass should appear lower on the frequency plane than the kik, or vice versa. It really doesn't matter whether the kik appears to be below the bass or the bass appears to be below the kik. That decision should be made based on which you think is more effective for the track. What matters is that you consciously create a low-end separation between the two instruments.

Sometimes this is an easy decision. If you're given a recording of a five-string bass in conjunction with a punchy kik drum that has a fundamental low-end push at 100 Hz, your kik drum is going to go above the bass—that decision was already made by the recordist and producer. While you certainly have the power to alter the low-end relationship using EQ and phase coherency techniques, there's no point in overriding a decision that already works. For less obvious decisions, you need to consider where the kik and the bass are most effective within the context of the mix. If the bass part is strong and integral to the mix, this should get first consideration, particularly since it's harmonic in nature.

The easiest way to throw a bass into a lower-frequency space is to combine the DI track with the amp. If you don't have both a DI and an amp track, you can't use this technique. Fortunately, it's rare to only get one or the other. Placed in their natural time-stamped positions on the recorded session, the amp will naturally be slightly behind the DI track in time. If you zoom in on the two bass tracks in your DAW, you can visually see this delay. By combining the two signals, phase coherency will affect the basic low-end space that the bass part occupies. Furthermore, if you reverse the polarity on the DI track, you'll probably notice a tremendous shift in the overall tonality of the bass. Depending on the relative balances of the DI and amp tracks, reversing the polarity on one of those signals can make the difference between the bass occupying the space above or below the kik.

There is no way to get absolute separation between the kik and the bass, nor would you want that. As much as you're looking for separation, you're also looking for a certain marriage between the parts. It's not an accident that bass players and drummers tend to design parts that work directly together. Your goal is to create enough separation so that the two parts don't totally compete with each other. If they do compete, you'll have an undefined, muddy mess at the bottom of your mix. Every successful mix either has the bass appearing above or below the kik. There *must* be some overall low-frequency separation between the two, and that separation often needs to be massaged and manipulated.

If you've been given both a DI and an amp track, you have several options. You can mix them together as they are. You can reverse the polarity of one and mix them together. You can nudge the time position of the amp (or the DI) in order to improve the phase coherency between them. Or you can dump one of them. You'll likely use every one of these options over the course of your career. There's just no way to predict which method will work best for any given track.

As you place more parts into your mix, you're going to get a much clearer idea of how to approach the kik-bass relationship. You could very well initially decide that the kik works best under the bass, only to change your mind once you bring in the rest of the parts. Therefore, spending an inordinate amount of time on the bass before you have more information is a waste of time. Once you have all your parts in the mix, you'll have a much clearer understanding of how well the bass part cuts through. Mixing bass isn't just about massaging a robust low end. The bass supplies the musical foundation of a track, and therefore it's important for the listener to be able to hear the movement of the part.

Once your other parts are in the mix, and you've determined the low-end space your bass will occupy, you then have to deal with how the part works musically in the mix. A great bass part can really make a track sing, and you want to do everything you can to make that happen. How difficult a prospect this is depends on the overall density of the track. It's usually quite easy to deal with bass on a sparse track. When there's very little going on in the mix, you have massive amounts of space, and there's no better candidate for filling that space than the bass. It's the dense tracks with busy bass parts that can be exceptionally challenging.

One way to be sure that the notes on the bass are easily heard is to make sure there's plenty of midrange information, anywhere from 1 to 6 kHz. If you sweep within those frequencies and adjust your Q appropriately, you can find overtones on the bass that are an octave of the fundamental. The denser the mix, the more midrange you'll likely need from the bass. Unfortunately, too much midrange will make your bass sound thin and stringy, and there is a point of diminishing returns. Fret and finger noise also become considerably more apparent due to excessive midrange information. The trick is to get a reasonable balance between the upper harmonics and the fundamental note.

On the right production, you can get a bass to sing with absolutely no string noise whatsoever. So adding midrange is not necessarily the best, or even only, solution. Furthermore, if the bass goes up to higher octaves, the bottom can fall out from underneath your mix. This can make a compromise difficult at best, and impossible at worst. On those occasions when you find a reasonable EQ compromise to be problematic, you might have to split the bass and provide unique processing for different sections of the part. This is not a preferred option, certainly not by me, but we must do whatever is necessary to make the mix great.

Bass is an interesting instrument in that you can often distort the living shit out of it without it being audible within the context of the track. Sometimes you can hear the distortion, and that's fine too—distortion is a mixer's friend; we love distortion. With the right kind of distortion, you can make the notes and movement of the bass audible without boosting unwanted, stringy artifacts. This methodology is especially effective on bass parts where the upper harmonics and string attack don't really exist.

The whole purpose of using an amplifier in the first place is to add distortion to the tone. If all you have is a bass DI, or if the amplified bass is particularly clean, you might consider adding some distortion for the benefit of the track, regardless of the genre. Surely the genre will dictate how much, and precisely how audible you make that distortion, but it's a technique worth investigating, particularly if you want to improve the overall audibility of the part.

Distortion comes in many varieties. You can distort a bass (or anything, for that matter) a number of ways. You can overload the output of an analog compressor or the input of a module on a mix desk. You can distort a bass brilliantly by running the signal through certain mic pre's. You can use a SansAmp—the hardware variety or the software variety (which I call a *sans* SansAmp). And there's a whole plethora of plug-ins you can use for this purpose, including bass amplifier emulators, tape saturation emulators, or even chorus, flange, and phase effects. The kind of distortion and how much you use will vary greatly depending on what you're trying to achieve, and there is no way to describe the optimal distortion for any given situation. Your best option is to experiment. That's what I do, even to this day, and especially when I get my hands on an unfamiliar piece of gear. You never know how a particular piece of gear will distort until you actually try it.

Lastly, there will be times when you have absolutely no choice but to ride certain bass notes. It's a pain in the ass, but the recording sometimes requires it. There are a number of factors that can cause inconsistencies that can't be contained with compressors and limiters alone. Often this happens when there's a resonating frequency in an insufficiently sized room, but the bass or the player can just as easily cause this phenomenon. Regardless of the reason, it's your problem to deal with come mix time, and if compression alone isn't enough to control inconsistencies in the bass level, you're going to have to do some rides.

Monitoring Levels

When you're working on the bottom of your mix, you'll need to pump some air. You can't make decisions regarding bass at low monitoring levels. How much air you push is up to you, but at a minimum, you should push around 85 dB as measured from the mix position. 85 dB happens to be the SPL in which our hearing is relatively flat. At times, you might even want to monitor at higher levels, but be forewarned: extended periods exposed to high-decibel levels can, and will, cause ear damage over the long haul. If you want to understand precisely how loud 85 dB is, go to Radio Shack and purchase an SPL (sound pressure level) meter. As a general guide, a single person talking generates 60 dB of sound, and our threshold of pain is reached at about 100 dB. While 85 dB is a reasonably safe volume in which to work for extended periods, you don't want to work all day at that level. In fact, you should evaluate your mix at a variety of volumes throughout the day, if for no other reason than translation.

How your mix works outside of your room is called *translation*, and you want your mix to translate well in as many places as possible. Frankly, monitoring at a variety of levels is far more beneficial to translation than mixing on multiple sets of monitors. Both the low end and the high end respond differently depending on how much air you push from the speakers. You must reach compromises on your balance decisions based on how the mix reacts at different volumes. I promise, if you monitor at high volume all day, your percussion levels are going to end up outrageously loud in the context of the mix. If you mix at low volume all day, your low end is going to be completely fucked. Just as you should monitor at a variety of levels, you should also evaluate your mix on more than one set of monitors.

I can mix an entire album on a single pair of monitors, but I've been doing this for a while. A second pair makes mixing far easier, and when you're learning how to mix, I recommend you use at least two sets of monitors. This alone will help tremendously with translation outside of your room. Your mix is going to react differently in each pair of monitors, and compromising between them will give you a higher likelihood of successful translation, especially if you switch between a small set of near-fields and a larger set of midfields, both of which we'll discuss in the next chapter.

Ideally, you want to mix for every kind of system there is. Your mix should work just as well on a cheap boom box as it does played on a high-end stereo system. This is where the biggest head-fuck comes in, because if you listen to your mix on a variety of different systems outside of your room, you're only going to confuse the living shit out of yourself. Your mix will react differently in every system. This is a given. What's relevant is how your mix works on a system when compared to other mixes played on that same system. So before you change your mix based on how your snare translates on a boom box with four-inch speakers, you first need to listen to other productions on that same boom box.

Given this, you're far better off having your own outside reference system—one that you're completely familiar with—than running around town playing your mix on all your friends' boom boxes and car stereo systems. The last thing you want to do is make decisions based on how the mix responds in an uncontrolled environment. Frankly, as long as there aren't any debilitating translation issues, your room should be your best reference. The whole purpose of building an acoustically treated, sound-isolated room is to provide accurate monitoring. I'll go into great detail about monitoring in the next chapter, but your room should be the place where you can safely make critical decisions about your mix. It's not where you get a rough estimate just so you can fine-tune the mix based on the stereo in your best friend's basement. If his basement is more accurate than your room, then mix there. All that said, if you must use an outside reference for evaluating translation, you should pick one system and stick with it. Seeing as you probably listen to music in your car, that would be a good place to start.

Bring in the Parts!

With our bass and drum frame in full effect, it's finally time to bring in the other parts. If you're not having fun yet, you will now. This is my favorite part of the mix. The song is fresh. The parts are fresh. Each track unfolds one at a time. It's almost like reading a novel. Every new track is a surprise. This is what mixing is all about! So have fun with it. Bring up your parts, listen to them, evaluate them, and place them in your frame. If you think a track needs EQ, give it some. If you believe a part needs limiting, go for it. Don't consider, don't ponder, don't debate yourself; just process, pan, and move on. If you're not sure about a part, mute it temporarily. You're not looking to make permanent decisions. You want to build a frame in which you can interchange any and all parts in and out of the mix.

Whatever you do, don't get bogged down on any particular part. You want to work fast. Deliberations at this point are just a waste of time. You need a better grasp of how all the parts work together first and foremost. Your early decisions are based purely on the instrumental bed. Until you've heard the lyrics, the melody, and how the production works as a whole, you really can't start to finalize decisions.

Not to be a downer at this moment of great excitement, but I should warn you that if the recording is particularly atrocious, working fast isn't even an option. You're in for a long, laborious day. Hopefully it's at least a good song. Unfortunately, the recording isn't the only potential hindrance. An unfocused arrangement can be equally time-consuming.

A highly focused track delivered by a producer who has a clear vision is a blast to mix, especially when it's a great song. If the producer or the band got confused somewhere along the way and thus deferred some decisions, those deferred decisions are now *yours* to make. No big deal, really. Of course, if the producer, the artist, and everyone but the singer's girlfriend completely lost the plot and caught a nasty bout of *Arrangementus Diarrheaus*, thereby deferring as many decisions as humanly possible on the track you're about to mix, I'm sorry.

A track suffering from *Arrangementus Diarrheaus* is nothing short of a pain in the ass (could I really pass up that pun?). Your mixing pace will likely come to a grinding halt, and by the time you're ready to start automating your mix, you'll be absolutely exhausted. I can assure you, it requires a staggering level of concentration to sift through scores of parts in order to come up with a single workable production. And you wanted to be a mixer. Sorry, too late—you've gotten too far into the book to return it now.

Arrangement issues can occur for a number of reasons, including disagreements over vision, seemingly random attempts to solve a perceived problem, or a collective case of losing the forest for the trees. Worry not! There's a way to deal with all these unwanted tracks, and it's called underdubbing.

Underdubbing

Whereas overdubbing is the process of adding parts for the purposes of improving a production, underdubbing is the removal of those parts that fail in this regard. The more confused your clients became in the recording process, the more underdubbing will be required. Sometimes the most rewarding mixes are those that start out with an absolute lack of focus. This serves you well as the mixer, mostly as a result of lowered expectations. A confused client and an unfocused track will often give you the best opportunity of saving a mix and thus offering the possibility of a big payoff with minimal risk. It's precisely this kind of mix that can procure you a massive supply of mix capital, and it's always good to mix this kind of track relatively early in the process, particularly with new clients.

Of course, a track of a great song with clear vision and stellar performances is far more likely to come out great than one in need of saving. And while there's nothing quite as rewarding as knowing that you saved a track, it's quite easy to personally mistake a great rescue job with a great mix, particularly in the short term. There's a big difference between the two, although it can be all but impossible to gauge this at the time of the mix. The brain has trouble discerning between true greatness and our own contribution to great improvement. Really, the only way around this is to let your mix age.

Once you've managed to forget about all the brilliant mix decisions you've made, once you can actually listen to the mix as a finished work rather than as a work in progress, you'll no longer compare the mix to the disaster you were first given. Now you get to compare your mix to every other production in existence. You see the problem here, right? You could have delivered the greatest mix humanly possible given the circumstances, and it can still be nothing more than mediocre in comparison to everything else. Sad, I know.

When people listen to your mix, whether they're punters or even professionals, they have no clue what you brought to the process. They don't know all the parts you sorted through, and they don't know the genius processing you performed on a lousy recording. The listener has no idea how you contributed, and they never will, because they don't get to compare the before and after. If your average punter actually *does* start to notice the mix itself, you've made a bad mix. All the listener should hear is the song, and if all goes well, they'll want to hear and sing that song over and over again. So sure, enjoy yourself when you have the opportunity to be the mix hero, but understand that the chances of your mix standing as tall as a track that practically mixes itself are remote at best. It makes no difference if you improve a track tenfold if there's nothing worthwhile to begin with. Ten times zero is still zero.

That's not to say you can't deliver a stellar mix of your basic *Arrangementus Diarrheaus* production, one that will stand up to the test of time. You can. I can think of several right off the top of my head. Confusion within the track doesn't mean you're dead before you've begun; it just means you have a challenge before you. Of course, when you're learning how to mix, everything is a challenge. When you get good at mixing, you begin to welcome challenges—embrace them, even. Besides, the absolute worst attitude you can bring to a mix is one of defeatism, as that will surely result in a self-fulfilling prophecy.

The moment you realize you have more tracks than you know what to do with, it's time for some basic detective work. Everything that was recorded should provide you with clues to where your clients have struggled. If you can make some sense of stranded parts—that is to say, parts that seemingly don't go with much else in the production—you may be able to figure out what your clients were trying to achieve in the first place.

Most parts are recorded to achieve a specific purpose within the arrangement. You'd think that any part that failed in that purpose would have been deleted or erased, but that is not always the case. Unlimited tracks coupled with inexpensive storage tend to interfere with this commonsense procedure. So if you bring up a part, and it does nothing good for the track, provides no worthwhile countermelody, serves only to distract the listener's focus from what's important, or offers no valuable rhythmic support, it's a stranded part, one that should have long ago been removed from the session. Underdub it.

Every now and then, I have a client tell me about some genius part that works phenomenally well if it's placed so cleverly in the mix that you can't even hear it. Bullshit. If you can't actually hear a part in the mix, it has no purpose other than to take up space. Merely taking up space is not a good purpose for life in general, so it's certainly not a worthwhile purpose in a mix. Surely you'll have parts that are balanced lower than others—that's a given—but a part needs to be audible in order to actually achieve some purpose. Even if that purpose is nothing more than to fill in the lower midrange, a part can't actually achieve that goal if it can't be heard. So don't confuse smartly subtle with totally inaudible.

An individual part can have a profound effect on how a track makes you feel. For instance, the right kind of cello part could add a melancholy feeling to an otherwise upbeat song. That may or may not be a good addition, depending on the production. So if a particular part is lacking prosody (producing a feeling that's somehow at odds with the lyrical content), then you should seriously consider the ramifications of keeping that part in the production. I'm not going to tell you that such a part needs to be muted, as there are times when producing a feeling that works counter to the song's content can be an effective tool. But you should certainly evaluate what each and every part is bringing to the production, the song, and the mix. If a part isn't providing something beneficial to at least one of those entities (preferably all three), then you should contemplate abandoning the part entirely.

Some parts will amount to nothing more than overkill, such as a part that repeats the same function as another, or a part that the artist and producer fell so in love with that they peppered the entire production with it. (They might have even put the part in other songs!) Don't feel obligated to use a part everywhere it's been recorded. It could be pure genius in a momentary break in the song, and pure crap everywhere else. Give yourself permission to use the part where it works, and abandon it where it doesn't.

Unfortunately, not all underdub decisions are easy ones. Some parts can leave you torn, particularly when you find yourself choosing between two parts that serve a similar function within the mix. These sorts of mix decisions are highly subjective in nature, and can result in considerable debate. You should get used to having that debate with yourself before you engage in a discussion with your client. If you decide to remove a part, there should be a reason, even if it's purely philosophical in nature. Without a definitive reason, you'll be unable to defend your decisions when it comes time for mix notes. Sometimes a decision is based purely on preference, and that's certainly a legitimate reason for making a choice, but doesn't help you when it turns out to be a point of contention between two members of the band. Whenever possible, it's best to have a concrete reason why you chose one part over another.

Since the vocal (or melody) is the most important part in a mix, you should make the preponderance of your tough decisions based on how a part affects the vocal. Just so we're clear, if a part helps the track, and doesn't negatively affect the vocal, then that part has helped the vocal. Remember, at all times you're attempting to push the listener forward, manipulate their focus, and cause them to have an involuntary physical reaction to the music; this will cause the listener to sing the song, which consequently will lead them to want to hear the track again. None of these goals competes with any other, so if a part, or combination of parts, seems to best accomplish your mix goals, those parts would be good candidates to keep.

Not to state the obvious or anything, but the worse the case of *Arrangementus Diarrheaus*, the more possible combinations of parts there will be. For this reason, it's not a bad idea to allow a little bit of randomness into the equation. One of the things I love about mixing on an analog desk is how quickly I can blow through mute buttons to put together different combinations of parts. This opens my discovery process up to random combinations, which aren't nearly as easily arrived at with a mouse and computer.

No part should be immune from a momentary mute in the discovery process—even parts that are fundamental to the mix. Just muting the drums might provide you with an insight that you wouldn't otherwise have. You might even discover a section that works best without the drums at all, or you might find that the song works best with the drums gone completely. Of course, your clients aren't going to appreciate you completely changing every arrangement they've given you. That's not the purpose of listening to random combinations of parts. It's just that creative decisions can't always be planned, and sometimes your best path to brilliance is to allow happy accidents to occur.

As you work your way through the underdubbing process, make sure to consider your five planes of space. For instance, how your mix fits together from a frequency standpoint could be a good reason for choosing a particular part. Suppose you have two similar parts, one played on a guitar in the lower midrange, and one played on a violin in a register two octaves higher. If both of these parts offer similar benefits to the track rhythmically, then it would be reasonable to consider how the parts work from a frequency standpoint. If the mix is packed with high-end and upper midrange information while lacking in lower midrange information, your path is clear: you should probably use the picking guitar. If, on the other hand, the picking guitar doesn't cut properly through a mix laden with lower midrange parts, then you should probably choose the violin part. If the two parts work best together, then by all means, use them both.

Where you place a part in the stereo field can greatly affect how it works in the mix. For instance, a busy tambourine located on the same side as a busy rhythm guitar will likely cause the parts to mask or even rub against each other. Placing them away from each other could prove considerably more effective. The opposite could be true as well. The tambourine and guitar could work in an interesting manner if placed together. It's not enough to merely place a part in the mix and decide it works. There needs to be some exploration involved. You can't listen to two parts on opposite sides and magically know that they'd be better together. You have to hear it for yourself. I don't mean to hammer on this relentlessly, but the discovery process with underdubbing requires some random experimentation. That's how you actually *discover* things about your mix.

Parts

Parts is parts. Regardless of the instrument, a part has a certain function in an arrangement, whether as melody, countermelody, rhythm, harmony, response, or any combination of these. Melody should be the loudest part in the mix. Contrary to John Cage's assertions (he produced a "song" of silence), the bare minimum an arrangement must provide is melody, which can be performed by a single instrument. Everything else in the mix is there to support the melody. It doesn't much matter if you've never dealt with a seemingly exotic instrument; that part will still have a specific function in the mix.

That said, different instruments have different challenges, and once you understand the most common challenges, you'll be able to recognize similarities, regardless of what instrument you happen to be dealing with at the time. We've already discussed the drums and bass. Let's take a moment to discuss some of the more common instruments and their unique challenges.

Electric Guitar

There are as many different guitar/amp combos as there are stars (okay, there's actually billions less, but you know what I mean). Tones vary from sickly distorted to ultra-clean, and while you can shape the sound, the overall tone comes from the hands of the player. There's usually way too many guitars on any given rock track, and using two mics to record a cabinet is usually one mic too many. Eight times out of 10, you should mute one of the mics and several of the guitars.

Every now and then, you'll get a recording of an electric guitar's direct signal. When you do, it means one of two things: Either your clients couldn't make up their mind on the virtual amp setting (which should be a crime), or the recordist didn't consolidate the session properly. Before you spend the better part of an hour perusing your own collection of amp emulations, find out how your client had been monitoring the track. I can promise you, they weren't listening to some anemic strumming of an electric guitar.

The first time a client gave me the direct signal from an electric guitar, I mixed it in the track as-is. Of course, come mix notes time, my client asked me why the hell I didn't put an amp on it, which I replied to by asking the same thing. At the time, I couldn't even fathom someone actually leaving the *amp* choice up to me as the mixer. Guitar tone is integral to a production. How could that decision possibly be deferred to the mixer? Apparently, sometimes it is—although it shouldn't be.

If you're ever given a direct guitar track, you should ask your client to provide you with a consolidated version of the part as they were hearing it throughout their session. I can nearly guarantee you they weren't listening to it without a plug-in, and if you can get some clue as to what your clients were monitoring as they recorded, it'll make your life considerably easier. Not only will their amp choice likely be the best choice—particularly since they're used to hearing it that way—but you'll also have some basis of comparison should you decide to change the "amp" setting.

It should be exceptionally rare for you to place an electric guitar anywhere but hard left or right in a full production, even when there's only one guitar. You want to keep that center territory open as much as possible for the vocal. Hard-panned guitars give you the full advantage offered by the stereo field, and you'll get more apparent loudness out of them without dwarfing the drums. Even guitar solos can be effective hard-panned, especially when the solo is designed to transition from the main guitar track, as opposed to an obvious overdub. That said, guitar solos certainly work great in the center position.

If there's nothing more than an electric guitar and a vocal on a track, you should probably let the guitar take up more space in the stereo field. Sometimes a single guitar in the center can be beneficial for a short period, especially if you come out of that treatment to two guitars panned hard. This will offer the illusion of going from small to large, which can be a dramatic and effective contrast.

Acoustic Guitar

There are a number of issues to be aware of where acoustic guitars are concerned. They're relatively easy to deal with when it's just guitar and vocal, but they can be quite problematic in a big track. For starters, they tend to dwarf the drums. An acoustic guitar is an instrument you can hold in your hands. A drum kit requires an actual patch of real estate, and is capable of producing decibel levels beyond the threshold of pain. Yet in a mix, a full-range acoustic guitar can take up a ton of space, and if placed prominently in your mix, it can make drums sound unnaturally small in comparison. It can be quite disconcerting to the listener to hear an aggressively played drum part in a large room dwarfed by an acoustic guitar. Reduce the balance of the guitar in relationship to the drums, and consider limiting the overall body of the guitar by cutting the low end and lower midrange. Both balance and EQ will greatly reduce the apparent size of the instrument.

On dense tracks, the space an acoustic guitar eats up can also be problematic. If the purpose of the guitar is to offer rhythmic high-frequency information, you can once again reduce the overall body of the guitar. You can also boost the upper midrange and high end in an attempt to make the guitar strumming more aggressive. Either way, this sort of treatment will allow you to more easily tuck the guitar into a dense mix without losing the rhythmic benefit of the strum.

Acoustic guitars on large tracks won't necessarily sound good in isolation. Radical EQ and compression are often required to make the instrument cut properly in a dense mix. It would be far better if the guitar were recorded in a manner that fit the needs of the track, but it's rare to find a recordist who is comfortable recording tones that seem to be lacking when evaluated out of context.

Many artists sing considerably better when they play their instrument, and it's not uncommon to have an acoustic guitar recorded at the same time as the vocal. Given the close proximity of the guitar and vocal mic, it's likely you'll have all sorts of comb filtering and phase coherency issues. This is especially true if the artist is expressive on the mic. There's really nothing you can do about shifting phase coherency between the vocal and guitar mic, and it shouldn't even matter. So the vocal's a little swirly. If it's a great vocal, who cares?

If you want to reduce the phasiness that occurs when an artist plays and sings at the same time, you can do so in the recording process by using a pickup on the acoustic guitar. Unfortunately, most pickups sound like shit on acoustics. Personally, I'd much rather deal with a swirly vocal than the awful, distorted pluckiness of a direct-signal acoustic. There is, however, a pickup that can help with this. It's called the Mag Mic, and it features a tiny mic within the pickup housing. A thumbwheel on the unit allows you to adjust the blend of microphone to pickup. This system will greatly reduce both the coherency issues and negative artifacts of the guitar pickup.

Lastly, I've never heard a single acoustic guitar that sounded good recorded in stereo. Resist the urge to spread two close mics placed on one acoustic guitar across the stereo field, even if the tracks were delivered with this intention. The phase coherency issues alone should be enough to prevent you from doing this. Remember, you never want people to notice the recording, and a single acoustic in stereo is going to wrap itself around the listener's head, among other potential problems. Besides, *it's not even stereo*. It's just out of phase. If you really think the guitar sounds best with a blend of two mics, by all means mix them together. Just be sure to combine them as a mono source in your stereo field.

Piano and Keyboards

Pianos are great big space eaters, as are most organs. It's quite common for pianos to be recorded in stereo, but unless it's the featured instrument, a piano could very well work better as a mono sound source, especially in rock productions. Frankly, there's nothing more problematic as a mixer than having to deal with an inordinate amount of stereo tracks. The strength of the stereo field is the space it offers for the entire mix, not the individual parts within the mix. Keyboards that fill up the entire stereo field eat up immense amounts of space. Sometimes this is the desired effect—in which case leave the track stereo; otherwise, consider combining the signals to create a mono source somewhere within the stereo image.

Mixes with multiple mono sources split across the stereo field are far more focused and interesting than mixes that combine many stereo sources. This may seem like a personal preference, but it's not. This is about framing a strong track, and your track can be weakened considerably by the excessive use of overly symmetrical *faux* stereo instrumentation. Aside from stacked synths designed to create a more complex and textured part—which would technically function as just one part where the arrangement is concerned—any more than one keyboard filling up the entire stereo field is usually overkill.

Piano is similar to acoustic guitar in that a great tone isn't always what's best for the track. Sometimes the best piano recording comes from sticking an SM57 right above one of the holes on the sound board. I can promise you, this technique provides an absolutely wretched tone when evaluated in isolation. It's also a tone that can work quite brilliantly when placed in the context of certain productions, especially when overcompressed. Of course, as the mixer, you aren't in charge of the recording. Your only option is to aggressively mangle these sorts of inappropriately recorded parts.

Phase coherency issues can be especially problematic with pianos, particularly when tracks are delivered by a relatively unseasoned recordist. A phase coherency issue will exist regardless of whether you combine the mics to make a mono source. Using just one of the two mics can be equally problematic given that half the piano will be distant from either mic at all times. This is especially true when the mics are placed just above the hammers.

There *is* one piece of gear that can be quite useful for disastrous phase coherency issues. It's called the IBP Phase alignment tool, and is designed and produced by a boutique company called Little Labs, owned by Jonathan Little (a well-regarded LA tech). There's both a hardware and software version of the unit, which allows you to alter the relative phase relationship between two signals anywhere from 0 to 180 degrees. I can't adequately explain to you how extraordinarily handy this can be, although perhaps that proclamation alone will manage to get the point across.

Percussion

One of my favorite tools for percussion parts is the mute button. I don't say this based on some misplaced hatred or fear of percussion parts, and I don't mute percussion as a matter of course. It's just that there often isn't much thought put into these sorts of parts, especially when they're recorded as time is running out on an exhausting session. Percussion recorded in this manner is usually nothing more than an afterthought, and afterthoughts rarely make the cut come mix time.

If you're not sure whether to discard a particular percussion part, ask yourself the following question: Does the part make the track better? If you can't answer that with a definitive "yes," it's probably a good candidate for an underdub. Your clients will rarely be attached to percussion parts that obviously fuck up the production.

In some genres, like most Latin music, percussion is an integral part of the production and should be prominent in the mix.

Percussion can also appear prominently in pop and smooth jazz tracks, particularly those tracks that don't contain a tremendous amount of cymbal information. Percussion in pop music is often programmed. This bodes well since the act of programming generally requires your client to put some thought behind the part.

Percussion that adds high-frequency information to a mix already saturated in high-end information can be problematic. The simplest option is to mute the percussion, but that's not necessarily the best option, especially if the percussion parts happen to enhance the internal rhythm of the track. In such cases, radically reshaping the percussion instrument's fundamental frequency is a reasonable option, particularly on tambourines and shakers. An aggressive boost in the presence range of 1 kHz (and below), in conjunction with a possible high-end cut, can be an effective compromise for this situation. While there's no doubt that this sort of heavy processing creates an interesting tone, such treatment is highly genre and track dependent, and therefore may not be a viable option.

Lastly, if you spend your day monitoring at considerable volume, you'll most assuredly place the percussion too loud in your mix. You always want to make your percussion balance decisions at low monitoring levels. Excessively loud percussion parts can be distracting and exhausting to the listener. If you find yourself regularly getting tired as you mix a track, it's quite possible that the percussion parts are placed too prominently in the mix.

Science Experiments

"Science experiments" are those highly effected, wacky sounds of unknown origin (from the perspective of the listener). Science experiments are great until you find yourself involved in one while mixing. Then they pretty much suck, mostly because they bring your mix session to a grinding halt. A science experiment executed during the mix phase amounts to nothing more than a time-consuming overdub. There is nothing worse than performing an overdub when you're mixing. Ninety-nine times out of 100, I'll take a long break and allow my assistant to record the overdub. If you don't have that luxury, then not only is your mix stalled, you'll be completely thrown out of the proper mix mind-set.

It is a well-established phenomenon that your last overdub will be the most prominent part in any given rough mix. This will happen even if you're aware of the phenomenon, and the only effective way to combat it is to take an extensive break between the overdub and the rough mix. As you might imagine, this principle doesn't change just because you happen to be working on a final mix. Given this, you want to avoid overdubs during your mix session.

If you can't get out of an overdub, then I suggest you inquire how many other overdub sessions you can expect over the course of the project. If there are other tracks in need of overdubs, you should take a day and do them all. The best option is to ask your client to work on the remaining overdubs somewhere else as you continue to mix, but that's usually not a viable option. If it were, you wouldn't be asked to perform them in the first place. Save yourself some time and misery and immediately schedule an overdub day.

Most bafflingly, there will be occasions when your clients will ask you to recreate a science experiment that already exists (somewhere other than in your session). I can promise you, your clients spent many hours in their recording session creating that perfect, unique science experiment, and the only reason they're not giving it to you is because they think that's part of your job. There is nothing more retarded than trying to recreate a sound that already exists in another location. Don't waste your time recreating a science experiment. Tell your client you can't beat it, and have them retrieve it for you; you'll make their day.

Referencing Other Mixes

Once you have a strong frame, and the overall mix is doing good things, you'll want some basis of comparison. Referencing is especially important when you're in an unfamiliar room. Regardless, you've been listening to the same track for an hour or two or three—it's time to listen to something else for a moment.

It's impossible to compare different mixes of different productions. You can only compare frequency curve and impact, and even that can be difficult at best. I prefer to reference my own mixes, only because I'm intimately familiar with how they react in different environments. If you don't have quality mixes of your own to reference, then use tracks that you're extremely familiar with, both in your room and out. When comparing frequency curves, it's good if you can get a track that has a similar makeup. Comparing an R&B reference to your rock mix doesn't help you much since the rock track will likely have a far more pronounced midrange.

Impact is the other comparison that should concern you when referencing other program material. In particular you want to evaluate how the mix grabs you. It's okay that you're comparing a finished mix to a static frame. You're not looking to beat the finished and mastered mix of a completely different production. That wouldn't even be possible to evaluate. You're just trying to gauge how far you are from a strong, cohesive mix. If you want a more relevant comparison, this would also be a good time to listen to the rough.

Rough Mixes

Some people prefer to listen to rough mixes before they begin. Hell, I don't even like *making* roughs, let alone listening to them. As the producer, I prefer to avoid the band or label personnel falling in love with certain balance decisions, most of which are made on the fly after an overdub. As I pointed out, the loudest part in a rough mix is almost always the last overdub. On rare occasions, this can result in a rough that's pure genius. Usually, it will only cause me fits later.

In general you should wait until you're through with the discovery process before listening to the rough. Listening to a rough only serves to influence the mix, and you want to control when that particular influence comes in. Therefore, it's preferable to go into the mix completely blind and allow the tracks to unfold before you. If you're uncomfortable with this methodology, then bring up all the tracks in your DAW and take a listen first. It's okay to hear the tracks and the production; it's listening to the rough that you want to avoid so you have the ability to read the tracks without bias. Bypassing influence gives you the opportunity to make great discoveries you might not otherwise make. Of course, sometimes there's no avoiding the rough, particularly when there's a need for diplomacy.

Regardless of whether you heard the rough before, there's no doubt you'll want to compare it to your finished frame. It's really the only bar you have to make any kind of comparison. If your frame isn't seriously smoking the rough in how it makes you feel about the song, you have a problem, and you'll need that rough mix to help guide you.

Hopefully, your mix will shit all over the rough, and if it does, you're in good shape. Of course, if the opposite is true and the rough is beating your mix, then you need to figure out why. No matter how good a mixer you are, this can happen. It's why I recommend listening to the rough after you've framed the mix. Once your frame is complete, you've made your judgments, you've chosen your parts, you know how they work, and now you get to see how your vision stacks up against your client's.

If your client's mix feels better, it's usually because there's some combination of parts that's hitting just right. This can happen because of balance decisions, but it often has to do with the parts you've chosen. You haven't wasted any time, so don't beat yourself up over a disappointing frame. Fix it and move on. Your client will never be angry because your mix is similar in arrangement to the rough. They'll be happy! Now, if your frame and the superior rough are identical in arrangement yet the rough is somehow superior, this is usually an indicator that your mix doesn't sing.

Make the Mix Sing, Pop, and Gel

A mix that sings is one in which everything works together to generate an undeniable energy. Sometimes I refer to this as a mix that "pops," since the mix seemingly jumps out of the speakers. This isn't a function of monitoring volume, as a mix that pops will get your attention and draw you in at any volume. You can use the terms "sing" and "pop" interchangeably. They're the same principle as far as I'm concerned.

Getting a mix to sing can be the most elusive part of mixing, and is probably the most difficult to explain. Whether the mix sings or not isn't measurable in any real way, other than by how it makes you feel, but if you find yourself listening to a flat, uninspired mix, it probably isn't gelling. This usually has to do with EQ and compression.

If you get too much separation between your instruments, your mix won't gel. Separation in a mix is usually a good thing. We strive for it. Separation allows us to hear all the different parts. There's a line, however, and if there's too much overall separation between the instruments, your mix won't gel, which will have a negative effect on how the mix sings. If your mix has so much separation that it sounds like five different players as opposed to a single band, then your mix won't sing. You want the listener to perceive a unified performance. If the individual parts are only serving to distract the listener, then you're not directing their focus properly.

Your band (whether programmed or otherwise) is supposed to sound as if they're working together, not as if they're each doing their own thing. That's the difference between a band that sounds musical and a band that sounds like they're playing the same piece of music. With any luck the producer has done her job in this regard. Regardless, it's part of your job to create an apparent unity of purpose within your mix. The fact that you're dealing with individual tracks certainly doesn't help matters. Neither does the usual recording methodology in which most parts are performed as overdubs. Typically, we're just creating the illusion that the musicians played together.

How your mix gels has everything to do with how you use your planes of space. For instance, if you have a guitar/vocal production and you pan the vocal hard left and the guitar hard right, your mix isn't going to gel. I realize I have recommended that you make full use of the stereo field, but that includes filling in the middle.

Balance issues can cause gelling problems too. While you certainly don't want an overly proportional mix, you can't get the track to gel if parts are popping out indiscriminately all over the place. Inconsistency in balances destroys the overall integrity of a mix, especially on the bottom. If the kick level is wholly inconsistent, and the bass is blowing up the speakers on some notes and virtually disappearing on others, your mix won't sing or gel, and it definitely won't pop. This is what makes compressors and limiters such important mixing tools. They allow you to control consistency.

Don't confuse the well-placed dynamic of an accented kick with that of an inconsistent one. The 16th pickup before the downbeat is a perfectly natural place for a drummer to put a dynamically lighter kick. This works to accentuate the downbeat and is a musical dynamic, which will serve to make your mix sing more. Musical accents have been all but eradicated from much of modern music, but that's not because they don't mix well. Don't concern yourself with the deliberate and musical inconsistency of a well-placed accent by a consummate professional. It's the unmusical inconsistency of a lesser player that must be dealt with aggressively.

Compressors have a number of uses. While controlling volume dynamics is the most common purpose, compressors are often used for effect. Depending on how you set your attack and release settings, you can make a part breathe. The ultra-aggressive placement of a compressor on a cymbal can completely eradicate the initial attack, allowing the listener to hear only the long, slow release of the cymbal increasing in volume. Compressed room mics can create the illusion of a far greater space than might have existed during the recording by extending the reflection time. When implemented in an aggressive manner, you're basically using compressors to shape tone as much as control dynamics. There are, however, risks involved in overcompression—you can make your mix small.

I'm not going to argue against ruthless compression techniques. Used well, even ultra-aggressively, compressors are quite handy in shaping the sound of your mix. But if you compress and limit too much across the board, you will eradicate all dynamics from your mix. This will often result in a small, lifeless mix.

The best way to make your mix sing is to use a 2-bus compressor. We'll discuss this further in the gear section of this book, but a good analog 2-bus compressor is essential for dealing with balance inconsistencies in your mix. Not only will the 2-bus compressor control the bottom of your mix, but it will also make it gel. Be careful, though. If you hit your 2-bus compressor too hard, you once again risk making your mix small. If you hit it too lightly, your mix won't sing due to distracting inconsistencies on the bottom. There's a sweet spot on your mix bus compressor, and if you can find that spot, your mix can be both tight on the bottom and big too. The combination of a tight and big bottom goes a long way toward delivering a mix that jumps out of the speakers. So if your mix isn't singing, the first place to look is your overall compression. If that doesn't do it, then you need to examine frequency balance.

How you fill the frequency spectrum can greatly influence how well your mix sings. If your mix is mostly high and low end, then you're missing the brashness that the upper midrange offers, and the meat that the lower midrange offers. If your mix is light on the low end, it won't appear big. If your mix is too dark, it will seem flat and uninspired.

The overall frequency curve of your mix is largely dependent on instrumentation and genre. Rock music is typically far heavier in the midrange than R&B, due to the nature of electric guitars. But if you have an obvious glut in a particular frequency range, one that isn't for contrast purposes, then your mix probably won't sing.

If you find yourself with a frame that has too much separation, the first thing you have to determine is whether the problem is self-inflicted. For instance, if you go through your EQ settings and find that you're radically cutting the lower midrange on just about every channel, or if you find that you're boosting the upper tiers of the midrange on most tracks, it's highly likely that you're causing the problem yourself. Overly thinned-out tracks not only won't gel, they won't have impact. This can be fixed by backing off on how much you EQ the parts.

Arrangement choices can also cause frequency gluts in your mix. In my experience, this is a fairly uncommon problem, but it does happen. If every instrument in the production is packed into the upper midrange and there's seemingly nothing to occupy the octave just above the bass, this can leave a very uncomfortable hole in the lower midrange. The only real fix for an arrangement issue of this magnitude is to overdub a part to fill it. As we've already discussed, this is a drastic suggestion to make as a mixer, and one you should reserve as a last option.

Getting your mix to sing is about getting everything to work together in such a way that the mix is undeniable. It's as if you're hitting a certain note with your mix. You won't get the maximum amount of pop out of your track until you've finished automating, but you should be well on your way by the time you complete your frame.

Automation

Alright! You've gone through discovery, you're familiar with all the parts you've been given, you've made the large majority of your arrangement decisions, you've framed your mix, which sings. It's time to automate!

There are two unique balance functions within the context of the mix that must be reconciled. First, there are the balances that are relative to one another at any given moment within the context of the mix. These are the balances that determine whether the overall mix sings. Then there are the balances relative to what comes next in the mix. These relative balances are what generate excitement and push the listener forward through the mix.

A good way to start—which will greatly simplify the mixing process—is to work by section first. Work the intro (or whatever the song starts with) so that the balances within the section itself are working. Move through the song section by section, setting your balances with automation. This, of course, includes placing your vocal.

The Vocal (You Didn't Actually Think I Forgot About the Vocal, Did You?)

Ah, yes. The vocal. Without it, there are no words. That may seem almost absurdly self-evident, but if it were such an obvious statement, I contend that no one would ever bury the damn vocal. Yet time and time again, people do.

I've purposely left the vocal for the automation portion of the book because this is the point in the mix when you're going to focus on the vocal. Up to this point in the mix, all we've been concerned about is framing a solid foundation. Now it's time to marry the vocal with the track.

The goal is to get that vocal to sit rock-solid in the track. If the vocal is too dynamic, you'll have no choice but to make it loud just so the listener can make out all of the lyrics. Furthermore, if the vocal is constantly popping out on certain words and phrases, your mix will be severely weakened, and therefore won't sing. Essentially, you want to manipulate the track around the vocal, and place the vocal solidly and consistently in the track.

The typical battle regarding the vocal occurs between the record company exec who wants to hear every word regardless of the cost to the track, and the mixer (or producer) who wants a track with some fucking strength. Although I'm definitely a huge proponent of a strong track, the vocal is what gets us all paid. The vocal contains the lyrics and the melody. It *is* the song. Still, there's a middle ground, one that should make everyone happy. You just need to know where that is—but then, that's what this book is for.

So how does one reconcile the opposing forces of a strong track and a loud vocal? Well, we've discussed a lot of this already. For starters, you've left a huge, wide-open space in your mix by using your entire stereo field. Only the kik, snare, bass attack, and the center cymbal information should be competing with your vocal in the middle of your stereo plane. That's a good portion of the battle right there. You've spent the early part of your mix sorting through your parts, maximizing strengths, and minimizing weaknesses. You've underdubbed superfluous parts that compete with the vocal, which prevents distractions and helps keep the listener's focus on the vocal. You've made your mix sing, which means the bottom of your track is under control and is giving you the kind of foundation you need for a strong vocal. You've used processing to make your track gel, without sacrificing separation. Now all you have to do is fit that vocal right into the sweet spot of the mix. You want to be sure the vocal stays in that sweet spot from the top to the bottom of your mix, and you want it loud enough to keep the listener's attention.

The listener needs to make out every word; otherwise, you might as well replace the vocal with a synthesizer. Remember, your goal is to get the listener to *sing*, and if they can't make out the words, they can't sing the song. Of course, your other goal is a secondary physical reaction, and you often need the track for that. This means that the vocal needs to sit just above the track, enough so that every word is audible, but not so much that you weaken the track beyond all usefulness. As with any rule (and that *is* a rule), there are exceptions to mixing a prominently placed vocal.

There will be times when the track will be more important than the vocal. This is particularly common with dance music, since the main goal of the song is to get people to dance, not sing. Sure, we sing as we dance, but what the hell are we singing about? Moving to the beat?

Buried vocals are also commonly found in the indie genre, although one could argue that indie bands might be a bit more mainstream if they'd only bring up the fucking vocal. So I don't buy that particular genre-based argument. Of course, there will be those times when you're given a vocal so awful, so unbearable, so intolerable, and so unlistenable that you actually fear for the overall well-being of humanity should the song ever break through. In that case, you have my permission to bury it. Otherwise, turn up the vocal.

If you want to keep the vocal loud and the track strong, then your vocal must sit perfectly in the mix from top to bottom. Compressors and limiters are the first step toward accomplishing this— vocal rides are the second. The more aggressive you are with the compressor, the less vocal rides you'll need to automate. Aggressive compression on a vocal brings out breaths, sibilance, lip smacks, foot shuffling, rustling, and any other noise the mic happened to pick up during the recording process. Sometimes all that noise is perfectly acceptable for the production—desirable, even—in which case you can be as aggressive as you like with your compressors. This will have the added benefit of saving you all sorts of time in the mix. If, on the other hand, compression artifacts are undesirable for the production, then you'll need to perform vocal rides.

I don't think I've ever done a mix that didn't have vocal rides. Even when the vocal is well compressed, you'll have to ride certain lines. How well your limiters contain the vocal has a lot to do with how dynamic the vocal is that was delivered to you. A vocal comped together in a haphazard manner with wide variances in level and tonality can be exceptionally problematic come mix time. This is usually the result of a lazy recordist. I actually ride and, if necessary, EQ, my comps to tape (or into the computer) just so I don't have to deal with it come mix time. Unfortunately, most recordists don't put this kind of care into their comps.

It's also not uncommon to get comps with obvious changes in tonality. This is always loads of fun, as you will be forced to match these tonality differences with unique compression and EQ settings. Typically, you won't have to worry too much about the slight tonality changes caused by a singer's movement on a large-diaphragm condenser mic. This is normal, and there's an acceptable range of tonality change. Unfortunately, if the tonality changes are obvious, enough that you can't find an EQ compromise that works for the entire track, you'll be forced to perform vocal splits.

I hate vocal splits. A vocal split means I've probably just added an hour or more to the mix. Unfortunately, if I can't find a workable compromise setting for the vocal throughout, I have no choice. Worse still, once I make the decision to split the vocal, I'll likely be splitting it again, and probably again after that.

Problematic changes in vocal tonality can occur for a number of reasons, even if the recordist was particularly attentive. An unavoidable change in mic or preamplifier will most assuredly cause tonality problems later. Performances from different days certainly doesn't help matters. Even the mic selection itself can be the problem. Dynamic mics, for instance, are susceptible to the tiniest change in position by the vocalist, and can require vocal splits. Yet there are times when a dynamic mic is the best choice for a vocalist, and not all vocals recorded on a dynamic will have tonality issues. So I am by no means criticizing a dynamic mic selection. Changes in tonality just happen to be one of the possible pitfalls of that particular selection.

Often these kinds of tonal issues don't become apparent until you've processed the vocal for the mix. Creating separation within the mix, compressing the vocal, and placing it prominently often exposes problems that would otherwise be unnoticeable or, at the very least, ignored. If you find yourself pulling your hair out as you repeatedly change the EQ and compression settings over the course of the song, then you probably need a vocal split. You'd think that this sort of problem would become obvious well before you reach a state of near exasperation, yet oddly, it doesn't. Once you realize you've repeatedly made the same EQ adjustment at the same spots in the track, you can reasonably assume you'll never find an EQ setting that works for the whole song. At this point, it's time for a split.

It's quite common to get a vocal that's considerably hotter in the chorus than it is in the verse. Given this scenario, if you set the compressor for the verse level, your chorus is going to get a bit strident in tone. If you set the compressor for the chorus level, your verse vocal is going to be too inconsistent and will require an inordinate amount of vocal rides. In this case, a vocal split for the verse and chorus will allow you to set your compressor input appropriately for each.

The more apparent loudness the vocal has, or the more it cuts through, the further into the track you can balance it. Apparent loudness has to do with frequency response and how we hear. We tend to have the easiest time hearing in the range of 2–3 kHz. This means that a strident vocal will actually sound louder to us, particularly at higher monitoring volumes. A singer belting out a line in their upper register can absolutely rip the listener's head off if you don't deal with the balance in conjunction with the track's apparent loudness. That said, you have to be careful just how far you ride down this kind of vocal. There is an inherent compromise between ducking a line because the singer is belting, and ducking it so much that it loses the energy and lift it's designed to provide. Part of this compromise lies in how you deal with the EQ. If you can soften just how strident the singer becomes through compression and EQ, you can keep the singer's energy up without causing the listener unwanted pain.

Whether you're doing your rides with a fader or by drawing automation trails in your DAW, the process is the same. Ride up the words and phrases you're having trouble hearing in the context of the mix. Ride down the words and phrases that are popping out of the track. You can see why an aggressive compression and limiting treatment might be desirable, particularly from the standpoint of your time. But you can only compress so much before you get obvious artifacts, and if the artifacts of robust vocal compression aren't a sum positive for the purposes of emotional impact, then your only other option is to ride the vocal. Usually, you'll implement a combination of the two—a healthy dose of limiting in conjunction with vocal rides.

I often spend an inordinate amount of time riding the vocal in my mix. I want that vocal to push the listener forward, and manipulate the listener's emotions. In order to achieve this, the placement and balance of that vocal must be entirely deliberate at all times. Since the vocal is the main focal point, I can manipulate the illusion of dynamics by how I place it in comparison to the track. If the vocal is well above the track in the verse, and then just above the track in the chorus, the band will appear to get louder to the listener, even if there is no actual change in dynamic. Keep this sort of relativity in mind as you place the vocal.

Compression

The amount of audible compression artifacts present on vocals goes in and out of fashion. The current trend is to put massive amounts of tuning artifacts on the vocal, in such a way that it actually sounds like a synthesizer. This would be akin to spraying your whole house with popcorn plaster to cover up a sloppy wallboard paste and tape job—a great idea in theory, but not so great in practice.

While I certainly understand the temptation to stay within current fashion trends, you're better off making these kinds of decisions based on the song and the production you're given. If the production calls for a breathy, spitty vocal (and many productions do), or if an Auto-Tune synthesizer effect seems like the right call to make, then by all means hammer the vocal, mix the track, and spend the rest of the day at the beach. I'm all for it! What I advise against is using an effect merely because it's in vogue, rather than making such choices based on the needs of the song and the production. No one is going to pass on purchasing a song because it doesn't fit within certain production and mixing trends.

If you're going to hammer the vocal with a compressor or limiter, whether you use an analog or digital one, you're probably going to bring up the *s*'s. Overbearing sibilance is distracting to the listener. What meets the definition of "overbearing" I'll leave up to you, but you're probably going to want to use a de-esser.

A de-esser is basically a compressor that is side-chained to a particular frequency. Sibilance falls between 5 and 16 kHz. The de-esser allows you to compress the fundamental frequency of the *s*, which greatly reduces the sibilance. Most de-essers allow you to listen to the keyed frequency, allowing you to sweep and locate the most offensive part of the sibilance.

S's are best dealt with during the recording process, but for some inexplicable reason, recordists rarely place vocal mics by ear. Poor mic placement will only serve to make the *s*'s worse, and the moment you start compressing or limiting, you'll likely have a severe *s* problem on your hands. You might actually need more than one de-esser to deal with two different frequency spikes on an excessively sibilant vocal. Use as many de-essers as you need to; just make sure you're not making the singer lisp. If you can't find a setting that works for the whole song, guess what? You need another split.

I'll say it again. I *hate* vocal splits. They cost time, and if I can avoid a split, I will. You should too. Unfortunately, added time is pretty much irrelevant. If the vocal changes tonality, or if different compressor settings are required, you really have no choice but to split the vocal. Since vocal splits put the vocal on multiple channels, you should consider placing a bus between the vocal and the output. This will provide you with a module that you can use as a vocal master for both processing and automation.

So if you're sitting here thinking to yourself, "Jeez, how many compressors or limiters does this guy put on the vocal?" the simple answer is as many as it takes. The more complex answer is that it depends on the mix medium and the overall quality of the recording. I don't need nearly the amount of processing in the analog domain as I do using a DAW. That doesn't mean you can't do a fine job mixing the vocal in a DAW, but to date, plug-ins don't react quite the same as analog processors.

If you have good converters, and you have external compressors and limiters available, you might consider running your vocal through an analog compressor and re-recording. If you have inserts on your converter bridge, then use *them*; just realize you're complicating your recall abilities tremendously once you do.

Regardless, you'll save yourself considerable time by using analog limiters and compressors on your vocal. If you don't have analog processing available, don't worry; it's not critical for good results. It just means you'll have to work harder. But then, there's nothing wrong with a hard day's work!

Finding Compromise

The first goal in the automation process is to whip your sections into good shape, preferably without dismantling what you've done previously. That's easier said than done. As you set balances in sections, you'll undoubtedly illuminate issues with your processing. Every time you make a processing change, you also alter your earlier decisions. For example, if you set your bass EQ and compression for the intro, and upon reaching the chorus you decide to give the bass more definition in the upper midrange, guess what? You may have just negatively changed how your intro works. Welcome to mixing.

This is where the tail chasing comes in, and it's normal. In processing each part, you're seeking out the compromise setting that works for the entire song. As you define each section of your mix, as you put the mix in more focus, you'll find it necessary to tweak your processing. Every processing adjustment you make will affect the entire mix, especially when you find yourself changing the bottom of your mix. The moment you take some low end off the bass, not only have you directly affected how the kik drum sounds, but you've changed how your 2-bus compressor reacts. Now that adjustment may very well translate perfectly across the whole mix. But if it doesn't, then an adequate compromise must be reached. There's almost always a good compromise. You just have to find it.

Any change in processing on one part will affect other parts in the mix. For instance, if you decide to roll off some low end from the guitars, it's possible you'll need to add some low end to the bass. If you add top to the electric guitars, you may have to bring up the vocal to compensate.

As you mix each section, consider the focal point and make sure it's placed prominently enough to take on that role. If there are response parts, they should pick up the focus of the listener when the vocal goes tacit. The moment the vocal returns, it should reclaim that focus. If the response overlaps the vocal, make sure the transition is seamless in the transfer of focus.

Not all arrangements use musical response as a tool. Typically, the busier the vocal is, the simpler the arrangement. A momentary pause in a busy vocal often serves as a welcome breath for both the singer and listener alike. Don't feel compelled to make something happen in those spots unless one of the players takes that moment to insert a musical word (which functions as response). The track is probably plodding along quite nicely and will automatically grab the focus of the listener without any additional work on your part.

As you progress through the track section by section, over and over again, you should also begin to examine the big picture—in particular, how each section affects the next. Balance doesn't just affect the mix as it relates to the moment, it also affects what's coming up, and it is within this context that you manipulate the listener and push them forward, particularly where payoff is concerned.

The Payoff

In modern music, the payoff is often synonymous with the chorus. The chorus typically occurs multiple times in the song and has identical lyrical content. It's the section of the song that is the most identifiable, the most likely sung, and what we all look forward to in a great song. A great song and arrangement will push us toward the chorus by design, and we want to be sure our mix does everything to enhance both the journey and the payoff alike.

If the listener doesn't get a big payoff from the chorus, all is lost. As with just about everything we discuss here, the majority of the payoff should come from the song. The stronger the payoff is from the songwriting, the less important it will be to pull the payoff from the arrangement and mix.

In AC/DC's "Highway to Hell," the verse is nothing more than drums, vocal, and a single guitar playing short choral bursts in unison with the bass. When the chorus comes in, a second guitar enters playing fully held power chords, along with an entire chorus of vocals. Not only does the song offer us a great melodic and lyrical payoff that's fun to sing, but the arrangement and the mix actually enhance the payoff using contrast.

The chorus doesn't have to get bigger in order to provide payoff. Take Led Zeppelin's "Rock and Roll," for instance. In this song, the refrain actually breaks down in order to set it apart from the rest of the song. In the first chorus, the guitar stops playing for the refrain. If the guitar didn't drop out, the payoff line "...been a long, lonely, lonely, lonely, lonely time," wouldn't be nearly as effective. In the second and third chorus both the guitar and the drums drop out, further setting the line apart. This offers contrast, and contrast enhances payoff. Those dropouts also serve to buy another 16 bars of the same repetitive riff.

The chorus by no means has the corner on the market where payoff is concerned. Any given song could have more than one payoff, including the bridge, the guitar solo, or even the outro. Take Pink Floyd's "Money," for example. There really is no chorus on this song, and what would normally act as the chorus is more of a turnaround to get us back into the hooky verse. It's a great turnaround, but the big payoff comes from the reverberant, climactic guitar solo, which comes down in dynamics to continue on a bone-dry track, only to climax once again before the track returns to the original groove. Each guitar solo section sets up the next, helping to maximize payoff and push us forward through the song. The changes in reflectivity and density only serve to enhance the payoff through contrast.

All of your planes of space relate to contrast and relativity. The more contrast you have, the bigger the illusion of dynamics. For instance, let's say your mix breaks down to a single dry and radically filtered electric guitar in the center position. This sort of breakdown offers you the opportunity for an explosive re-entry in every way possible. When the band returns, the track (and in particular, the guitars) opens up to the entire frequency spectrum. Your stereo imaging explodes from a mono guitar to two hard-panned guitars. There's a massive change in track density, and with a giant room on the drums there would be an enormous increase in reflectivity. Contrast is occurring on every other plane, which gives you the illusion of dynamics without ever using more than 4 dB of actual dynamic range.

This doesn't mean you have to use every available dynamic all the time. There are many great songs that purposely don't make use of mix dynamics. I mean, if you think about it, if every song was a wild ride of explosive dynamics, this would be boring in its own right. Some songs are designed to keep us in a certain headspace. As long as the track and vocal draws you in as the listener, the forward motion can be delivered purely by the vocal and lyric. Enhance that forward motion with contrast when it's appropriate, but don't go out of your way to create a dynamic that's not necessary. Remember, you always want to follow the song and production.

If you think about your balances in terms of how they set up the coming balances, you're going to have a far easier time arriving at an effective mix. When you bring up a part, you *must* consider not only how it affects the mix at the moment, but also how it affects what's coming up. If you negatively affect the payoff because of a mix decision in the verse, you are not serving your mix well. This is critical thinking when it comes to mixing effectively.

Refining and Enhancing

As you make your way through the mixing process, as the hours of chasing your tail pass by, your adjustments will become finer, your attention to detail will become greater, and your perception more refined. By the end of a mix, you should be able to hear even the most minute internal balance differences, all the way down to 1/10th of a dB. At the very least, you'll think you can hear differences that small.

I'm convinced I can hear an internal balance change of 1/10th of a dB when I'm toward the end of a mix. Whether I can or not is irrelevant, and I've never bothered trying to measure my own sensitivity at that stage of a mix, partially because I'm too tired to bother, and partially because it just doesn't matter. There's no way anyone is going to hear a 10th of a dB change other than in a hypersensitive state. So if you find yourself making adjustments this small, and I've done it, you're probably wasting your time.

Which brings us to the question, "Just how small of an internal balance change is a reasonable one?" That depends on your attention to detail. By the time I'm finishing a mix, half a dB reduction in the vocal is the difference between the singer appearing just on top of the track and slightly in the track. This is a rather large perception change for such a minute adjustment, and it will greatly affect how the listener feels about the track. Conversely, at the beginning of a mix, half a dB change won't even register as significant. The track is in too rough a state for you to hear the real effect of such a minute internal balance adjustment.

It's the tiny details that make a mix great, particularly as they relate to the big picture. Simply boosting a fill before the chorus can increase an already existing payoff. These sorts of enhancements help you to squeeze out every bit of forward motion you can from the track. The further along you get in the mix, the more you have to think along the lines of the whole mix. As you get toward the end of your mix, you're going to refine and enhance. Look for opportunities to improve your mix anywhere you can. It can be the difference between a really good mix and a great one, and that distinction is worth the time.

Finishing Your Mix

I've been toward the end of mixes that were seemingly a total disaster, in which just one or two key moves completely focused the track. I know it sounds weird, but a finished mix can completely sneak up on you, although admittedly, the completion of a mix is typically a little less random than that.

I usually know I'm near the end of the mix when I can't stop singing and moving. I mean, think about it. If I can make myself sing after many long hours of working on the damn song, it *must* be a good mix. There are other indicators as well. If I can't seem to make adjustments to the mix without rejecting them outright, I know I'm getting close.

It's almost as if you get a mix to near completion, and everything locks up on you. If every move you make seems to completely destroy the integrity of the mix, you're probably done. At some point you just have to admit you can't improve it any longer.

Then, of course, there are those times that you just give up. Hey, that's a perfectly reasonable way to finish a mix, particularly if you feel you can no longer offer any improvement. Granted, it's always better to feel good about your mix when you print it, but you're at the mercy of what you've been given. You can only bring a production up to its fullest potential, and that potential might not be especially satisfying. If you can't make yourself sing and move, you didn't necessarily fail as a mixer. I realize it can be difficult to distinguish between your own failure and that of your clients, but as you mix longer, this becomes more apparent.

It's critically important that you develop a sense of when your mix is finished. It's ridiculously easy to go past the mix, and the moment you do, you're on a path of diminishing returns. Once you get the big picture working in your mix, you must be exceptionally careful about the changes you make. If you suspect you're close, start saving often and with unique file names so you can get back in the event you do go past the mix.

Mix Notes

Mix notes is the time when your client gets to go through the mix with you. Let's face it, by the time you're ready for your client to hear the mix, you could use some input. You've been working on the song for anywhere from six to 12 hours, maybe more, and you need a fresh perspective.

By the time you're presenting the mix to your clients, you should know what parts happen where, when, and why. There should be very few ideas regarding the mix, and in particular the arrangement, that you haven't already considered. There will be occasions when your client offers some wacky idea that you hadn't considered. But when it comes to the basic integrity of the mix, there should be little that hasn't already come to mind. Frankly, by the time the band and producer listen to the song, you should actually have a far better understanding of the track than even they have.

If this is the first mix of a project, be sure your mix is spectacular before you play it for your clients. Certainly, there are times when you can seek your client's input before you're completely done with the mix—the first mix just doesn't happen to be one of those times. If you blow your clients away, you set the stage for the entire project. Even if you're only mixing one song, you still want to wow them. There could be more mixes in the future, so think long-term in this regard.

It's always a nerve-wracking experience to play the first mix for a new client. You have no way to gauge what the reaction is going to be, and you have no idea if your session is going to be an easy or a difficult one. Unknown situations are always stressful for everyone, not just you. There are some steps that you can take to relax your clients. For starters, you can lower the lights and shut off the computer monitor when you first play the mix for them. Reducing light creates a more relaxing listening environment and enhances everyone's hearing. It's far easier to hear emotional impact when the lights are low, mostly because there are no visual distractions. The lack of visual stimuli allows your client to visualize the mix as they hear it. Just as this is beneficial to you as the mixer, it's helpful for your clients as well.

Shutting off the computer monitor is a must on the first play-back, since it can be exceptionally difficult for your client to resist watching their mix rather than listening to it. You don't want your client to have fair warning of what's coming next in their own mix (or dismayed by what's been muted); you want them to get the full emotional impact of the work, evaluated from the perspective of the listener. Granted, your clients are hardly in a position to experience the full impact of a first listen, but they're far fresher than you are come the end of a mix. While your clients are intimately familiar with the arrangement, they've never heard it in a near-finished state. If you can impact them with the mix, then you've done your job well.

For unattended sessions, the mix notes process doesn't typically happen on the day you mix the song. The unattended process requires you to print your mix and send it to your client for evaluation. Personally, I can't stand not having the client there with me, but sometimes there's just no other option. Since the mix notes process will entail ending mixes with changes, consider naming your mixes consistently. For instance, I always label the first print of a mix "Song Title Print 1," and name the session the same. I do this because it can be extremely easy to forget which mix goes with which session. This can result in the disastrous error of sending the wrong mix to mastering, particularly if every mix is named "Final." Final Mix. Final Final Mix. Final Final Final Mix. I can promise you, that kind of naming protocol will eventually bite you in the ass.

Often the most useful information you'll get from the mix notes stage is confirmation. There will be all sorts of things in the mix you'll still be on the fence about. You don't have to actively seek this confirmation. Your client is fresh come mix notes time, so if they don't notice something that you're worried about, it's likely not an issue. Of course, if it's still bothering you and the client hasn't mentioned it, you can always bring your concerns to their attention.

Since most of the mix notes process involves personal interaction, I'm going to go into the strategies involved in the Dealing with Clients section of the book. As a process, there's not much to it. Get notes, make changes, move on. The problems occur when you lose control of the mix notes phase of the session, and that has everything to do with interpersonal skills and little to do with process.

Printing the Mix

When mixing in the analog domain, it's normal to print the mix the moment you're done with it, mostly because you have to tear it down and start the next one. In a DAW you don't really need to print until all the mixes are done and you're ready to wrap up the project. Regardless of whether you're working in the analog or digital domain, you should print alternate versions of the mix. The most common alternate mixes are as follows: Vocal up, vocal down, TV, instrumental, a cappella.

I realize DAWs have perfect recall, and it might seem superfluous to print alternate versions, but while you may be able to recall the mix precisely today, that won't necessarily be the case in a year—in fact, it probably won't be. Updates to your software require updates in plug-ins, and your mix likely won't recall identically the moment you do this kind of update. Even if your clients don't need the alternates now, they may years down the line, and part of your job is to give them everything they need. Besides, do you really want to print alternates for your client a year or two later? Do you really want a call from your client while they're in mastering asking you to print a vocal up of a song? Print the alternates and save everyone on the project all sorts of hassle.

Vocal up and down mixes are typically delivered in half dB increments. For a focused and effective mix, a half dB difference in vocal level should be relatively significant. It's possible you might favor a full dB adjustment, and I know mixers who do quarter dB increments on their alternate vocals. You'll have to find the increment that you feel works best for you, and it might even change over time. Only you can provide the answer for this based on what makes a difference for your mixes.

Some people like to have six different vocal level alternates—three up and three down. To me that's overkill, even in the analog domain, but at least there's an argument for it in that scenario given the difficulty of recalls. When I'm working in a DAW I usually only print one alternate, and it's almost always a vocal up. Until you've been mixing for a while, I recommend two alternates—a vocal up and a vocal down. If you start to print a vocal down, and you're convinced the vocal is way too low for the mix to ever be useful, then print a second vocal up.

On those occasions when the vocal arrangement includes double tracks and harmonies, a decision must be made. If you raise only the lead vocal, you change the balance relationships within the vocal mix. There will be times when you want to keep that relationship intact, in which case you should raise all the vocals for your alternate mixes. Just make sure you label your mix clearly with either an "all vox up" or "lead vox up," as you'll never remember which you did later.

The TV mix has no lead vocal. Harmonies stay intact, and double tracks are optional. The purpose of this mix is for those occasions when the singer must perform without a band—which is a common occurrence for TV performances; hence the name. You can also call this the "karaoke" mix. Hey, if your mix makes it into karaoke machines, that means it was a huge success; good for you.

The instrumental has no vocals whatsoever. This track can be quite useful for editing purposes, particularly if your client wishes to prepare a radio edit after the fact. If an edit needs to be performed where there's a vocal overlap, the instrumental can be used in conjunction with the a cappella (vocals only) in order to make the edit. In some genres, like hip-hop, the instrumental is often included with the single, although that practice is diminishing given the rise in online sales. Still, you never know what the future holds, and instrumentals could one day be offered as bonus tracks with online purchases.

The a cappella is a vocals-only mix and can be quite handy for edits and remixes.

Saying Goodbye Is Hard to Do

Finishing up a mix project is always weird. You'd think it would be a big event with a definitive ending, but it's more like a petering out. Even this chapter feels like that to me. What, we're done? Well, no. Not the book. We have plenty more to discuss, but once the mixes are done and printed, that's it. It's time to move on to the next project, meet new people, and deal with new challenges. I don't think I'll ever get used to the end of a mix session. It's sort of like being an obstetrician without all the blood and placentas. You just helped your client give birth to their new child. Sure, your client's pregnancy is over, but now they've got to go raise and nurture their child. Meanwhile, you have another baby to deliver tomorrow. Say your goodbyes and move on. Don't worry. You'll see them at mastering later in the book.

You didn't think you were going to just leave mastering up to chance, did you?

Chapter Four

Gear

*Gear used on a mix are tools that will make
your life either easier or more difficult; they are
not what makes a mix good or bad.*

If you've spent any time at all on any of the various Internet audio discussion boards, you've probably noticed a nearly insatiable appetite for discussing gear. I'll save you some time. Asking a group of strangers their opinion on a tool as common as a compressor or limiter will result in nothing more than useless information. Here let me answer some of the more common questions for you:

What's the best compressor for under $100?
You get what you pay for.

Should I buy a [Universal Audio] LA-2A or an 1176?
You should buy both.

Yeah, but which one will be more useful?
They're both useful. Which will be more useful on what?

Which will be more useful on vocals?
Who the fuck knows? That depends on the vocalist!

If you're guilty of asking these kinds of questions, or even if you enjoy opening up these kinds of threads in order to read the many varied opinions of mostly anonymous strangers (and I was one of those anonymous strangers for a time), then I have some questions for *you*. Exactly how is a piece of gear supposed to provide you with the sensibilities necessary to construct a killer mix? Which piece of gear is going to sort and underdub your parts? What unit is going to maximize the payoff in the chorus? Which box is going to determine where the listener's focus should be? What piece of gear is going to cause people to sing and dance? The answer, of course, is none.

All technology, and all tools (and tools are technology) are by design intended to make life easier. If a common tool falls short of that goal, then it's probably the wrong tool for the job. For instance, if you put an 1176 on a vocal, and it makes that vocal sound worse, should you throw away your 1176? But it was great on the last few vocalists! What happened? Should you spend the next few hours fighting the negative effects of the 1176, or should you perhaps try using an LA-2A instead? I suppose that depends on whether you have one or not.

I mean, I can use either an LA-2A or an 1176 successfully and beneficially on a vocal somewhere on the order of 99 percent of the time. If the 1176 doesn't sound good, the LA-2A usually does, and vice versa. If I don't have one of those two limiters available to me, then I'm going to either need to get one or use something else. Asking which one is better isn't relevant. They're different. Oh, you have more questions? I have more answers.

What's the best DAW for chopping up and reconstituting a lousy drummer?

Well, all DAWs can do that. Is this the most important function in your DAW? Do you spend the preponderance of your day editing inconsistent drummers? If you do, it's quite possible you're editing that many drummers *because* of the gear that you own.

Which DAW can I work fastest on?

Now there's a worthwhile question, but don't go running to the Internet to post this inquiry, because only *you* can answer it. Of course, you'd have to become adept at each and every available DAW in order to make such a determination—a highly unlikely and somewhat useless endeavor, given the scope of the task. Besides, it really depends on what you do most. If chopping up drummers is of little to no interest to you, but mixing is, you should probably base your DAW choice on what makes mixing easier. At all times you want to choose your tools based on what is going to make *your* life easier—not someone else's. Therefore, no one else can answer this question but you.

Does the Bomb Factory 1176 sound like the real thing?

Is anyone even using that piece of crap anymore? Er, I mean: Not even close. Of course, if that's all you have available, you should use it.

Does an SSL G384 plug-in sound just like the real thing?

Uh, no. In fact, there isn't a single plug-in designed to emulate an analog piece of gear that's even remotely accurate in that role. Not a one. Does that make them useless? Not necessarily. Does it make them look good? Absolutely!

Too often gear is viewed as some magic bullet: so powerful that it will be the difference between you delivering a great mix and a mediocre one. That's not true. Your collection of gear is your collection of tools, and if you only have certain tools available, those are going to have to do. The beauty of plug-ins is that once you own the package, you can have as many of them on your mix as your processing power will allow. One analog 1176LN is only good on one channel. Not so with the 1176 plug-in. Of course, if you're an innovative kind of person, you might come up with the idea of re-recording a track (or two) through the 1176, freeing it up for something else.

This is by no means an argument that a plug-in package is better than that single 1176. You should still have at *least* one analog 1176 in your arsenal at some point. Still, when it comes down to making a purchase decision for right here and now, if the sheer number of limiters available to you is more useful than the sonic benefit of a particular one, then it seems to me it's the plug-in package that will make your life easier.

I can safely say that you will never own so much gear that you won't need anything else. At all times your purchases will be made based on priority, and that priority should be based on what tool will make your life easier now, and more than any other tool. If you can accurately determine this, then your next purchase decision is an easy one.

My favorite trite audio Internet argument regarding gear is this notion that a good carpenter never blames his tool. Yeah, well, a good carpenter doesn't buy a hammer made of plastic, either. Picking the tools is part of the overall job, and there are certain minimum requirements if you wish to mix effectively. A DAW, a computer, and some monitors may be the bare minimum necessary to mix, but they aren't the bare minimum necessary to mix effectively or successfully.

Take world-renowned violinist Itzhak Perlman. If we were to provide Mr. Perlman with a student violin, there's no doubt in my mind that he would make that instrument sing like no one else could. But if you were to give him his favorite Stradivarius, not only would his tone improve markedly, he'd also have a far easier time playing the instrument. This in turn would allow him to concentrate purely on his performance, rather than delegating a portion of his brainpower to overcoming the shortcomings of the student instrument. The Stradivarius would no doubt make Itzhak Perlman's life easier.

Monitoring

Whereas a particular compressor or limiter can make your life easier, poor monitoring will only serve to make your life more difficult. Your monitoring is so critical to working effectively that certain deficiencies cannot be overcome with skill.

You can't possibly deliver a proper mix if what you're hearing from the speakers is so out of whack that it will retain little to no similarity outside of your room. As we discussed earlier, how a mix works outside the control room is called translation. If your mix doesn't translate properly, you can't possibly mix. Unfortunately, you can't necessarily blame translation issues on your speakers alone. The acoustic space that contains those speakers plays just as important a role as the speakers themselves.

There are two kinds of translation issues—those that can be overcome, and those that can't. If you're mixing in a room that has a bit too much bass in the mixer's position, your mixes will translate oppositely and reproduce too little bass outside of your room. Basically, any linear frequency issue you might have will translate in an equally opposite manner outside of your room. If you know this, then you can adjust how you hear in your own room. After a while, your brain will automatically adjust for any mildly out of whack frequency response issues. All rooms, no matter how well built, will have these sorts of anomalies, and they are relatively easy to deal with. The problems lie with room translation issues that can't be overcome.

I wish this were as simple a fix as changing your monitors. Unfortunately, your speakers don't sit in a vacuum. The sound that comes from your monitors exists in a room, which means there is going to be reflection. If your room has acoustic issues that make it impossible to hear certain frequencies, you will never be able to overcome this issue with brainpower alone.

The single biggest expense of any properly implemented mix room is the build-out. A poorly treated acoustic space will prevent you from even being able to mix, as nothing you do will make any sense in the outside world. From a visual perspective, it's like painting in a pitch-black room—your results will not only be unsatisfactory, they'll be completely unpredictable, and no amount of comparison outside your workspace will ever allow you to fix the problem, because you'll have to go right back into your pitch-black room to make any changes. If there's no semblance of translation, and if there is no similarity between what you hear in your room and out of it, then how are you going to fix the problem?

This sort of monitoring issue doesn't automatically mean that you have to spend a fortune on your acoustic build-out. It will, however, either require some financial investment in your current room, or a move to a properly built one.

There's plenty of information on the Internet on how to deal with the acoustic problems of your mix room. As with anything on the Internet, some (if not most) of that information is completely bogus, and you'd do well to carry a nice big grain of salt when you're researching the subject. The best solution is to hire a well-regarded room designer who has a track record of successful build-outs. Pictures and firsthand testimonials from legitimate studios would be a good start toward confirming the qualifications of a room designer. This kind of professional isn't going to be cheap, but then neither is a full-blown DAW, or a great mixer, for that matter.

If your room doesn't translate well, that needs to be fixed before you're going to get good results mixing. I don't care how adept you are at evaluating a room by referencing program material you're familiar with. If you're not hearing certain frequencies because your control room is nothing more than a bedroom with a desk and speakers in the middle of it, you're never going to be able to make it translate. Your favorite mixer can listen to 1,000 reference mixes over the course of 20 days, and still will not overcome certain acoustical problems.

I used to switch to a different mix room every other week, and I became insanely adept at quickly deciphering and compensating for a room's translation issues. Now these were all professionally built rooms by some of the most respected acoustic designers in the world, so they weren't by any stretch of the imagination broken. Stick me in an acoustically untreated bedroom, however, and you can forget about translation. It's not going to happen. The bottom line is you can't compensate for what you can't hear.

What you plan to do with mixing will likely determine how much you're willing to spend. If you're seeking to mix your own music, and only your own music, spending $100,000 on a build-out in your rented apartment is clearly a nonstarter. I really can't tell you whether the current crop of Internet-savvy, self-proclaimed acousticians can really help you fix your room. None of the acoustic panel makers seem to agree about anything regarding their expertise, despite the fact that they all sell similar products. Let's face it, these guys don't make their money on consulting; they make it by selling you their acoustic panels, which leaves one to question what you're actually buying.

I'm not suggesting that the boutique panel manufacturers are unscrupulous. Depending on how much is broken with your room, acoustic panels could be the best option for fixing your problems without investing a fortune. It might be worth throwing $1,000 at the problem just to determine if you need to throw 10 or 20 times more at it to create a reasonable critical-listening environment. Just make sure you go to someone reputable who doesn't argue with the basic premises of this book all over the Internet. If the owner doesn't understand mixing, then he can't possibly understand your needs in the studio. I would start with a company called GIK Acoustics if you're going to try the acoustic panel and bass trap route.

All I know is, you *must* deal with how your room translates if you have any hope of mixing successfully—even if you're only mixing for yourself. So the first thing you have to do is fix your monitoring.

Monitors

The other half of the monitoring equation is the monitors themselves. Studio monitors come in all different shapes and sizes, and selecting the one that's right for you is a personal choice. This fact would tend to render any specific recommendations from me as nothing more than useless, although as someone who has mixed on many different monitors, I can offer you some valuable insight on this subject. Good news, to be sure!

If you're new to mixing, then I would suggest you have more than one set of studio monitors available. There are three basic styles of studio monitor: bigs, midfields, and near-fields.

The bigs are typically soffit mounted and require a rather large build-out in order to accommodate them. If you get yourself just about any audio magazine you'll usually see the picture of a control room with the bigs prominently displayed on the sides of the studio glass. My good friend and producer Peter Bunetta calls them the "adult" speakers—I suppose since I generally don't use them until he comes to listen to his mix. I guess I have some growing up to do! Occasionally, I might check out the bigs just to listen to the low end for a moment, but overall I find them completely useless as mix monitors. They're great for listening to as you print your mix, or for group listening parties, but that's about it. If you don't have the room or the money to install bigs, don't worry; you'll be fine without them.

Near fields are small speakers with six- to eight-inch woofers. They typically sit on the bridge of your console or production desk. In my experience, a good near-field accentuates the midrange, mostly because it doesn't have the woofer size to accurately extend to the full bottom. For the better part of 20 years, the Yamaha NS10 was the industry-standard near-field monitor. NS10s are absolutely awful monitors where the actual enjoyment of music is concerned, but are brilliant as studio monitors, as long as you can overcome the learning curve. NS10 woofers can't take much abuse and need to be replaced regularly; otherwise they get exceptionally floppy, but I expect this is probably an issue with just about any near-field monitors, given the inadequate woofer size. NS10s are no longer made by Yamaha, and given the overall unavailability of replacement woofers, I would recommend finding a different near-field. Besides, a 20-year reign is long enough.

Midfields are bigger than near-fields, and carry a woofer from 10 to 15 inches in size. By design, midfields are supposed to be placed six to eight feet from the mix position. This offers some distance between you and the speaker, which allows the low end sufficient space to properly develop. That said, I almost never put midfields behind the console. I prefer to treat them like near-fields and put them on the bridge of the desk. There is no right or wrong regarding this, just what works for you in order to get accurate translation.

Auratones, or your garden-variety boom box, are often used for checking mixes. These sorts of speakers are often referred to as the "lowest common denominator" where reproduction is concerned. Personally, I don't use them, don't understand the need for them, and prefer not to waste valuable horizontal bridge space in order to house them. Don't let that stop you, though. There is certainly a valid argument for a boom box check, and if you find it useful, then by all means include them in your monitoring. My only caveat is don't actually spend any time balancing on them. Use them purely for evaluating how your mix translates when compared to your other monitors.

Ideally, you want to have a pair of near-fields for their accentuated midrange, and a pair of midfields for their full range. This way you won't feel like you've been ramming an ice pick into your ears all day by working exclusively on near-field monitors. If you only have near-fields, then you can consider using them in conjunction with a subwoofer. When the subwoofer is on, they'll act more like midfields, and when it's off they'll work like near-fields. I've used NS10s with a subwoofer on more than one occasion, and this can greatly relieve some of the fatigue issues.

Switching between studio monitors as you mix offers the benefit of constructing a compromise that works between them. The compromises that you make between monitors will mostly deal with frequency and balance decisions. For instance, a snare that sounds awesomely obnoxious in a midfield monitor can be exposed as overbearingly obnoxious in a near-field monitor. By adjusting the EQ and balance of the snare in order to come to a compromise that works in both sets of monitors, you will increase the likelihood that your mix will translate well outside your room.

After a while, you may even perform certain mix functions on certain speakers. You might, for instance, carve out your low end on the midfields at high volume, and do your vocal rides on the near-fields at low volume. You might get all your balances in the near-fields, and do all your rides on the midfields. You might do most of your mixing in the near-fields, and use the midfields as relief. How you use your monitors is up to you, but until you're an expert mixer, you should definitely use more than one variety of studio monitor.

Choosing your studio monitors is a personal choice, one that should neither be arrived at lightly nor by chance. There are scores of studio monitors on the market, and given the supreme importance of translation, this is not the place to skimp. Personally, I like monitors that make me work hard. That may seem counterintuitive from someone who is so insistent on mixing fast, but I can promise you that you don't save yourself any time in the long run by mixing quickly on monitors that tend to disguise the truth of the matter.

Monitors that make everything sound nice, with a scooped midrange, are going to bite you in the ass. It's far better to use a pair of monitors that readily show all the warts. This will make it harder to mix, but will also reduce translation issues. Say what you want about NS10s—and I swear to you I fucking hate them—with the right amplifier pairing and in a well-designed control room, I can mix like the wind on them. That's because I know exactly how they translate, and they tend to reveal all the warts in the midrange.

Seemingly every studio monitor manufacturer will tell you that their monitor is "flat." In theory, a flat monitor responds evenly across the frequency spectrum. In practicality, there's no such thing as a flat studio monitor. All you need to understand is how your monitors respond in your room, and how that translates outside of your room.

Monitor Varieties

There are two kinds of professional monitors—passive and active. Passive monitors require an external amplifier, one that should be carefully paired with the speaker. This too is a matter of personal taste, and in general the better the amplifier, the better the pairing is going to be. The power of your amplifier is also an important consideration, as improper power to your monitors will cause them to operate inefficiently. I'll leave this research up to you, but in the end, you need to actually make this decision yourself by listening to how they work together. Purchasing an amplifier that's meant to make your local audiophile happy will generally prove to be useless in the studio, and will only be a waste of money.

Active monitors have the amplifiers built into them. This design offers a number of advantages. When you get into the upper tier of biamped monitors, the amplifier is matched specifically to the speaker. If you don't like the amplifier-speaker pairing of an active monitor, you don't like the monitor. That makes life simple. Active speakers also travel well, although they can be ridiculously heavy. If you find yourself traveling to another room, your active monitors will remove a major variable from the equation. There's no doubt that they'll react differently in every room, but that will be the only difference. I say don't bother fucking around, and get yourself a high-end pair of active midfields; but then it's always easier to spend someone else's money.

Monitors, particularly midfield monitors, also have a few options where the tweeter is concerned. Some monitors are designed with concentric tweeters, in which the tweeters sit right smack in the middle of the woofer. The thinking behind this design is to time-align the top end with the low end, as they're emanating from the same focal point. Supposedly, when the tweeter and woofer are separated, the high-end information is slightly out of sync with the low-end information, which causes skewed imaging. Imaging, shmimaging. Yeah, I agree that the imaging isn't quite as accurate on non-concentric monitors, but I've mixed extensively on both, and you can make mixes translate on either variety.

Some monitors implement ribbon tweeters, which tend to soften the high end a bit. This offers the added benefit of reducing fatigue. Again, it's pointless for me to make a recommendation regarding this, because all that matters is what works for you in your room.

The only real concrete advice I can give you regarding what style of monitor is best for you is don't buy them without trying them in your room first. It doesn't matter to me if you're in the middle of Alaska; you're wasting your money buying a pair of monitors if you don't try them out in your room first. Professional monitors can cost anywhere from $1,500 for a relatively inexpensive pair of Tannoy speakers to $7,000 for a pair of Meyer HD-1s. Spend the money on shipping and insurance to try out your monitors. Most vendors will let you return them within 30 days if they're not to your liking. Just be up front with the vendor about your intentions, and they can tell you the best way to proceed.

One last consideration, and one that shouldn't be ignored, is how your near-fields and midfields pair up. If you can't switch between your monitors without completely confusing yourself, then that's not a good pairing. You should be able to easily switch back and forth between your monitors and not be shocked by the difference in sound. While I admit it's rather shocking to switch to NS10s after working for an hour or so on just about any pair of midfields, there are some combinations that can cause a mind-fuck of epic proportions. When you come across this, you'll know it. Besides, I already told you not to get NS10s. What the hell are you even considering them for?

If you really want to mix, it's essential to get the monitors that work best in your room and for you. You need at least one great set of monitors, and they're probably going to cost you several thousand dollars. If you love Tannoy concentric monitors, you might be able to get some cheaper, but price really shouldn't be your main consideration. If you can't hear the way you need to, mixing day in and day out is going to be nothing less than miserable. Take the time necessary to find just the right monitor for you and you won't have to make that purchase again for many years to come.

Summing

As much as I prefer to mix on an analog console for a multitude of reasons, it's the summing that offers the critical difference, one that skill alone can't overcome. As of the writing of this book, digital summing is wholly inadequate for mixing, and I really don't expect that to change any time soon. To go back to our Itzhak Perlman metaphor, digital summing would be akin to providing Itzhak with a two-stringed violin and expecting him to perform at his usual high level. While I'm certain he'd still be able to do amazing things with the two-stringed instrument, he'd be so limited in what he can perform that a person of lesser skill with a fully functional instrument would likely produce a more usable result. There is a point where skill cannot overcome the shortcomings of our instrument.

DAWs have been around since the late '80s. I recorded the entire first Pharcyde album on a DAW back in the early '90s. By the early 2000s, DAWs were commonplace in studios, and they've now taken over as the main platform for recording and mixing. DAWs have improved considerably over the course of their 20-plus-year history. Plug-ins have gone from abysmal to downright usable. High-quality converters—which have been available for many years now—have come down considerably in price. There's one place, however, where DAWs are still dreadfully lacking, and that's digital summing.

That's right; I'm telling you that your DAW in its stock form is going to make life not just difficult, but untenable as it relates to mixing. That doesn't mean you can't make your clients happy (we all have clients that are easy to please). It certainly doesn't mean that you can't come up with an amazing arrangement. It means you're facing a limitation so severe and so critical to mixing that your main instrument is essentially broken. Your results will remain severely compromised until you fix the problem.

I can't tell you why. I can't tell you how. I can't even prove what I'm about to tell you, and I can assure you that the DAW manufacturers, particularly Digidesign, will not only reject this claim but will actively try to persuade you otherwise through flawed white papers that most of you can't understand and bogus comparisons that most of you wouldn't know are bogus.

All DAWs bog down at the 2-bus.

The 2-bus is the path by which all of your audio is summed together. Forgive the obvious statement, but as mixers we take many tracks and bring them down to two: the left and the right. You might recognize these as outputs 1 and 2 of your DAW. If you're mixing internally to your DAW, all of your audio is being digitally summed through those two outputs, which happen to be your 2-bus.

The more audio tracks that are summed digitally, the more choked the audio gets. DAWs don't combine audio well, and they never have. Some people on the Internet will argue that DAWs somehow combine audio "perfectly" (and they'll even use that word), it's just that we, as humans, somehow prefer the "flaws" of analog summing better. Yes, and a student cello made of balsa wood emits sound perfectly; we just prefer the wonderful flaws of that old Stradivarius. Ahem. Digital summing isn't good enough. Sorry.

This doesn't mean you have to start shopping for a six-figure large-frame console any time soon. There's a more reasonable and affordable fix to this issue, and it's called a summing box.

A number of summing boxes are available on the market. They wouldn't even exist if there wasn't a clear need for them. That doesn't seem to stop people who don't know what they're talking about from debating the issue, though. I'll leave you to do the research on which summing box is best for you, but I use the Dangerous 2-Bus, which I settled on after extensive real-world testing. This is not meant as a testimonial for the product, although you can be certain I wouldn't be using anything on my 2-bus that wasn't of the highest quality. It is, however, a summing box I'm intimately familiar with, and as such, it's the one I'll use for my examples.

The Dangerous 2-Bus is essentially an ultra-simple analog console consolidated into a convenient two-space rack unit. It has no faders and no pan knobs—just 16 static analog inputs that sum the audio down to two outputs. If you have a Pro Tools rig with at least one 192, you can easily integrate a summing box into your system, and if you want to give yourself a shot at delivering great mixes, this is as necessary a purchase as the DAW itself.

Good analog summing will provide you with a more extended high and low end, wider mixes, more punch, and most important of all, more depth. As much as gear manufacturers use adjectives like this to regularly to sell their products, I'm not a gear manufacturer. I'm a mixer. These are legitimate adjectives that make sense to anyone that mixes. The difference between a mix summed analog and one summed digitally is so obvious that once you switch your outputs to multiple channels of the summing box, you'll notice an immediate overall improvement in your mix.

It's important to keep in mind that digital summing degradation compounds. In other words, digitally summing four channels isn't nearly as problematic as digitally summing eight (although the density of the program being summed also tends to be a factor). This means that you can get away with *some* digital summing; you just want to reduce it as much as possible, preferably without breaking the bank. While one Dangerous 2-Bus could very well be enough for you, two of them will give you even more flexibility and should be considered, if not in the short term, then in the long-term.

Although the most ideal scenario would be to have one analog channel for every output (which would mean you've managed to eradicate your digital summing completely), that's probably not necessary, particularly when evaluated from a pure cost/benefit standpoint. I personally use two Dangerous 2-Bus units, and while three would be better, it's likely not going to benefit the mix enough to warrant the expense for my situation, particularly when we bring converters into the equation. Besides, it's pretty rare that I have so many tracks that I actually need more inputs. Even on productions that have more tracks than outputs, there are almost always parts that play in different sections. As a consequence, it's unusual for me to end up with any digital summing whatsoever.

Since the concept of analog summing and how summing boxes are configured is likely a foreign concept to many reading this book, I'm going to offer specific examples of how one might set up their summing box. We'll start with a one-box setup.

Let's say you have one Dangerous 2-Bus and one MOTU 192 in your room (a 16-channel converter box). Unless you're mixing to an external device or unless you have external stereo converters, you'll only be able to use 14 converters from your 192, since two of them will be required for actually monitoring the mix. With 14 analog outputs available, you should be able to limit the digital summing substantially. Here's an example of how you might set up a rock mix through a single Dangerous 2-Bus.

1 Bass (mono)

2 Kik (mono)

3 Snare (mono)

4 Vocal (mono)

5–6 Drums (other than kik and snare)

7–8 Guitars

9–10 Keys

11–12 Percussion and FX Returns

13–14 BG Vocals

While this configuration with one Dangerous 2-Bus isn't perfect, and there will most certainly be some digital summing involved, the majority of your summing will be done analog, and outside of your DAW. The more summing you can do outside the DAW, the better.

As your mixes improve, you'll probably want to expand your external summing abilities. The configuration as laid out above is really nothing more than the bare minimum for overcoming digital summing issues. Since Dangerous 2-Bus units can be coupled with multiple others, you can easily increase the number of available analog inputs. I use two summing boxes, which provides me with a total of 32 inputs. Since I have 24 converters, two of which are used to monitor the mix, I can send a total of 22 outputs to the Dangerous boxes. Fortunately, that's usually enough.

I'll give you an example of how I might configure my outputs for the same basic rock mix:

1 Bass (mono)	11–12 Guitars 1 & 2
2 Kik (mono)	13–14 Guitars 3 & 4
3 Snare (mono)	15–16 Keys
4 Vocal (mono)	17–18 Background Vocals
5–6 Toms	19–20 Percussion
7–8 OH's	21–22 FX Return
9–10 Rooms	

As you can see, there is considerably less digital summing with 24 converters and two summing boxes than there would be with 16 converters and one summing box. With two summing boxes, digital summing is nearly eradicated for all but the biggest of mixes. This is good.

There's one caveat where summing boxes are concerned. The quality of your converters and clock will greatly affect just how much you gain. The better the converters, the more improvement you'll get from analog summing. I use Radar converters in my DAW room, which are considerably better than your stock HD 192 converters. You would be hard-pressed to find a person who has used both who would argue with this statement. That said, there's no doubt that you're better off with a stock Pro Tools rig and a Dangerous summing box than a stock Pro Tools rig alone.

You're going to see all sorts of claims from people on the Internet that they hear no difference when they use a summing box. Mark my words (assuming they're not just making it up), those that make this claim either don't have the monitoring necessary to hear the difference (let alone mix in the first place), or don't have the converters necessary to make the extra conversion worthwhile.

Frankly, you've got to have some pretty crappy converters for this hybrid system to work worse than a pure in-the-box (ITB) mix.

After 20 years of mixing in analog studios, and various attempts throughout those 20 years to put together a system that can compete with analog mixing, and after countless failures on this front, the hybrid system I'm prescribing here has been the only combination that's proven acceptable. In fact, it's better than acceptable. I can get no better results outside my private hybrid mix room, including in my favorite analog rooms. While I prefer to mix through a large console and with a plethora of analog outboard gear, that preference is based purely on speed—not ultimate quality of results. And although I argue that speed makes you a better mixer, the ability to leave a mix and go on to another seems to counterbalance this particular issue.

Testing Your Summing Box

If you're going to try a summing box out for yourself, and I highly recommend that you do, there's a specific procedure that I recommend. If you mix a song to completion, and then you put it through a Dangerous summing box, you're going to have a difficult time with the evaluation. The summing box *will* change your mix. Even though the mix will be far better in some ways, it will also be different. It's difficult to get past the inherent balance changes that will occur from such a radical change in your summing. Therefore, you don't want to test a summing box on a finished mix, as it's really not a comparison that you can accurately evaluate. There is really only one way that I can figure to fairly and accurately judge what a summing box can do for you.

Start by installing a summing box into your system. Run the analog outputs from your converters to the inputs of your summing box. By running all of your audio through the first two inputs of the summing box, you remove the sonic nature of the summing box itself as a variable when making your comparison. Mix a song in your DAW by digitally summing through outputs 1 and 2. Make your way through discovery, and frame a decent static mix. Go beyond the point where the mix is singing and you feel good about it, just to the point where you're beginning to struggle with the mix.

Now switch your channel outputs so that you're using all the channels of the summing box instead of just the first two. This switchover takes a few minutes, since you have to select new outputs for every channel. If you have a good summing box (and the only one I can vouch for is the Dangerous 2-Bus), you should notice a greater depth of field, considerably more clarity in the bottom end, a seemingly broader frequency range, and more overall punch. The difference should be night and day, and you should immediately find yourself struggling less with the mix.

Don't be put off by the changes in your mix. If there were no changes, it would be a useless and superfluous box. The whole reason for making the switch at the struggle point of your mix is that it's not going to cost you time. In fact, the mix should improve so much where impact is concerned that you'll likely find it considerably easier to mix.

Now, this isn't a scientific way of determining a difference. It's a practical one. You can't devise a scientific test to prove this for yourself or anyone else. For starters, you can't perform the switch in real time. The reason you can get away with performing a listening test in this manner is because it's meant to reveal how much easier it is for you to mix on an operational and process level. It's not meant as a subjective listening test, although you'll likely think your mix sounds better. Regardless, if you're finding it suddenly easier to mix, there's a reason for it. It's easier to mix when summing analog.

That said, I guarantee I'm going to get hammered on the Internet for this one (I might as well have sent out invitations). I mean, not only isn't the comparison blind, it's not immediate! So why would I recommend this? Because blind comparisons are overrated when it comes to mixing. Look, if you notice a big difference, you're not imagining it. There's a point in a mix when you know something has changed, and you know how that change has affected you. Making comparisons on a mix while you're *in* a mix shouldn't be performed blind. If the difference affects you, you'll know it. If it doesn't, then it's not a big enough difference to matter. We do comparisons a thousand times a day as mixers, and they're rarely, if ever, preformed blind. Do you need to perform a blind test to determine whether the vocal sounds better with an 1176 or an LA-2A? Do you need a blind comparison between EQ settings? Of course not. You're evaluating the sound within the context of a mix. These comparisons mean everything to your mix, and there's neither a reason nor the time to perform them blind.

If you want to set up the comparison blind, then set up two mixes, one using multiple outputs, the other using two outputs, and have someone help you switch between the mixes. But once you hear how much extension you get on the bottom end, you're not going to bother. Once you realize how much more depth your mix has, that summing box isn't ever going to get unplugged. You're in the middle of a mix; you'll know instantly whether there's a big difference or no difference at all. I'm sure I'll be challenged to pick blind by some Internet wannabe screaming about expectation bias. If you're one of the Internet wannabes, then by all means, test it blind. If you're on your way to being a bona-fide mixer, listen to the obvious difference and move forward on your mix.

Consoles Sum, Too

While a summing box is probably the best option for a mix suite, there's always the possibility of owning a full-blown analog console (complete with knobs and everything!).

Keep in mind that not all analog consoles are created equal, and unfortunately there are hundreds of consoles out there, new and used. Picking one that's right for you depends on a great many factors, including your budget and what you intend to use it for. If it's purely for mix work, there are a great many disadvantages to using a console over a summing box.

An analog console takes up space, so you're going to need a control room that can accommodate its footprint, which means you'll also need a build-out to go with the beast. Analog consoles also add in a smear factor from a monitoring perspective, in that the sound coming from your speakers reflects off the surface. I've been mixing with the reflective smear of an analog console for my whole career. I'm so used to it that it's not even an issue. In fact, it took me a minute to get used to mixing *without* sound reflecting off the console. You just need to be aware that this phenomenon exists. Of course, if you're merely going to put the console off to the side, like it's a summing box, then this isn't really an issue, but that's only a viable option for your smaller mix desks or your larger mix rooms.

Analog consoles, particularly used ones, are maintenance nightmares. Even if you have technical prowess, your recall abilities will be hindered greatly by the day-to-day differences in sound due to breakage and repair. And once you recap? You won't be able to recall any of the mixes you did before the recap job. Besides, all those movable faders and knobs are only hundreds of tiny possibilities for why your mix isn't coming back exactly as it was. These are not insurmountable issues, and if your session is attended, you can make sure that your client understands the importance of avoiding recalls by getting them to sign off on the mixes. You can even do this with unattended mixes, although your efficiency will depend on how quickly your clients can evaluate uploaded mixes. While the reduction in recall accuracy can be a drag, it can actually work toward avoiding most recalls, since it forces both you and your clients to make final decisions and finish mixes.

Analog consoles usually come with mic pre's (of varying quality), so they're a great addition to a tracking room. If that's a large part of your work, then a desk can be an exceptionally good option, and should most certainly be considered.

Although many of the prevailing analog mixing consoles from the '80s and '90s can be purchased today at bargain-basement prices, you need to think long and hard about whether this is the best option for your mix room. The two most common large-frame consoles are the Neve V series, which come with a variety of packages including total recall, and the SSL E and G series, in which total recall is standard. Both of these consoles come with a dynamics section on every channel, and while the compressors are semi-usable for certain parts, you wouldn't want to use them on every channel. In many cases (and I really can't believe I'm saying this) you could very well be better off using a good plug-in compressor over the ones supplied on these consoles.

These particular desks have massively large footprints, and require a separate machine room for the power supplies. They also use severely outdated computers for the automation systems: the SSL uses Bernoulli drives, and the Neve V uses a 286 computer. If you don't know what a Bernoulli drive or a 286 is, then you have some understanding of just how old these systems are. There have been some updates for these computer issues, allowing the implementation of more modern systems, but they're still antiquated at best.

Frankly, I would describe both of these consoles as nothing more than "usable" mixing consoles. I say this despite the fact that there have literally been thousands of successful and great-sounding albums mixed on them, including many of my own. The SSL uses VCAs on each automated channel, which has a compounding effect. As the number of channels with VCAs increases, the more degradation there is on your audio. The Neve V has an obvious buildup of 500–700 Hz, which can be bypassed through the simpler monitor path available, or compensated for with EQ. The V consoles run so hot you can literally fry an egg on them, which means your cooling costs will go through the roof, and you'll be recapping 60 channels at least once every five years, which is probably two years past due. As if all that's not enough, there isn't a decent mic pre between them, which means they're useless as recording desks, and will serve as nothing more useful than monitoring desks during the recording process. In my view, this issue alone negates one of the best arguments for purchasing an analog console in the first place.

My favorite mixing desk is the Neve 8068, but you can expect to pay more for one of these than most people pay for their house. Pretty much any Neve built before 1978 is going to offer great mic pre's, great EQ, great summing, and of course, endless hours of maintenance. Vintage APIs are amazing desks. Trident B series consoles are surprisingly decent desks for the money, but they didn't come stock with automation. Still, if you're using one for the summing, you don't really need automation.

In general you should stay away from any desk that was built or used primarily for live sound. Too many design shortcuts are taken in these sorts of consoles, as portability is of primary importance.

There might be some live consoles out there that are totally usable, but the perception issues alone make this sort of solution problematic. No one wants their mixes run through the same shitty console that was at the local club.

As of the writing of this book, there are still a variety of alternatives for a new analog console. These range from outrageously priced overgrown behemoths to reasonably priced, wholly usable sidecars. I can't possibly go through every console ever made, since I haven't used them all, and there are far too many considerations in this type of purchase for my generic opinions to be useful.

It's important to note, however, that adding an analog desk or a summing box into your setup does not automatically guarantee that you've improved your summing. There are a whole host of prosumer-grade analog solutions that fall well short of the quality necessary for good summing. If you're going to move to analog summing, you should seek out the highest quality possible within your budget. In general, the simpler the design and the higher quality the electronics, the better your summing will be. This is why I like the summing box alternative for DAW mixing. They're built specifically for this purpose.

Stereo Compressor

If you're mixing classical music, straight-ahead jazz, or any music that is best delivered with a dynamic worthy of only a dedicated listening room, a stereo compressor is unwarranted. If you're mixing any other popular genre of music, you need a stereo compressor, and you need a good one.

I've used the same stereo compressor on my 2-bus for nearly 20 years: the SSL G384, which is a one-space rack unit compressor modeled off the ones in the G series desks (although as of this writing I'm not able to determine how faithfully). When it comes to what goes on my 2-bus, I'm superstitious beyond the point of rationality. There are only a handful of compressors other than the G384 that I'd actually ever strap across my 2-bus, but I'd be hard-pressed to actually use any of them (hence my admission that I'm beyond the point of rational where this is concerned). If you're about to go online to find the best price on a G384, you'd best make your way to eBay. Solid State Logic doesn't make these particular compressors any longer—they now sell a "new and improved" version, and we all know what that means (HINT: It means it's not as good as the original model). So, if you want the SSL G384, you're going to have to purchase one used. I'm hopeful that this testimonial alone will raise the value of these compressors. As it is, I can already sell mine for more than I purchased it. Not that it matters. I wouldn't sell it—not even from my deathbed.

Your stereo bus compressor is the one compressor that you would be ill-advised to use in the plug-in form. This might be reasonable on a temporary basis as you learn (and earn!), but analog compressors are far better than their digital counterparts for the job. This is especially so when you directly compare the plug-in to the analog compressor it emulates. You can perform about 80 percent of the heavy lifting where compression is concerned with a hardware 2-bus compressor, but it'd better be pretty damn stellar at the job. If you get the impression that I freak out about everything and anything that goes on the 2-bus, you're right; and there's a good reason for this. The 2-bus affects the entire mix!

The Internet is a great place to get bad advice where your stereo compressor is concerned. The number-one myth is the notion that stereo compression should be left in the hands of the mastering engineer. While there's no doubt that mixing with a stereo compressor takes practice, and while it's quite possible that you'll fuck up several mixes in the process (can you say overcompression?), it's essential that you as the mixer—and only you—compress your mix.

Most mixes of popular music will need compression, particularly if you want the mix to work anywhere outside of an isolated listening room. As has been pointed out repeatedly, a dynamic range of anything more than 4 dB is unrealistic for the habits of today's music buyer. A wider range might have been acceptable 30 years ago, but today people tend to listen to music as they engage in other activities. This means that music must compete with external noise, and if the dynamic range is too great, sections will all but disappear from audibility in any real-world situation. Most music must compete with noise from cars, dishwashers, dryers, babies crying, hairdryers, etc.

So why *not* leave compression up to the mastering engineer? Simple: your balances will change far too drastically for this to be a reasonable option. Balance is your main weapon for manipulating the listener's emotions and focus. If you're going to spend hours upon hours getting those balance relationships just right, why would you find it acceptable for them to completely change come mastering time? If you don't compress the stereo bus while you mix, you're not delivering a mix. You're delivering some weird approximation of a mix, and it's not even that, since you can't predict precisely how the mix is going to change—and it *will* change.

One could certainly argue that EQ done by the mastering engineer will change balances, and although that's technically true, EQ adjustments work relatively uniformly across your mix. Your mix won't suffer from some minor EQ adjustments, and if it requires major EQ adjustments, then the mix was broken to begin with. Frankly, I take great offense when a mastering engineer puts a compressor on my mix.

You can certainly mix without an analog stereo compressor, and if your monitoring and summing have left your bank account depleted, this coveted addition to your mix arsenal can wait. But this will put you in the unenviable position of having to do all of your compression on the individual channels, which is time-consuming and nowhere near as effective as a stereo compressor on the 2-bus. One high-quality analog stereo compressor can make your life so much easier and mixing so much faster that the time you ultimately save (once you get past the learning curve) will pay for the unit in just a few projects.

Stereo compression is like adding glue. Whether you choose to use it aggressively as I do, to reduce the amount of individual channel compression necessary, or whether you prefer a more subtle approach, it's an invaluable tool for mixing.

In general, you should strap your 2-bus compressor onto the mix right from the start. But if you really want to get an idea of the power of a 2-bus compressor, take a moment to get your bass and drums mixed, and then strap on the compressor. The control it will supply over the bottom of your mix will be obvious, and you may never take it off your 2-bus again. I have mine strapped across the 2-bus even while I'm recording.

Most stereo compressors have a sweet spot. If you hit the compressor too hard, your mix will become too compacted and your low end will be neutered. Both of these symptoms will actually make mixing more difficult. If you hit the compressor too lightly, you won't get the gluing benefit, and your bottom end will be inconsistent at best. I'll warn you now: mixing with a compressor strapped to your 2-bus can be nothing short of frustrating, and can give you a whole new appreciation for the overall tail-chasing experience that is mixing. Even after you get past the learning curve, you'll still find yourself adjusting the threshold when the mix is getting close. Reducing or increasing the threshold of your 2-bus compressor at any time during the mix, even by the tiniest margin, will completely change your internal balances and overall EQ curve. That said, a threshold adjustment can also be the one change that brings your mix into perfect focus.

The ratio you use on your stereo compressor is up to you. I typically use a 4:1 ratio, as I find 10:1 far too aggressive for the 2-bus. Pick whatever ratio works best for you. Your attack and release settings really have more to do with the program than anything else. These should be set purely by ear. When you hit upon the best attack/release settings for the track, your mix will immediately start to sing, so avoid getting into the rut of using one setting for everything that you mix. Once you've figured out the best settings for your mix, don't change it! Otherwise I fear you'll be cursing me until the day you retire for having convinced you to strap a compressor onto the 2-bus. We wouldn't want that to happen.

There's one other way to gel your mix, and that's by slamming your 2-bus with your mix. This method allows the electronics on your 2-bus to act like a limiter. If you're mixing in the box, this isn't an option. You have to have an analog 2-bus to do this. Furthermore, not all 2-buses are created equal. The 2-bus on an SSL will crumble in short order, yet you can absolutely hammer the 2-bus on most of the 80 series Neve desks to the point that the meters are pinning at all times as you work. If you find yourself on a vintage console, try it, and see how far you can push it. You might find it makes your life easier.

The DAW

In all likelihood, you already have a DAW. It's even more likely that your DAW is your main axe for mixing. If you've got a 2-inch tape machine and a killer analog console, more power to you. Unfortunately, the rest of the world is now working in DAWs, and when your client delivers tracks in digital format, this is where you'll be working, too. I suppose you could print the tracks to 2-inch, but I would generally advise against this, since any benefit the recording might have gotten from tape is long gone. If you want the benefit of tape, and I'm here to tell you that you do, you'll have another shot when it comes time to print the mix.

Which DAW is best for mixing is hard to say. I'm currently using Logic in my mix suite, partly because I have no need for the subpar converters that come with Pro Tools. It amazes me how much money people spend for that system given its remarkably obvious shortcomings, but it's what you'll find in every major studio, so I guess there's some reason for it—although I've never been able to quite figure out what that is. If it pisses you off that I have such a low opinion of Pro Tools, take a break from the book and come back to it. You can't learn in this state of mind.

ANNOYANCE INTERMISSION (play music now)

Welcome back.

If you're performing the lion's share of your automation and processing in the box, then you're going to need to investigate some plug-in packages. Don't expect emulation plug-ins to sound anything close to their hardware counterparts, and if you have no basis of comparison regarding this, then judge the plug-in purely on its own merits. I'm not sure what you gain by limiting your overall control to matching that of a piece of analog hardware, as it seems counter to the power that a DAW is supposed to be offering you in the first place. In other words, a plug-in that emulates a three-band EQ only has three bands of EQ. If it doesn't actually sound the same, and it doesn't, wouldn't you rather have seven bands of EQ? For this reason, I suggest you stick with plug-ins that are designed to be their own thing, or choose emulation plug-ins that combine multiple units into one, like the URS packages. The URS Console Strip Pro is an emulator, but we have no idea what's actually being emulated, and the package offers a rather large number of possible combinations. Whether those combinations are true to the unnamed original hardware is irrelevant. They offer different tones and are worth investigating as a package.

The Brickwall Limiter

Brickwall limiters, like the Waves L2, are regularly used in the mastering process. The brickwall limiter shines in its ability to reduce dynamic range, thereby achieving higher playback levels from your CD. I'll get into the whole loudness issue later, when we discuss mastering.

Brickwall limiters flatten peaks and prevent your mix from passing a certain threshold (like digital 0, for instance). Technically, you could brickwall-limit every track if you wanted, but I'll warn you now: your mix will suck. I'm not going to tell you never to use these kinds of limiters on tracks in your mix. They can be useful tools on occasion, so go ahead and experiment with them.

Of course, given my missive regarding the necessity of a stereo compressor, it will surely only be a matter of time before you get the brilliant idea of strapping a brickwall limiter across the mix bus. I can promise you that's not even remotely brilliant for a number of reasons.

While compressors will drastically alter your internal balances (and for this reason it should pretty much piss you off whenever a mastering engineer puts a compressor on your mix), brickwall limiters don't tend to alter internal balances, at least not until they're being abused. That fact alone is argument enough for leaving the brickwall limiting to mastering, but there are other compelling reasons.

You can't undo what a brickwall limiter does to your mix, not without actually recalling and reprinting the mix. While this might not seem like a big deal if you're running a DAW, it can be exceptionally problematic when your client goes to remaster the original mix some years down the line. Sure, you can instantly recall it, and have a new mix in 10 minutes flat, but will you be able to recall the mix 10 years from now? Hell, you probably won't be able to recall your mix in five years. Since recalling the mix has a technological statute of limitations, and since brickwall limiting will add artifacts, which restrict the amount of EQ that can be used, and since you will generally tie the hands of any mastering engineer who attempts to sweeten your mix, it's advisable to forgo the brickwall limiter. Your client will surely appreciate having a master he can actually do something with in the unforeseeable future.

As if those reasons aren't enough, you're too tired at the end of the mix to make that kind of judgment call. If you're thinking you'll combat this by strapping an L2 across the mix bus right from the jump, consider what it's like for a singer performing with an Auto-Tuned vocal in their cans, and you'll have some idea of the mayhem that will surely ensue. There's a reason someone touches up the mix after you, and there's a reason why it's not you. A fresh perspective, specialized equipment, and a different monitoring environment are just a few of those reasons. Besides, you're too close to the mix to have any kind of clarity where minute enhancement is concerned.

If you wish to brick-limit the reference mixes you send off with your clients, that makes sense. Most artists find themselves completely befuddled by mixes that don't play at a competitive level—even after you explain to them why they'll have to turn their stereo system up. In fact, the issue of clients evaluating mixes that haven't been brought to level can be so problematic that I actually *advise* you to put a brickwall limiter on your reference mix as you consolidate it for your client. Be careful, though. You want to be sure you're giving your client something representative of the actual mix; otherwise, you're going to have a whole different set of problems, including some new mix notes that have no basis in reality. For this reason, it's unadvisable to use aggressive brickwall limiting on your client's reference mixes.

Be sure to label the file name in a manner that lets you know you've added limiting. You'll want to compare your raw mixes to the properly mastered mixes, not your limited versions, and if you don't label well, you'll have to engage in mix forensics to determine which is which. For your more knowledgeable clients, it's not a bad idea to give them a mix with and without limiting. If they prefer one over the other, they'll let you know that.

Analog Tape

These days, tape machines are probably the most misunderstood pieces of mixing gear. If you've never used a high-quality 2-track tape machine, then I recommend you borrow or rent one before you print your next mix and hear for yourself what it does.

The difference between a mix that's hit tape and one that hasn't is similar to the difference between videotape and film. From a musical perspective, it's the difference between five individuals playing a track, and a band performing a song. I have personally demonstrated the value of tape to countless clients, and I still have yet to come across a single one that didn't immediately recognize the enormous benefit that tape supplied the mix.

There is probably no analogy that I can come up with to adequately describe what good analog tape will do for your mix. The difference is so staggering, and the result so pleasing, that it can actually cause you to wonder how you listened to your mix without it for all those hours. Tape is the finishing process for a mix. It congeals the mix, glues the parts together, widens the mix, offers more depth, provides more nuance, and most important of all, it's what finishes the mix.

That said, not all tape machines are created equally. As if that's not bad enough, there are different tape formats, widths, alignment specifications, and headstocks (which can perform poorly when worn). All of these factors will dramatically change your results. An improperly aligned tape machine alone will render it unusable for its intended purposes. Furthermore, many people are under the false impression that tape will reduce your high-end response, and this impression is largely due to how digital tape emulators respond. A properly aligned tape machine with well-applied levels can provide tremendous fidelity to the original source. In fact, the tape print done properly will give you a more accurate representation of the mix than most converters, and in those cases where the converter might be more accurate, the tape usually just sounds better.

There are many professional-grade 2-track machines out there, including ATRs, Studers, MCIs, Otaris, etc. There's also a whole host of prosumer-grade analog machines, and I'll refrain from denigrating any specific manufacturer here, but in general they're not good enough for your mix. ATR Services is pretty much the only company I'm aware of that offers professional-quality tape machines today. Anything else you're going to have to purchase used, and you'll probably need to budget for some maintenance and head relapping (depending on the head wear).

If you're just starting out mixing, then you don't need a tape machine. Even if you've been mixing for 10 years, you don't need one. I, on the other hand, always print my mixes to tape. Ultimately, if you want to compete with me, then you're going to need one.

Some people like half-inch tape for their 2-track masters, some prefer quarter-inch, and my friend Ron Saint Germain prefers one-inch for his masters. There's no right or wrong where varieties of tape are concerned. There are only your likes and dislikes. I personally use an ATR-102 half-inch machine for my mixes, and I use ATR tape. These days I don't tend to store my mixes on tape, so I print and transfer into the DAW and essentially deliver digital prints of the tape playback. Since I have good converters I can do this without losing too much in the transfer. If the budget exists, I'll store the mixes on tape, and that's what I'll deliver to mastering.

If you read about analog tape on the Internet, you'll find some of the stupidest and consequently largest threads out there regarding this subject matter. In most cases, the people arguing that digital offers more fidelity than analog tape don't even know what they're talking about. Unless you spend time using tape and get over the learning curves involved, you have no way of arguing this, and I promise you that 99 percent of the people arguing that cheap digital is more accurate than tape are either deaf or have never actually printed a production onto a good 2-track machine.

My purpose here isn't to convince you to run out and purchase a tape machine. In fact, that's the last thing you should do. You can't purchase a tape machine until you actually know what it is you like. If you can find anyone in your local area that has a good analog machine, see if you can borrow or rent the machine for printing mixes. Make sure it's someone who's exceptionally familiar with using and aligning analog machines. Otherwise your results really won't be very reliable.

If you're mixing completely ITB, you could always bring your session and iLok to another studio and print to their tape machine. Even if you're mixing through summing boxes, you could pack up your entire rig and bring it to another studio. If it costs you 100 bucks in studio time and another $90 for a reel of tape, it's money well spent just for the experience alone.

Reverbs and Delays

While reverbs are useful for creating the illusion of reflectivity, they also tend to wash out detail and smear clarity. Oddly, as much as digital reverbs provide the illusion of space, they can also eat up space within your mix, particularly if you use too much. Excessive reverb will make your mix sound like a globular mess. In many cases, you're far better off forgoing the reverb and using a repeating delay to add a tail. Repeating delays in the 250 ms range can actually sound like reverbs without taking up nearly the amount of space and without destroying the overall clarity of your mix. That's not to say you should never use digital reverb. You just need to be aware of the potential costs of doing so.

Frankly, digital reverbs leave much to be desired. They drive me crazy, mostly because I have some basis of comparison, given all the great plates and chambers that have been at my disposal over the years. Capitol Studios has several amazing chambers below their parking lot, and these are far more appealing for providing reflective space than any digital reverb. Organic reverbs tend to eat up less space, and react in a more nonlinear and natural manner.

If you have a recording room, or if you have a space that's a reasonable distance from your control room, then you can use that room as a chamber. All you need are two well-placed speakers and two equally well-placed mics. If you create a stereo image with your monitors in the room, and mic the reflectivity of the room itself, you have yourself a chamber. The quality of your chamber will depend on the quality of the speakers, the mics, the room, and the mic placements, so keep that in mind as you put this together. If you want to make the room appear bigger than it is, you can use compression to get more excitement and decay time out of your room.

You can use any size room as a chamber, even your bathroom, which can be handy since it's usually quite reflective in nature. This makes for a great "small-tiled room" effect, which you might find in your digital arsenal. Stairwells also make for great chambers, particularly the concrete ones you find in multi-floor office buildings. I can tell you, if I had a studio in my house, I'd have every room wired up for this purpose.

EMT 140 plates are large and cumbersome and must be tuned by someone who knows what they're doing. They also require their own special sound-isolated room, as they will pick up nearby external noise. That said, there's nothing quite like a good-sounding plate. Digital plates don't react at all like the real thing. Notice I use the term "react," and not "sound." That's because I've never actually heard two plates that sound the same. Plates are more like musical instruments in that they each have a unique quality about them. For whatever reason, when you put a good plate on a track it seems like it's a part of it. I've yet to feel that way about a digital emulation of a plate.

Spring reverbs can be quite handy too, particularly on guitars. Springs evaluated on their own merits sound pretty ratty, but then that's the whole point of them. Sometimes you want that ratty spring reverb sound, and the best way to get it is to use an actual spring. You could probably put together an entire room of spring reverbs for less than most plug-in packages, although you really only need one or two.

Digital delays also leave much to be desired, although they're considerably better than digital reverbs. If you have a tape machine, you can use this for delay. There's an inherent delay between the record and playback heads on any multi-head tape deck. By slowing down the playback speed, you can extend the length of that delay. If you want repeats, all you need to do is feed the return of the tape machine back into the machine again. Just be careful: you're actually creating a feedback loop, and if you lose control of that loop the results can be unpleasant at best and disastrous at worst. You can also find some vintage tape delay units on the used market. Roland made several tape loop units that offer a variety of other effects (including chorus and reverb), and of course there's the Echoplex, which I've used on many occasions.

When I was at the California Science Center I came across an enormous metal tube used to demonstrate how slowly sound travels. The flexible (but stationary) tube was probably about 10 feet in diameter and 150 feet long, and weaved its way around the giant room from ceiling to floor like a big snake. When I spoke into one end I heard my voice return about 300 ms later. This was the time it took for the sound of my voice to travel to the other end (which was capped), and then return. I actually went straight to Home Depot that night and purchased 60 feet of corrugated flexible plumbing tube. This was awesome for creating very short analog slapbacks (given the limited size of the tube). Frankly, it was a major pain in the ass to bring everywhere, but it was always fun to use, and produced some very nice delays. At the very least it was a good conversation piece.

Now, this isn't to say I don't use digital reverbs and delays. I do, and there are some very nice ones out there. Just be aware that they don't react like analog reverbs and delays, and there's an entire universe of these kinds of effects at your disposal. With a little creativity you can create your own, and although they do take up physical space (which is an obvious consideration), they tend to be relatively inexpensive additions to your arsenal.

There are all sorts of other effects processors out there. Frankly, there's no reason for me to go over all the different kinds of choruses, flangers, phasers, filters, and anything else you can think of. They're all used for effect, and there are a million possible reasons for using them. As with all gear, if it helps your mix, use it. If it doesn't, don't. Hey, what could be more Zen than that?

Dealing with Clients

Working the room, keeping people happy and relaxed, is half of mixing successfully.

As much as you'll find yourself alone in the room for long stretches at a time while you mix, you're one part of a team. Sure, you're being brought in for your mixing expertise, but you generally don't have the power of veto, and no matter how passionately you feel about a particular decision, there's more than one person who can override you. How you deal with people can make or break the mix, and for that matter, the entire mix session. If you're incapable of expressing yourself in a manner that is logical, well thought out, and persuasive, you're going to have a difficult time mixing effectively, particularly at those times when you must deal directly and personally with the clients.

The more comfortable you can make the artist, band, and producer feel about the mixing process, the easier it is to do your job. Mixing skills alone aren't enough. One of the best ways to make your client comfortable is to make them feel important. You're essentially being handed someone's creative child, which is likely viewed as the culmination of a lifetime of work. If you don't give the client the impression that their project is the most important project on your plate, you risk alienating them.

The most effective way to help someone feel like they're important is to actually treat them that way. That may seem self-evident, but if you're on the phone half the day trying to line up your next job, or if your clients see you working on another project during their allotted mix time, even if it's for just a moment, the client is going to wonder how you really feel about their project—and rightly so! No one wants his or her brainchild in the hands of a mixer who doesn't appear to give it any kind of priority. Perception is reality, and you have some control over how you're perceived. Not only do your clients expect your full attention, they deserve it. Your clients want to feel like you're into their music (at least to some degree). If you're not, they'll know it, and if you take on every project that comes your way without investigating it first, I can guarantee you'll mix something you hate.

Declining Projects

As a professional mixer, you're being paid for your mixes, not your time. This is an important distinction, because you don't want to compete against other local studios for time. There are likely several studios in your market that operate from this position, and trying to compete directly with them will only drive down the price of studio time. Once you're able to deliver high-quality mixes with some consistency, you should charge for your skills, not your time. Your skills are what make you more valuable than your competition.

One of the best ways to build up your discography with high-quality mixes is to be selective in what you accept. This is a difficult pill to swallow, because no one wants to turn down money. Unfortunately, if you take every loser project that comes your way, your results will suffer, which in turn could make you less valuable. Therefore, it's always best to listen to rough mixes before accepting a project, and you should decline those sessions where there's no chance of a decent result. Of course, there are several other reasons for declining a session, including the size of the budget, the quality of the songs, and in some cases, even the quality of the recordings.

Everyone is crying about their budget come mix time. Get used to it. Unfortunately, if you accept $250 per mix (which is abysmally low regardless of your market), then you're worth $250 per mix. I mean, if you really are worth only $250 a mix, then fine. But if your skills make you more valuable, then you're not doing yourself any favors by accepting that kind of money.

Personally, if I were somehow compelled to mix a project regardless of budget, I'd rather mix on spec than for $250 per mix. At least on a spec project I have a chance of making my full rate if the band gets signed, and I could be rewarded for my gamble with profit sharing. Making $2,500 for 10 songs would put me in a league with all sorts of people who normally can't compete with me.

The "perception is reality" rule applies here—not only are you going to be underpaid if you accept that kind of money, but you're going to be treated in a manner appropriate to your pay scale. Anyone who specifically wants a mixer isn't looking for a bargain. They're looking for the best mixer they can get within their budget. Your expertise will still be weighed against your pay scale, and the lower that pay scale is, the less respect you're going to get from your client.

So what, you say? Well, if all you care about is getting paid no matter how much that amounts to, then you might as well get a corporate job with full benefits. If your goal is to become a premier mixer and to build a successful business as such, then you need to act like one, and you can't act like one if you're not paid like one. There is a very basic rule in life that applies here: when you pay peanuts, you get monkeys. Unfortunately, in this particular metaphor *you* become the monkey, and I can guarantee that not only will you be treated like one, you'll feel like one too.

I can't tell you where the line is regarding this. The money you can command depends partly on your market, your discography, and your ability to sell yourself. If you're in a small town in a tiny country, that will likely dictate your pay scale more than any other factor; that is, until you're able to grow beyond your local market. That, of course, is why the Internet was invented.

It's pretty simple: If you don't like the music, then you pretty much don't understand it, and if you don't understand it, you certainly won't be able to mix it. Now, you can mix projects that you don't love, but you can't mix a project that you hate. In fact, you don't serve anyone by mixing a project you hate—least of all yourself. You'll lose those clients permanently, and it will probably cost you future clients as well. Besides, it becomes a lot easier to decline a project for budget reasons when you think the songs are mediocre at best.

Mark my words: The day you mix a song in which you can find absolutely no redeeming quality is the day you'll have no idea how to mix, no matter how good a mixer you've become. Just keep that in mind before you accept a project based purely on money. It'll happen. We all have to pay bills. When it does, you'll know what I'm talking about, and you'll likely never do it again. Listening to the roughs before you accept a project saves everyone time and heartache.

Occasionally I'm sent roughs that are so badly recorded there's absolutely nothing I can do with them. This is a far trickier reason for declining a project, and there are other factors that affect such a decision. I can tell you, if the songs are absolutely brilliant, you should be interested no matter how bad the recordings are. Great songs will always transcend shit recordings, and if they're arranged halfway decently, you'll probably be able to make mixes that get the songs across well. In the worst-case scenario, you can discuss re-recording some parts in the hopes of saving the project. The politics that exist with the producer will determine whether you can even make this sort of overture, and it's probably best to mix a song or two before you even broach the subject.

The general personalities of your potential clients could also have some bearing on your decision to accept or decline a project. If you've determined your potential clients are despicable, a low-budget or poor recording makes declining a no-brainer. The last thing you want to do is take on a potentially challenging project with people that are unreasonably difficult, or worse yet, delusional. You can certainly *improve* a bad recording of bad songs, but you're ultimately limited by what you're given, and any improvement will be incremental at best. You can't make the glorified bedroom demos of a producer-less band sound like they made a record at Abbey Road with Sir George Martin. Even if the music is great, you have to seriously evaluate whether miserable people are really worth the effort. Only you can determine your own personal threshold regarding this.

Obviously, you can't be so picky that you never work, and while I've spent the last few paragraphs giving you reasons to decline a project, you probably won't come across a high percentage of projects that require a pass. Just because a song doesn't inspire you doesn't mean there's nothing redeeming about it. If you think the lyrics are awful, mix the vocals by syllable as if it's in a foreign language. Lose yourself in the music. Really, a project has

202 Zen and the Art of Mixing

to be particularly atrocious in order to find absolutely nothing redeeming about it. As long as there's something positive to grab hold of, you can mix the project.

Dealing with Problem Clients (and Winning Them Over!)

No matter how fortunate you are, if you work in this business long enough you're going to come across some problem clients. If you just managed to spit your coffee all over this book, I apologize. Clearly, you already know that's a bit of an understatement. That said, I don't want to be perceived as someone who thinks that all clients are problematic. I don't even want to be perceived as someone who thinks *most* clients are problems. But as my friend Peter Bunetta so adroitly puts it, it's not who you know in this business, it's who you avoid. Unfortunately, avoidance is not 100 percent effective, and a few bad experiences with slimy people over the course of your career will be enough to cause you to implement strategies for dealing with them. I'm full of strategies. Just understand that the advice in this section isn't meant as a prosecution of all clients in this business. Consider this more of a "Break Glass in Case of Emergency" section.

Making music can be an emotional process. The mixing phase can be exceptionally stressful, partly because it's the most expensive phase, and partly because it's the end of the record. As Michael Jackson put it, "this is it," and we all know how that turned out. It's difficult to accurately evaluate an unmixed song, and in many cases, no one on the project is sure what they've got. They have suspicions. They have hopes, and they want you to bring those hopes to fruition. It's important that you be sensitive to this, because a problem client might very well be a nervous one.

The beauty of life as a mixer (aside from all the babes) is that you're in and out of a project. You don't have to deal with the day-to-day drama of the artist, and if you do, it's for small periods within a relatively short time frame. Of course, it doesn't take long for an artist who loves drama to bring that element into your life. Please excuse the obvious word of caution, but it's advisable to avoid the drama. You don't serve anyone well by getting emotional, no matter how hysterical those around you become. Not that you won't occasionally get sucked into the drama—you will. You're human, and hopefully you're passionate about what you do. But the better you become at ignoring the emotional outbursts and instigations of a drama queen, the more effective you'll be as a mixer, and the less problems you'll have completing a challenging project.

Of course, the most effective way of combating the effects of an overbearing client is to get them out of your way as much as possible. Which brings us to your alone time in the control room. There's a reason I called the control room the Womb in *The Daily Adventures of Mixerman*—it's our only warm, safe haven from the madness outside. If you can limit your time with problem clients to little more than the beginning and end of a given mix, you'll have a far easier time staying out of the fray.

You should do all that you can to claim the control room as your domain, and in a manner that doesn't alienate your clients. You never want your clients to feel even remotely unwelcome at their own session, but the control room for the mixer is no different from the recording room for the performer. The last thing you need is to have someone fidgeting nervously behind you while you're trying to perform. Hell, that's the last thing *any performer* needs, and the most overbearing artist will have a deep appreciation for this comparison. Believe me, when you're in the headspace necessary to mix, negative energy can and will be felt, and it doesn't help. So explain the process and ground rules for your clients. Set your boundaries in a friendly manner, and use the results of a kick-ass mix as your backup.

Even with clear and effective communication regarding the sanctity of the Womb, you'll have those boundaries tested repeatedly. There's usually that one client who thinks he's immune to the rule, whether it's the singer or the producer. Sometimes the producer wants to hang in the room, and you'll be hard-pressed to kick the producer out, particularly at the beginning of a mix. Still, you need the producer to come in fresh to help evaluate the impact of the mix. It's impossible for him to evaluate the mix in this manner if he's been pounded by it for hours right along with you.

Of course, good explanations aren't always enough. Sometimes you need to employ enforcement strategies. You'd be surprised by what you can get away with saying when you do it with a smile. "Okay, I need my alone time now," said with a smile, will usually result in an empty and quiet control room.

Backseat mixing is problematic at best. The person in the back of the room really has no idea what you're concentrating on at any given moment. The hat could be insanely loud, and if you're intently focused on the bass, you could very well be oblivious to this particular balance issue. Meanwhile, the client is in the back of the room going nuts wondering why you're mixing the hat so loud. This can have a negative impact on trust, particularly if it's the first mix.

Aggressive mixing is also difficult when your client is with you at all times. If your clients have a very clear picture of what they want, they'll be closed-minded. If they're not sure what they have, they'll be nervous. In either case, your aggressiveness will only serve to scare the living shit out of them.

As you work on your mix, particularly through the discovery stage, you need to be open to any and all ideas available to you. One of the great advantages of hiring a third-party mixer is the inherent lack of preconceptions. If the client cringes every time you try something radical, or begins pacing every time your mix falls apart, you're going to be in for a long and difficult afternoon. This happens to be the most effective case for getting your clients out of the control room.

You need the freedom to try out bad ideas in order to find the good ones, and you most certainly don't want the artist sitting in the back of the room having to endure that! Admit that you have lots of bad ideas. Tell your client that it's your process for finding the good ideas. In reality, bad ideas are a part of everyone's process, so the artist is going to understand this. Explain that you'd hate to be influenced away from pursuing a certain path just because it doesn't seem immediately fruitful. The best way to achieve your client's goals is to have a firm understanding of what you have and how it all works together. Experimentation is the best way to accomplish this.

By couching your reasons for alone time in a manner that addresses the best interests of your client, you stand a far better chance of avoiding a confrontation, or worse yet, hurt feelings that could ultimately turn into resentment. Addressing your client's interests is always a good way of presenting an argument, particularly when tensions are high. Remember, until you've delivered your first kick-ass mix, your clients will likely be on edge. Expect this, and make sure that you take the steps necessary to prevent negative energy from affecting you. Otherwise the mix will suffer, and then you won't gain your client's trust. Don't be afraid to gently nudge your clients out of the control room when you need time to work. If you don't, you risk losing the job entirely.

Even if you disagree with my contention that you need alone time, or if you're the rare mixer who's such an extrovert that you can't bear the thought of more than an hour alone, you must at the very least establish control of your domain. It's not reasonable for your client to make mix adjustments. Frankly, this is less of a problem in a DAW than on an analog console, which can be physically reached by your client. There will be times when a problem client warrants that you relinquish the controls for a short period of time, but you should allow this as a last resort and only with strict supervision. You cannot mix if you don't have full physical control of your own mix. One change will set off the need for other changes. It's bad enough that you spend your time chasing your own tail; you certainly don't need a second tail brought into the equation. Keep your clients off the mix, and force them to communicate effectively with you.

Equally as debilitating as an aggressive client is a passive one. While your overall goal is to deliver a great mix that your client loves, it's not in your best interest to have no input whatsoever. A lack of useful input can be baffling, to say the least. This usually comes down to a client who is either intimidated by the process (or even you), or is too easily pleased. On the surface that may seem like a dream job, but critical input and notes only serve to improve the mix. Lack of critical engagement by your clients can affect your overall aggressiveness. It could cause you to work under-aggressively, as you have no critical backstop, or over-aggressively, as you'll have no boundaries to worry about. Neither one of these mind-sets is good for the mix.

On those occasions when I find myself with somewhat passive clients, I tend to get more animated, more personally aggressive, and more provocative. I do this to keep the energy up. A session lacking excitement and energy risks a lackluster mix. You set the tone of the session, and you have to do it within the confines of your client's personality. If you need them to be more engaged, engage them. If you need them to be more reserved, get them out of your way so you can do your job properly.

Establishing Trust

The first mix of an attended project is of paramount importance. Even if you're normally capable of pushing out two mixes per day, you should take the whole day for the first mix. You might even leave it up overnight before you engage in mix notes. There are a few reasons for taking a little extra time. For starters, the first mix has to be set up from scratch. There's no EQ, no processing, and no effects set up. All you have are raw tracks and an empty mix palette (or desk). There's a certain amount of janitorial work that must be accomplished before you can even begin mixing, even with mix templates in place. Much of that setup work will be used throughout your mix session, which speeds up the process considerably on subsequent mixes.

The first mix sets the bar, and if you want the rest of the session to go smoothly, you want to set that bar nice and high. That may seem counterintuitive, but the point is to relax your clients, not play expectation games. If you don't set a high bar from the start, it can be cataclysmic to the session. Add in an unfamiliar room, and/or clients with whom you've never worked, and you'll most certainly need time to get your bearings on both fronts. As much as I advise you to mix as fast as possible, there's really no room for error on the first mix. By the time your clients come to listen to the mix, you want to absolutely rock their world. If you do, you'll have their trust.

Trust is critical in mixing. Without your client's trust, every decision you make will be second-guessed. The artist and producer will be less willing to leave you alone for hours at a time. You won't be given nearly the leeway that you want on the arrangement, and seemingly fruitless experiments will be cut off before they've fully developed. Nothing is more destructive to a mix session than lack of trust, and if you don't have it, you must acquire it as early in the process as possible.

If a client doesn't trust you as a mixer, they're not going to trust the mix. If you have a track record as a mixer, this becomes a less common problem, although it can happen regardless of your discography. Some people are only impressed by the biggest names in the business. In those cases, gaining trust could very well be all but a lost cause. Your only chance is to knock their socks off.

If you're mixing an entire album, try to choose a song that has a ton of potential, but low expectations. In particular, you want a song with a well-defined and focused arrangement. If you pick a song that requires too many parts decisions, you'll have no gauge on your artist or producer, how they work, and what they like. It's far easier to be aggressive with underdubbing when you have an overall understanding of the people involved, and particularly once you've established their confidence. Choose a song that's got some room for improvement, but isn't in need of a complete over-haul. If you want to be the hero (don't we all?), wait until the third or fourth song—that's when you'll have the most leeway to do anything you want.

I'll warn you now that by the three-quarter mark of a successful mix project, your clients could become so enthralled by the concept of underdubbing that they might begin to insert themselves into the process. This means you'll have the client in the control room right from the start of the mix. Worse yet, they'll attempt to help you make parts decisions. It's often difficult to get out of this other than to point out the pitfalls of abandoning a system that has been proven to work. Sometimes this is a welcome development, particularly if you have a good working relationship with the producer. Sometimes it's a nightmare, because you are no longer allowed to operate in an aggressive manner. All you can do is revert back to your "alone time" arguments, and hope that works.

It's possible, if you're working on a DAW, that you prefer to have many mixes in various states of completion. While this is a perfectly legitimate way of working for an unattended mix session for out-of-town clients, it can be problematic for an attended one. Even if the producer is a longtime client, you're going to want to make sure that everyone on the project is on the same page. The best way to achieve that is to finish a mix. Every artist has preferences. You can easily accommodate these once you've determined what they are. For instance, if you discover on the first song that the band prefers their background vocals to actually be louder than the vocal (I just mixed a project where this was the case), it's likely that they prefer this treatment uniformly across the album. The process of completing mixes provides the opportunity to gather this sort of time-saving information. Besides, you still need to gain the band's trust, no matter how much they love their producer and no matter how much their producer loves you. Unless you're familiar with everyone involved in the project—this includes record company executives—finish at least the first few mixes to build rapport and establish a working methodology.

Picking and Choosing Your Battles

There will be times when your clients will start to engage in exercises in silliness. For instance, I've had clients, producers, and artists alike continually make mix suggestions involving a 10th of a dB. Whether they can actually hear that difference is moot. I've already admitted that I can hear this small a change in a hypersensitive state, and it's quite possible that your client is afflicted with the same debilitating condition. That said, as much as bringing up the guitar a 10th of a dB is probably just a waste of time, I have no problem participating in such ludicrous adjustments.

It's difficult to make an argument against a change that can't possibly make any real difference. I mean, how can you possibly protest an internal balance alteration that has no real effect on the impact of the mix? If it has no real effect, then what exactly is the problem with doing it? If it makes your clients feel better about the mix, then I say it's completely worth your time. Obviously, if you find yourself spending an exorbitant amount of your day randomly bringing parts up and down by 10ths of a dB, you need to have a reality-check conversation with your client regarding time/benefit ratios. The mastering process will most certainly cause a greater quantitative change in internal balances than 10th of a dB increments at the mix stage.

You have to determine where the line is regarding this, but you should always try to err on the side of the client when it comes to inconsequential mix notes. Your concern should lie with the big picture, not with generally superfluous minutiae. The big picture where the art of mixing is concerned lies not just in how your clients feel about the mix, but also in how they feel about their mixer.

Picking and choosing your battles is essential to a smooth-running mix session. As much as a healthy ego is wholly congruent with effective mixing, you don't want to let your ego get in the way of a happy client and a great mix. If a request by the client doesn't diminish the overall impact of the mix, then there is absolutely no justification for spending any time debating it. You only weaken your arguments on more essential matters. You have limited capital to spend with your client, and if you waste it on bullshit that makes no difference to the mix, you may find yourself out of that capital when it really matters. You're the mixer, you're there to make the mix, but if your clients aren't completely happy with it, then as far as they're concerned you delivered a bad mix. What might seem to you the stupidest, most inconsequential complaint about your mix can make the difference between your clients loving or hating their own record.

That may sound silly, but if your client is cringing every time they hear the mix for something like a clap track in the bridge, then what are you gaining by keeping the claps in? Now, if you feel that the claps are so crucial to the overall impact of the mix that they warrant a discussion, you should engage in one. But you need to have a concrete argument as to why the mix feels so much better with eight bars of claps. This sort of debate can't be about your ego. It must be purely about how the decision actually benefits the overall track.

When you have a single artist, these sorts of debates are far easier than when you have a band. Bands disagree, and the more personnel in a band, the more elusive consensus becomes. This can put you in a tough spot. If the drummer and the bass player hate the clap track and everyone else loves it, what are you supposed to do? The safest and wisest decision is to default to the producer's wishes. He was hired to arbitrate these kinds of decisions, not you. Unfortunately, sometimes the producer is unwilling to commit, which is probably why you were given that contentious clap track in the first place. Hell, there might not even be a producer on the project. Either way, this puts you in the position of negotiating a solution.

All bands have a power dynamic. There are very few bands in which everyone has an equal say, and in those rare cases of a true band democracy, an up or down vote is usually effective for these sorts of disputes. The more people there are involved in the mix, the more you have to consider potential problems. If, for instance, you discover early on a point of contention regarding a part that exists on the rough, you need to make sure you have the opportunity to determine what your own opinion is before you insert yourself in the debate. You shouldn't even entertain this sort of discussion until you've pretty much finished the mix. Difficult split decisions often become non-issues when presented within the context of a fully focused mix.

It's easiest to demonstrate what a controversial part does to the overall impact of a mix once it's near completion. Of course, if the part in question has been mixed in such a manner that it's sorely missed when muted (or conversely, is uniformly revolting when unmuted), you've managed to sell your decision without having spent any capital whatsoever. Don't construe this maneuver as some underhanded technique for getting your way in a mix. While you certainly have an inherent advantage in selling your vision just by how you put the mix together, this is a good thing for everyone involved, since it tends to prevent gridlock on your session.

If none of your solutions seem to resolve a particular issue (and you should have several plans regarding the resolution of any particular issue), then it might be best to express your strong opinion and allow your clients to work it out between themselves. Bands settle disputes on a regular basis. They should have the necessary infrastructure to deal with this sort of problem, particularly if they're making the decision based on a nearly completed mix. The happier your clients are with the overall mix as presented in the room, the easier it will be for each of them to accept a compromise.

A word of caution on this: There's an inherent risk in leaving a compromise solely up to a band. They might just come up with a solution that defers the decision even longer, by requesting two different mixes. *Avoid this scenario at all costs!*

Now some of you reading this might consider printing two mixes to be a reasonable solution. It's not. All you're going to do is bring more people into an already crowded decision-making process. Band girlfriends, managers, record company execs, promoters, fans, even friends of friends of the band are going to weigh in after the two mixes leave your room. If you think that mix isn't going to come right back to you a month later with camps even further entrenched than before, you're sadly mistaken. A request for two different mixes requires immediate and aggressive damage control.

This is one of very few instances when I will attempt to assert my own power of veto in a mix session. Unless you're a name mixer who was hired directly by the record company, you don't actually have veto power beyond threatening to quit the session. You want to avoid making that kind of threat either overtly or implicitly, as they might just take you up on it. Still, you need to exert some muscle occasionally, and this is one of those times. I put it to my clients as plainly as I can. "We're only printing one version of the mix—the best version—and we need to make the decision as to which that is right now. I wouldn't be doing my job if I let you put this off any further." This sort of proclamation may seem bold (telling your client "no" usually is), but it's absolutely necessary that you protect your clients from their own inability to make a decision. Insist on a resolution, and dissuade them from deferring it yet again.

There are times in a mix when you must stand up for the mix itself, and prevent your clients from working against themselves. This is one of those times, and why you don't ever want to spend your capital on frivolous issues. When you assert yourself in this manner, and only on an occasional basis, your clients will take notice. If you've been nothing but accommodating regarding the majority of their mix notes, your client will finally know what they already suspected—you have their back. Your clients expect you to have their back; otherwise, they'd mix it themselves by committee. In all likelihood, they're going to listen to you. If they don't, well, you get to print two mixes, alternate mixes for each of them (vocal up, vocal down, instrumental, etc.), and then you get to do it all again in a month, only this time you'll be reworking the entire mix all because of a stupid fucking clap track in the bridge. Good luck with that.

If you're thinking to yourself, "Gee, maybe I shouldn't let it get to that point," then you're beginning to understand. If the inclusion or exclusion of a part comes to the asinine solution of printing mixes that accommodate both, you've lost control of the session, and you need to regain that control as soon as possible. Look, if both mixes are viable, then what's the problem with picking one and going with it? And if one mix seems only marginally better than the other, then why not just pick one and be done with it? Plus, printing two mixes sets a dangerous precedent for future mixes. Once you've given your clients permission to get away with deferring a decision beyond the mix session, what's to prevent them from asking for three mixes of the next song? What's to prevent them from asking for stems? If you don't draw a hard line the first time it happens, you'll merely be drawing it on the next mix. So don't let the session come to this. Yes, your Zen Mix Master is freaking out. That should tell you how important this is. Take note.

Communication

I don't think I can adequately explain the importance of communication to a well-run mix session. Your job throughout the session is to facilitate communication, and you do this through leadership and example. All creative endeavors succeed through an open and honest exchange of ideas, but even that's not enough. There must be comprehension as well. You're wasting your breath if no one can understand what the hell you're talking about.

Sometimes I marvel at just how inherently broken human communication is. Discussions can become so circular in nature that they can make the mix process look simple in comparison. I've personally endured countless long, extended, meandering conversations over something as simple as a minute balance suggestion, like bringing up the vocal half a dB across the song. I realize that there are times when it can be difficult to put certain concepts into words, but asking for the vocal to be turned up doesn't seem to qualify. Of course, if that person doesn't actually know that they want the vocal up, that would explain the particularly babblative soliloquy on their part. But if you then turn to your confused client and ask directly, "Do you want the vocal up?" only for them to respond with a definitive "yes," you have a seriously compromised communicator on your session.

There can be a number of causes for poor communication. Sometimes an inability to clearly communicate is nothing more than a personality trait. Sometimes your client is uncomfortable with offering a direct solution. It's possible they're intimidated by your expertise where mixing is concerned. They might even be worried about offending you. They may not want to assert themselves in a manner that appears unyielding. Frankly, they may not even know what's really bothering them. Whatever the reason (and you may never know the reason), you (and your clients, for that matter) require usable input that produces results, and it's your job as the mixer to focus everyone in your session down that path.

The best defense against poor communication is the diligent use of cross-examination techniques. If a client on your mix session proves incapable of providing usable information in a reasonable amount of time, you must extract it from them. I suppose the first step of the process is allowing them to meander momentarily in the hopes of arriving at some starting point. Once you have some information, you can begin interviewing the client, and hopefully get to the bottom of their indefinable issue with the mix.

There will, of course, be times when your client's problem with a mix is complicated and can't be easily explained or fixed. In those cases, you'll know it, because your client will be exceptionally uneasy with the mix. Fundamental problems on a mix mean you've somehow missed the boat, at least from your client's perspective, which is pretty much the only perspective that matters. If the mix is fundamentally broken for your client, then you're going to have to go deep under the mix hood to ascertain the problem. I don't care how good a mixer you are, this will happen, and sometimes you can find yourself at a complete loss as to how to fix the problem. The first thing you need to determine is where the crux of the problem lies. Is your client unhappy with the arrangement or how the mix sings? If it's an arrangement issue, you'll need to go through all the parts with your client as if you're in the discovery phase. Chances are, if you made decisions on parts that are different from the rough, this is where the problem lies.

If you play the rough and your client is all smiles while you're wondering what the hell she's smiling about, there's a serious perception gap between you. Attempting to convince your client that your arrangement choices are the better ones is a useless waste of time. The best thing you can do is print your mix as it is (for your client's future reference outside the room), and make a new mix with your client's arrangement preferences. The purpose of printing the mix is simple; they might love it later.

Sometimes, your client just needs to go through the mixing process with you before they're open enough to listen to your mix. Sometimes you just need to determine how it is they think. This is exactly why I recommend against the first mix with a new client being a track that requires extensive underdubbing. You have no idea how they're going to react to radical arrangement choices on a first mix. It makes no difference whether your mix is great or not. Ultimately, your client makes that determination, and if you have no capital built up, you have very little room for error.

If the problem with the mix has to do with how it sings, and you completely disagree with your client, then you have to figure out where this discrepancy lies. This is the time to bring out reference material, in particular your client's favorite records, preferably ones that relate in some way to what you're working on. Your client might not be hearing properly in your room, in which case you need to help them acclimate to the space. You might also want to print the rejected mix and rough on a CD and bring it to your client's car. This allows her to hear the mix in a familiar system, and it gives you some understanding of her usual listening environment.

Of course, we can't reject the possibility that your client could be right; your mix might not sing properly (although you'd think the rough would illuminate this). Taking a moment to reference some other mixes could very well provide you with the needed inspiration for fixing a problem you didn't realize existed. It's also possible that your client prefers shitty mixes. Good luck with that!

The issue of a mix that's not singing is really only a major issue if it's an early mix. If you've established trust and a rapport, this isn't a big deal. Your client won't be falling apart wondering if she hired the right person, and you'll be able to work through the problem together. If you're working on a DAW, you can even move on to another mix and come back to it fresh later, but this isn't really a viable option on the first mix.

If you started out with 75 tracks, ended up with less than 24 in the mix, and spent 12 hours getting there, only to find out you've mixed the song completely differently from how your client wants it (despite having no definitive rough of the song), I'm not going to tell you that you won't be pissed. You will be. Seeing as your client refused to make any real decisions throughout the process of recording, to then reject outright your best efforts toward an effective arrangement can be nothing short of irritating. In such a case, anger would be a legitimate reaction. Personally, I'd be apoplectic at such a realization. Your best bet is to call it a day and come back fresh. This way everyone can focus on fixing the problem and not pointing fingers. Fortunately, this particular scenario isn't a regular occurrence, but then, I didn't invent it out of whole cloth either.

It doesn't matter why there's a problem with the mix, or for that matter, what the problem is. What matters is that you *understand* the problem. Understanding what your client is unable to explain can only be achieved through investigation and an in-depth interview. It's best to be unemotional when dealing with a mix catastrophe; otherwise your frustration will surely reveal itself. This will only serve to make your client defensive, or worse yet, emotional. Emotion evoked by any source other than the music itself only clouds communication.

Hopefully, your client's outright rejection of your mix will be a rare occurrence. If not, you either need more practice, or it's time to consider another career. Rather than end the book abruptly here, I'm going to assume you need more practice and continue onward.

Mix Notes (The Reprise)

I'm happy to report that the more common reaction will be your client's marked adoration of your mix. Regardless, there will usually be some notes. Notes are good. It's the details that make a mix great. While it's true that we must keep our attention on the big picture where the mix is concerned, it's the summation of all the tiny little details that creates the big picture in the first place. You can make a *good* mix in a relatively short period of time. It takes many hours to make a *great* mix, and the difference between them is in the details.

Once you've determined that your clients are on board with the overall mix, all that remains are those details. Fixing details is a simple procedure and can be dealt with in very precise terms. As I pointed out in the Introduction, I have a mantra for this time in the mix. "Part. Section. Up or Down."

"I was thinking, well, maybe when I listen to the first chorus— it's really good, don't get me wrong, the guitars are so strong, I really get sucked into the whole thing, and that snare drum, I love it, such great crack—but sometimes I'm left...I think it's a very strong vocal performance, you know? And..."

You could allow your client to go on endlessly, or you could help her out.

"Part? Section? Up or down?"

"Vocal, in the first chorus, needs to come up."

Ahhhhhhhh.

If your client has a clear idea what the problem is, don't let her beat around the bush endlessly. You're never going to figure out what the hell she's trying to say. Give her a helping hand. Part. Section. Up or Down. If it's something more complex than that, she'll say so. If it's not, you can cut out loads of time from the process by preventing a veritable verbal diarrhea of superfluous information. This also prevents your client from putting herself in the position of having to defend a mix adjustment regardless of whether it's actually an improvement.

If you can streamline the process and prevent your clients from getting bogged down in detailed philosophical discussions over something as simple as turning up the vocal, you'll be doing everyone a big favor. Until you actually make the mix adjustment, there's no point in speculating as to its effectiveness. Make the change, evaluate the change, and then discuss whether or not it worked out. In most cases, the move will prove itself as a sum positive or a sum negative instantly and without debate. If there's disagreement, at least you have something concrete to discuss, which can lead to a solution, whatever it is.

If you buy into the notion that your client's suggestions can be beneficial to the mix, and accept that you're a part of a team, it makes the mix notes process far more efficient and effective. By the time you're entertaining notes, you've been mixing for hours, and your client is now the one with a fresh perspective. Use their freshness to help you finish the mix. They're going to hear issues that you might not notice until the next day. If you can harness your client's feedback into direct, succinct communication, their notes will only benefit the mix. Of course, some things will require a bit of interpretation on your part.

When it comes to communicating with your client, your greatest and most effective weapon is to listen. Considering that you're attempting to increase your abilities where critical listening is concerned, you may as well include people in that development process. Of course, we've already established that there are inherent shortcomings in communication. Given this, many times you'll engage in the art of inferring what's being discussed.

For instance, if your client says, "The snare drum, whole song, sounds clacky," this is obviously a little less clear than the usual "up or down" instruction you've requested. The use of the term "clacky" probably means your client is hearing the artifacts of an overcompressed snare. Only your most knowledgeable clients are going to tell you directly that a part sounds overcompressed, so you need to pay careful attention to the adjectives they use. You're going to hear some wacky (and often paradoxical) adjectives where your mix is concerned, and you need to decipher these seemingly arbitrary words into a usable instruction.

Suppose a client says to you, "I think the vocal is too loud in the first chorus; the track isn't quite explosive enough." Your client has made a judgment on the mix, and offered you a solution. Yet there is far more than just one solution for the judgment she's expressed. While you've been provided with specific direction regarding the vocal, you've also been told that "the track isn't explosive enough." This part of the statement should tell you quite a few things.

First, your client only mentioned the first chorus, which means the second and third choruses are probably working for her. You'll be able to investigate this further once you've fixed the first problem. Second, if her problem is with the explosiveness of the track, then why would we automatically reach for the vocal? It's possible that the guitars need to come up. Or the guitars might need to come down to give the drums more apparent strength. Third, it's possible that the section preceding the first chorus isn't setting up the payoff sufficiently. Remember, how a section works in the context of the song is directly dependent on the preceding section, and if the chorus isn't "explosive," it might have more to do with the pre-chorus than the chorus itself. Fourth, your client could be absolutely right. The vocal might be too loud. Or your client could be right about the part and wrong about the direction. You might actually fix the problem by bringing the vocal *up*—the exact opposite solution to the suggested one. Fifth, it could be a performance issue in that the band just didn't hit that particular chorus with as much energy, although, if that's true, you should probably already be aware of this issue.

Depending on the tracks, there could be any number of other problems that don't require touching the vocal. If all you hear from your client is "I think the vocal is too loud," then you're accepting the diagnosis without actually evaluating the root symptom.

That said, you should probably start by bringing down the vocal. I mean, that's one of the potential solutions, and it would be nothing short of embarrassing to go through a 20-minute ordeal only to discover that the solution was exactly as your client suggested. If you're going to be so obnoxious as to state repeatedly: "Part, section, up or down" as a means toward getting your client to be more efficient, then you don't do yourself any favors by ignoring the simplest solution offered by your client. Even if you absolutely knew for sure that the vocal level wasn't the issue, it would be best to try your client's suggestion first. Then you can safely take a few minutes to seek out the root of a more complicated issue without looking like a hypocrite.

Sometimes you'll come across what I call the "paradoxical suggestion." When your client suggests the vocal is too loud, it's quite possible that the vocal is actually too soft. I can't tell you how someone can confuse up from down; I can only tell you it happens to everyone, even you as the mixer. This tends to occur most often at the end of a mix when you're making your most minute adjustments. I wouldn't describe this phenomenon as common, but it happens often enough that you should certainly be aware of it. If a reasonable and feasible suggestion is made, the implementation of which makes a problem worse, you very well may have received a paradoxical suggestion. Try the opposite.

Mix Notes by Committee

When you're only dealing with one client, getting notes is a relatively simple process. It's when you have an entire crew of clients that mix notes becomes a game of diplomacy. The person you should trust the most is probably the producer. She's the one the band hired to produce the album, and she's probably the person who hired you. In the absence of a producer, you should actively seek out the brainchild of the project. It's important to have at least one person on the project that you can rely on as a true sounding board.

Essentially, you want to create an unspoken alliance with the overall leader of the group. While there are certain political reasons for this, it's not the overall purpose of such a strategy. Frankly, it's not even really a strategy. It's just what happens naturally in the mix dynamic, but it's good to recognize the effect of selecting an ally in the room, if only to prevent you from selecting the wrong person for the job.

For starters, you want to keep the session on an even keel, and if you gravitate toward the guy who understands the least about the big picture, or worse yet, exhibits the most out-of-whack sensibilities of the group, either your mix is going to suffer tremendously, or you're going to piss off the people who actually matter in the equation—probably both. There's almost always one person in the group who has the overall picture in mind, and that's the person whom you must work with most closely. Usually they'll assert themselves in that role, but sometimes you need to figure it out for yourself. Not only does this person understand the musical goals of the project, she probably best understands the personal dynamic of the band, and likely has the greatest influence on the project. This is the person who will be next to you through the mix notes phase.

As you navigate your way through the mix notes with a large group of people, disagreements are bound to come up. Some of these will be old disagreements that have been deferred, some will be new ones caused by your mix. Either way, split decisions need to be negotiated to resolution. Usually, someone will back down, and that will be enough to tip the debate. Sometimes hard lines have been drawn, and the last thing you want to do is put your thumb on the scale, as you will only manage to piss off exactly half of your clients. If you weigh in on one side or the other of a difficult debate, you risk becoming the deciding vote. You want to avoid that if possible.

Obviously, you're going to have an opinion on just about any problem that comes up. You've made an insanely long series of decisions on your mix. You've literally had internal debates with yourself over certain issues. There should be very little about your mix decisions that you can't explain. You should know why you chose one part over another. You should know why you made one part more dominant. You should know the relative strengths and weaknesses of the production and performances, and how that played into your decisions.

Although your opinion is important, and in some ways you're being hired for your opinion, you're also being hired for your solutions. If you take a hard line on a solution, you become one vote of several. If you take a hard line on the problem, and offer multiple solutions, you have a chance of amiably resolving the dispute. You're not there to be a deciding vote; that's ultimately the producer's job. You're there to deliver a kick-ass mix, and if you can maintain a kick-ass mix while simultaneously solving any contentious issues regarding the mix and production, you will do yourself and your client a great service.

The best approach to coming to a resolution is to first identify the full scope of the problem. You can achieve this by listening carefully to the debate. You want to gather as much information as possible, and based on that information, consider alternatives to solving the problem at hand. The more alternatives you can come up with, the better your odds are of coming up with a satisfactory resolution.

In the beginning of the mix, you should remove all external factors and compromises from the equation. The end of the mix is the time to consider anything and everything that comes into play regarding the mix. For instance, suppose there's a saxophone solo on a hard-rock track. The producer put it on there and loves it; you might even like it yourself, but half the band might think it's weak. The debate is over whether the sax solo is weak or not, and the solution that's been bandied about is whether to get rid of it or keep it. But that's not the only solution possible. Adding distortion to the saxophone might be a compromise that makes everyone happy. Putting a radical flange effect on it might make it acceptable to the others. Running the sax through a distorted guitar amp might solve the issue. You could try giving the saxophone a radio effect, or you could try running it through an auto-tuner set to stun. There are all sorts of middle-of-the-road solutions to the problem that could very well deal with the root issue, and simultaneously please everyone in the band. It's your job to find these solutions where they exist.

The mix notes stage is the time when all compromises are fair game, and you want to find ones that work for as many of your clients as possible. Essentially, the six hours that you've spent on the mix were preparation for anything and everything that can and will be thrown at you come mix notes time.

I mixed an adult contemporary track once in which I was asked by the A&R rep to turn down the guitars because he was afraid the song wouldn't get played on radio. These were not outrageously loud guitars by any stretch of the imagination, and they weren't even distorted, yet they were placed prominently enough that he was worried about radio play. This is an external factor that shouldn't be considered at the beginning of a mix, but that must be addressed at the end. By addressing the guitar level at the end, the artist has some basis of comparison to determine how he wishes to proceed. It's between the artist and the A&R rep to negotiate this sort of compromise. As the mixer, I need to provide what I think is best for the song, production, and artist, and then if there are things I haven't considered (whether purposely or not), they can be addressed in the mix notes phase.

Now I suppose if all I ever mixed was adult contemporary, and I worked with this particular A&R rep all the time, I'd naturally place the guitars lower than usual, particularly since we were only dealing with a half dB difference. This goes for anything. The moment I know of an overall preference a client might have, I automatically compensate for that. If the client prefers the vocals about half a dB louder than I normally place them, I tend to mix with that in mind. Just don't confuse an overall minor preference with an external pressure. If you know how your client hears things going in, you can make the whole track work toward their preferences without compromising anything on your mix. In fact, you'll automatically do things differently in your mix to accommodate any particular preference.

In the case of the guitar on the adult contemporary track, we brought the tracks down half a dB, which wasn't enough to hurt the mix, but enough to make the A&R rep happy, which in turn made the artist happy. The large majority of your mix changes during the mix notes process won't negatively affect the mix.

"More Me" Syndrome

Even if you've only mixed one band in your life, you're probably familiar with the "More Me" Syndrome. Frankly, the better you are at mixing, the less this will come into play. A great mix is the best antidote for More Me Syndrome, as it should distract your clients from ever noticing themselves. That doesn't mean it won't happen, even on a kick-ass mix. Explaining the big picture to a drummer who thinks he's too low in the mix is typically an exercise in futility. He's just not looking at the big picture. You can try to explain it, and you should, but some people find their own work so distracting that they just can't hear the whole mix.

If you've managed to blow everyone else away, this shouldn't be a problem, as it's probable that the rest of the band will shoot down the drummer's protests. It would be great if you could just ignore drummers who want themselves louder, because the alternative would be to ignore the guitar player who wants himself louder after you bring up the drums. If you made a mix guitar-heavy rather than drum-heavy, there's probably a pretty good reason for it—the guitars did more for the production than the drums.

This is what it all comes down to. You only have the five basic arrangement functions regardless of what kind of parts you have: rhythm, harmony, countermelody, response, and melody. If the harmonic instruments are more effective than the rhythmic instruments at causing the listener the desired physical reaction, then they should be louder than the drums. If the rhythmic instruments seem to be more important, then they should be louder.

The players always think their parts are the important ones—and they are—but the context in which you place a part should not be an arbitrary one. It's a decision made based on where you want the listener to focus. You're not mixing with any particular bias, other than what's best for the mix and production, and it's always good to point this out.

When dealing with More Me, you need to put up clearly defined arguments. If the harmony is the strong point of the bed and not the rhythm, then this should be explained and if necessary, demonstrated. You just want to be sure that your client understands what they're listening for before you do. If you allow them to evaluate the change purely in terms of balance, you might well lose the argument over what is probably a purposefully unbalanced mix. If your argument is how the track makes you feel and what kind of physical reaction you think is most effective based on your unbalanced mix, you need to explain this before performing a demonstration. This way they're listening for the right things.

Ego

A healthy ego is important to any creative endeavor. If you're good at mixing, then you likely have an ego regarding your mixing abilities. The artist and producer probably have healthy egos as well. I'm not sure you can actually do something well without one, since it seems that ego is what drives us toward greatness. That said, an overactive—or worse yet, unrealistic—ego can get in the way, and it's sometimes important to check your ego at the door when you're dealing directly with the client.

Since the quality of the music and its emotional impact on the listener can be highly subjective, there will be times when you will find yourself in complete disagreement with your clients. Since it's your job to facilitate good communication, you must do all that you can to prevent being a hindrance to it. If your ego is so out of control that you can't accept the idea that you might be wrong, you're going to have a very difficult time dealing with clients on your mix. The best ego check of all is to keep in mind one simple fact: it's not your record (unless you're mixing your own record, in which case forget I mentioned it).

One of the big mistakes I see in the studio is the insistence by some people in arguing against an idea rather than just trying the idea in the first place. If your client presents you with an idea for the mix, the worst thing you can do is dismiss it as something that won't work. For starters, until you hear it, you don't really know whether it will work. Besides, if you're so sure that a new concept won't work, why not demonstrate it instead of arguing the point? You never want to engage in an argument that can be easily proved or disproved by demonstration.

For instance, let's say the client thinks it might be a good idea to put a full drop before the first chorus. You're going to argue against this before giving the idea a fair shot? For all you know, the drop could be brilliant. Why would you argue against something that has a chance of improving your mix? That would be your ego talking. Check it at the door.

Even if you thought of putting a drop in that spot, even if you tried it to no avail, there's no point in arguing against it. You can tell your client you tried it there. You can tell them it didn't work, but you should most certainly demonstrate why it didn't work. They just might be able to help you make it work. I mean, you're not the only one with good ideas here, and besides, *it's their record.*

Now if your client wants to spend half a day trying every wacked-out, crazy idea he can think of, you're going to have to put a stop to that. If your client wants to take two hours to work on a crazy science experiment that she should have worked on during the overdub phase, you're right to protest, particularly if it happens on a regular basis. But to refuse reasonable ideas that only require 10 minutes of your time? I don't think so. Arbitrarily shooting down your artist's ideas or relentlessly debating ones that can be implemented in short order is only going to cause resentment, and is most certainly not in the best interest of the mix or your tenure on the project.

Remember, as the mixer, you kick everyone out of the room when you want your time to experiment with the mix. It's possible that your client needs some time to experiment, and they don't need you shooting down their every idea, because you "know" it won't work. If you know it won't work, prove it to everyone in the room, including yourself. Further, you need to prove it without making negative predictions. You're going to make a prediction and then root against your client being right, all so you can be right? You're on the same team—you're all trying to make a great record together—you don't do anyone any favors by pitting yourself against your own team.

There will be many occasions when you'll be asked to do something in a mix that you've tried and rejected. While it's reasonable to inform your client that you didn't have much luck with their suggestion, such a statement should be followed with a demonstration, and then an explanation as to why you think the idea doesn't work. If you supply the demonstration, and the client hears the issue for themselves, they will likely never second-guess that decision in the future. If you don't demonstrate it, and they accept your word, they could wake up three years from now cursing you for not using their brilliant idea in the mix. I once left a particular decision up to Ben Harper, and he called me up years later to tell me he was pissed for making the wrong decision. Who do you think he'd be pissed at if I had made the decision for him? Give your clients the same respect you give yourself. Let them hear for themselves what works and what doesn't work, and always allow for the possibility that you're wrong.

That said, your clients are hopefully paying you more money than they might your closest competitor because you've established yourself as consistent and able to get the job done great the first time. Clients who attempt to negotiate your price based on the lower prices of others should be told immediately that it costs far more to do something twice than it does to do it right the first time. My point? They're hiring you for your ability to deliver great mixes, so they're interested in what you have to say. Don't be afraid to express your opinion. Your clients want to know it, and will generally follow your recommendations, as long as they're presented in a manner that they can understand and respect.

> *If the mix doesn't somehow, and in some way, annoy someone in the room, the mix likely isn't done.*

This is probably my favorite of all the 10 Steps. I can always tell who understands mixing and who doesn't just by how they react to it. The sad truth is that you will never uniformly please everyone involved on the project with your mix. Yes, you'll be able to get a reasonable consensus, but the band and producer and even you will all make compromises. Usually, you'll be totally happy with the mix, because you're the one coming up with the compromises. The same can't be said for everyone else. The people who are evaluating your mix are the ones who are, and have been, intimately involved in the project from the beginning. They don't listen to the mix like the listener, particularly at the mix stage. They might be able to hear the big picture after some time has passed, but the way the song really impacts the listener is going to be lost on them. There will always be something in your mix that bothers someone.

The way I figure it, if you're always going to annoy someone anyway, you might as well go out of your way to do it. Bold balance decisions are one way to accomplish this particular goal. Sometimes you just get a part in a track that's so outrageously awesome that you just have to put it insanely loud in your mix. This really comes back to balance again. If your mix is in perfect balance, it's not going to be an interesting mix.

Bold balance decisions will often annoy someone in the room, and the only way to avoid this is to make safe, non-controversial decisions. Of course, safe decisions are without a doubt the best way to make a boring mix that no one will react to.

The difference between an aggressive mix with bold balance decisions and an overly proportional mix is the difference between a mix where everything seems loud and a mix where everything seems soft. I always want everything in my mix to sound loud. Now that can't literally be true. Just as it can't literally be true that everything in a mix is soft. But for whatever reason the illusion of this is quite real. If parts in your mix seem to jump out at you and command attention without distracting from the vocal, you've got a killer mix on your hands. If everything just sounds soft, you have a flat, limp, unexciting mix.

A great example of this is the Soft Cell version of "Tainted Love." All the balance decisions absolutely jump out at you, whether it's the outrageously loud electric machine-gun effect at the beginning of the production, or the sonar pings in the verses, the synths, or even the background vocals. Every time a part comes in, it comes in nice and loud and grabs your attention without ever pulling you away from the vocal.

Given this, it doesn't behoove you to play it safe with balance decisions. If a part is interesting and it does something good for the mix, make it loud. If it's not, mute it. While I'm sure you'll find exceptions to that advice, it's still good overall advice, and I guarantee that if you follow it, you'll annoy someone in the room. This is a good thing. Don't shy away from it.

Money

The best way to fuck up a mix session is to talk about money while you're actively working on the project. The only advice I can give you in this regard is to get the money straight before you start mixing. Price should be established, your deposit should be paid, and then you mix. You can't be getting into money discussions with your client when you're actively trying to be creative. Money issues cause resentments on both sides when they're brought into the creative room. You get pissed off because you have to think about money when you're trying to create. Your client gets pissed off because it appears that you are thinking more about the money than their wonderful project. Believe it or not, your artist wants to feel like you'd be doing their project even if they weren't paying you. That may or may not be true, depending on the record, but in most cases your clients are merely deluding themselves. That doesn't mean it's in your interest to correct this delusion, and I promise you, if you talk about money while you're in the process of mixing the album, that's exactly what's going to happen.

Deal with the money up front. Set your terms, whether your price is based on the project, the mix, or the day, and make sure it's clear what's being paid and for what. Some mixers use contracts. Unless there's points involved, I wouldn't bother. Once you agree on a price and the number of tracks to be mixed, make an invoice for the whole amount with half due up front, and the other half due upon completion of the mixes.

You can run your business any way you like. I'm just telling you that engaging in money talk during the creative process can destroy the smooth flow of a mix session. The best way to avoid this is to have straightforward, clear terms that are agreed on in advance of the session.

It's Their Record

The better you are with your clients, the easier mixing is going to be for you. Your best bet is to accept that you're mixing *their* record. If you think along those lines, you'll serve your client's needs, and you'll make them happy. If you can make them happy and deliver great mixes, you'll be well on your way to a successful mix career.

Chapter Six

Mastering

Mastering is actually more misunderstood than mixing, and not just by neophytes. I personally know several well-regarded, well-paid mixers who will freely admit that the mastering process is completely foreign to them. They don't go to mastering sessions. They don't get involved in mastering, and I can promise you that the major labels couldn't be happier, mostly because record companies have long been under the false impression that aggressive mastering helps to sell more records.

As the mixer, you not only need to understand the mastering process, you need to actively involve yourself in it. This is your work that's being processed by someone else, and done improperly it can be to the absolute detriment of your mixes. A butchered mastering job can remove every bit of life from your mix, wipe out any semblance of depth, and alter your balances so drastically that you'll no longer recognize your own mix. You're going to leave this to just *anyone*?

Just in case that wasn't salient enough, let me put it another way: If your best path toward a successful music-making career is to put out a product with the most impact possible, then why on earth would you not see your project through to the very end? As a mixer you have a responsibility not just to your client, but also to your career to make sure that the end result is properly representative of the artist. Allowing your client to destroy everyone's hard work makes no logical sense whatsoever. Yet it happens every day.

Theoretically (and traditionally), the mastering engineer's sole job is to prepare the client's master for manufacturing while staying within the given parameters of the delivery medium—whatever that medium happens to be. All delivery mediums have parameters that must be adhered to for proper reproduction. A 12-inch vinyl record has a maximum run time in the neighborhood of 30 minutes and an optimal run time of about 15 minutes, depending on the bass level and overall volume of the program; a proper playback speed of 33 or 45 revolutions per minute; and a limitation on the amount of low- and high-end frequency information that can be reproduced based on the run time of the side. A CD has a maximum run time of about 72 minutes, with a bit rate of 16 bits, a sampling rate of 44.1 kHz, and a maximum level of 0 dBFS (decibels relative to full scale) before clipping. The mastering engineer's job is to take your master in whatever form you deliver it (tape, CD, WAV file, SDII file, etc.), make sure it conforms to the specifications and limitations of the destination delivery medium, and prepare the master for the manufacturing company. These days the master is typically delivered as a PMCD (pre-master CD), which is a sealed CD master that the manufacturing plant uses to press the final product.

The mastering engineer's role has expanded greatly over the years. These days, the mastering engineer also tends to make mix judgments, and attempts to maximize the impact of your mixes through the use of a processing chain. The processing chain can include any number of digital and analog EQs, compressors, limiters and faux tape-saturation devices. This may sound all well and good, but at some point, maximizing impact was confused with maximizing *level*. There was a time when the credo of the well-regarded mastering engineer was "do no harm." This noble sentiment has been replaced over the years with the "take no prisoners" mantra of a war—more specifically, a loudness war.

Loudness is the apparent level at which a CD plays through a consumer playback system. The louder the mastering engineer can make your CD, the louder your CD will sound in comparison to other CDs, and the louder your song will sound in iTunes (although the Soundcheck option will match the playback level of all your tracks in iTunes). Loudness began as a way to get a perceived advantage. If your CD played back louder than other CDs, then people would more readily take notice. It's the same principle behind the loud commercials we've lived with for so many decades. If the commercials are louder than the television show, they're harder to ignore.

Loudness is achieved mostly by reducing the dynamic range of a mix. On any CD in which the loudest parts hit digital zero, the overall dynamic range is determined by the extent of the low volume information. If the loud parts on a CD are played at a comfortable volume and the soft parts are so quiet that you actually need to be in a sound-isolated listening room to hear them, then that CD has an enormous dynamic range. As exciting as a large dynamic range can be, it's useless in any real-world environment. This is mostly due to the masking effects of the constant background noise in our lives.

Mixers and producers figured out the pitfalls of a broad dynamic range long before the mastering engineers put their thumbs on that particular scale. It was the classical music producers who were crazy happy over the increased dynamic range of digital reproduction, not the popular music genre producers, who were already engaged in a vinyl loudness war of their own.

The original loudness war from the late '70s and early '80s cooled down once CDs came out. The producers decided to take advantage of the improved dynamic range that CDs offered, and the mastering engineers on the whole kept the program level under −3 dBFS (other than perhaps some transients), mostly because early converters typically degraded the sound above that level.

It was the introduction of brickwall limiters like the Waves L2 that set off the current 15-year loudness war. A brickwall limiter will prevent any transients from ever passing beyond a set maximum level. Mastering engineers quickly realized that by smashing down the transient peaks into square waves, one could easily reduce the dynamic range without ever risking outright clipping. By pushing the loudest parts of the mix down with a brickwall limiter, the mastering engineer could reduce the dynamic range of the mix, which resulted in a CD that played at a higher average level than other CDs. CD players with jukebox turnstiles made these differences in level obvious, since the new loud CDs actually played louder than other discs. Record companies liked the idea of having their newest artist's CD play louder than other CDs, and it didn't take long before radio airplay became part of the justification.

Radio stations have used severely effective brickwall limiters for many decades. The FCC requires this because it helps prevent transmission bleed into other bandwidths. Once label executives caught wind that mastering engineers now had these "magical radio limiters" at their disposal (which they've always had!), it didn't take long before the mythological concept of "radio ready" mixes spread throughout the industry. In reality, there is no advantage gained by putting a severely brick-limited mix on a radio station that is already brick-limiting the signal. In fact, loud records actually sound much worse on radio, but that obvious disadvantage doesn't seem to alter the perception within our industry.

There are debates as to who fired the opening salvo in the digital loudness wars. I always jokingly accuse my good friend Charles Dye of starting it all with his mixes on Ricky Martin's "Livin' la Vida Loca," but I'll admit here and now it wasn't him. These days, I'm happy to report, Charles is actually active in combating loudness with his Turn Me Up organization (turnmeup.org).

While I have a pretty good idea who *actually* started the loudness war, it's almost pointless to lay blame on one particular person, as it was a relatively gradual occurrence. At some point, someone—a producer, record company exec, or mastering engineer—started pushing the envelope to gain an advantage. One man's advantage is another's disadvantage, and so the war was on.

The record companies began rewarding mastering engineers for their ability to maximize loudness. The louder the mastering engineer could make a CD, the more money she could charge the record companies. The major labels literally incentivized mastering houses to make CDs as loud as they possibly could, even if that meant obvious clipping at the reproduction stage. All bets were off once that happened, and by the time some mastering engineers were capable of charging $10,000 for a half day's work, sound quality was no longer important.

It wasn't long before mixers, who were also part of the profit-sharing infrastructure, and who could also reap the monetary benefits of loud records (albeit more indirectly), realized that their favorite mastering engineer could make the CD louder if they delivered mixes that used less stereo field and more upper midrange. And as if that wasn't enough, the loudest of the loud mastering engineers magnified apparent loudness by boosting the high frequencies of a mix. The end result was what we have now: overly bright, depthless, distorted records. And thus, the total annihilation of dynamic range and listenable music was complete.

Here we are at the crossroads. There is no more level to be gained. There is no way to make your CD louder than your competitors', since there's no way to make music louder. As an industry, we're already pushing the level past the capacity of the converters. We're well beyond reasonable EQ curves where brightness is concerned. With tempo fluctuations long eradicated, we've destroyed the last true dynamic we had available to us from a production standpoint. We've destroyed the impact and depth of an entire generation of productions, and we've rewarded the consumer for seeking convenience over quality by reducing sound quality to such an extent that it's become irrelevant. Nice, huh?

The great irony of the loudness war is the undeniable role it has played in changing how consumers listen to music. Whereas music was once a visceral and interactive listening experience—one that captured the full attention of the fan—loudness, brightness, and the consequential distortion has reduced music to nothing more potent than background noise. Ironically, the widespread production of music capable of cutting through all but the most overbearing background noise has had the effect of causing the average listener to turn their music *down*, not up. The rampant turning down of music has had the consequence of making music nothing more important than background noise, thereby reducing its overall relevance and value. While there are certainly other factors contributing to the metamorphosis of how people listen to records, I'm not sure music would have become the stepchild of the entertainment industry had the music industry not treated it like one first. (Although the overall swallowing up of record companies by the mega-entertainment conglomerates certainly didn't help matters.)

While it might be interesting to actually research (and divulge) who started what in the evolution of the loudness war, I fear that doing so would only serve to elevate certain producers and mastering engineers to an even more iconic status than they already enjoy. It doesn't really matter who pushed what envelope when and for what reason. It's human nature for us to compete. In modern times this causes us to push the envelope beyond all reason, and this is exactly what we've done as an industry.

Just so there's no misunderstanding, this loudness summation is basic at best, and doesn't provide the full breadth of the digital loudness war. To lay blame purely on the mastering engineers as a community would be unjustified. There are very few in this business with clean hands where loudness is concerned, and it's been a natural spiraling frenzy propagated mostly by greed. I provide this information so you have some understanding of the history, so you can hear for yourself the ramifications of apparent loudness on the effectiveness of a mix, and so you can understand what the hell your soon-to-be-fired mastering engineer has done when he delivers you a master that sounds as flat as a pancake.

As with any professional, the best measure of a mastering engineer is through the aggregate of his results. Absent that, your first line of defense in choosing a mastering engineer is to get some insight into what she *uses* to master records. The sensibilities come from the person, but the quality of playback comes from the gear, and the decisions are based on the quality of monitoring. If your new mastering engineer is working out of a bedroom using a Pro Tools rig with stock 192 converters and performing all processing with plug-ins, I don't care how great her sensibilities are, the monitoring, the playback, and the processing will be so atrocious that the gear will only serve to completely negate the mastering engineer herself. This is the one job in this business where it is best to judge the shop as a means to judging the person.

I'm not saying that the gear is more important than the person here. I'm saying that if the mastering engineer isn't diligent enough to put together a more-than-respectable playback chain, then they obviously don't have the necessary auditory sensibilities to be touching your mixes.

Since mastering can be achieved with a minimal setup, and since even cheap mastering can bring in considerably more money than expensive recording, there are far too many hacks out there willing to call themselves mastering engineers as a means of boosting lackluster recording and mixing revenues. Studios frequently offer mastering as a service for their clients, yet they rarely have the qualified personnel for the job. I'm sorry, but your records are far too important to leave mastering up to someone who doesn't make it their one and only profession.

If your mastering engineer doesn't have, at the very least, a designated room, a top-of-the-line stereo pair of converters, and a verifiable career as a mastering engineer, this is not who you want mastering your mixes. For starters, if you send your mixes to someone who does mastering on the side in order to help subsidize his recording and mixing work, you're sending your mixes and your clients to your direct competitor. Not to be overly protectionist about this, but that's probably not the wisest decision you could make.

One good indicator that you're potentially dealing with a professional mastering engineer is whether they have a high-quality tape machine in their room. Look for multiple-size headstacks, and ask if the mastering engineer can record something on his analog machine. The answer should be "no," since mastering engineers have no need for record electronics. Even if you're not bringing in tape masters, a tape machine is a pretty good indicator that you're at least dealing with someone who takes the gig seriously.

Now it's quite likely that I'm going to get some flak on the Internet for recommending you choose your mastering engineer based on her gear list, and I suppose you could consider this to be a preemptive strike in that regard. I can tell you, if I didn't actually regularly sort potential restaurants by the type of lettuce they serve, I might have abandoned the suggestion. Unfortunately, there are so many people in this field who don't have a clue what they're doing, that the gear list is one of the few concrete ways I can suggest to weed out the potential wheat from the chaff. Even with this whole gear list strategy, you're going to come across some hacks, so you can't choose based on gear alone. This is merely a way to save you a little time and heartache. I promise you, the brutal destruction of your hard work will cause you nothing *but* heartache; that is, if you actually give a shit about what you do.

To be clear, the goal isn't to find a mastering engineer who likes the same gear that you do. The goal is to find someone that has reasonably professional tools, whatever that means to you. If she's using converters you've never heard of, then you can't possibly judge her for that particular choice. It's just that the overall chain should give you some idea who you're dealing with here. Again, the gear list merely acts as an indicator to save you some time. It's not the way you choose your mastering engineer.

There's another way to determine the overall viability of a particular mastering engineer—look at the liner notes on your favorite CDs. Unfortunately, when you start making your calls, you'll find that the prices are all over the map. Seeing as the highest paid mastering engineers are typically the ones that figured out how to make CDs the loudest, a high price isn't a good indicator of quality. There are some mastering houses that can cost up to $10,000 per album. Now, if you happen to call one of those 10K butcher shops, don't think for a second they're going to turn down what little money you do have. All large mastering houses will have discount packages, which basically means the guy who was an intern just a few months before your call will now have the opportunity to practice mastering in the middle of the night on your music and your dime.

While an outrageous price tag isn't an indication of quality, a ridiculously cheap price tag probably is. If someone can master your album for $300, run. You're not going to be satisfied with the results, and neither is your client. Don't waste your time with deals when it comes to mastering.

You also want to stay away from shops that like to put together the entire package of mastering and reproduction for you. These shops usually have legitimate mastering engineers working for them, particularly if the main business is mastering, but they also typically use their learning engineers for those package deals. Not only will you be dissatisfied, but the mastering house most definitely won't bend over backwards for you, given the reduced rate.

What you're looking for is a particular mastering engineer who can accommodate you personally, who can give you feedback on your mixes, and who will be interested in giving you the best service possible—this is usually achieved by a mastering engineer who runs his own shop.

I've used Dave Collins for the lion's share of my mastering needs over the years, and I don't mind writing that here, mostly because it's pretty easy to discover that just by looking at my discography. I've worked with him for the better part of 15 years now, and although I've used other mastering engineers over those years, that's usually because an A&R executive or producer took the decision out of my hands. Such is the politics of major label mixing.

Sites like Allmusic.com are great for investigating a potential mastering engineer's discography. While Allmusic is notorious for inaccuracies, a working mastering engineer should have an enormous list of product on this sort of online database. At the very least you can determine whether she even shows up on the radar.

It's quite possible (likely even), depending on where you live, that you won't be able to find an appropriate mastering engineer within driving distance. While this isn't ideal, it's not an insurmountable problem. Personally, I always try to attend the mastering sessions, but it's not always feasible. If you have a good working rapport with a mastering engineer, you don't have to attend. That said, I recommend that once you find someone you like, you go to a few mastering sessions in order to develop that relationship and gain much needed experience. Ultimately, you want to find someone who complements what you're trying to achieve, and who makes your mixes better. It could take you years to find this person, but once you do, you'll never want to leave them.

Most mastering engineers will perform a test master on one song for you, particularly if the potential reward is a full album's worth of work. I would advise against sending a record to 10 different mastering engineers for a big shootout. For starters, it would be nothing short of slimy to perform that kind of cattle call without letting the mastering engineers know the overall scope, and if you're foolish enough to tell them all up front what you're doing, the good ones will decline. That means you'll be comparing mastering jobs from the bottom of the barrel, which is nothing short of a useless comparison. Besides, it's impossible to evaluate that many masters. I promise you'll do your head in like that, so don't even try. If you're going to do a shootout, don't include more than three mastering engineers, and that's probably two too many. Give the test to one guy, and if he does a good job, have him master the album.

How Do You Know It's a Good Job?

Honestly, it took me years to figure out how to properly evaluate a mastering job. I was literally brought to tears on countless occasions before I understood mastering. In actuality, it's absurdly easy to evaluate a mastering job, and I can save you quite a bit of frustration in this regard. Yes, I'm going to reveal my most treasured secret to you. Here it is:

If the mix is better after mastering, it's a great job. If the mix is worse, it's a lousy one.

Okay, I realize that may seem ridiculously simplistic, but it's also true, and it happens to be the only viable way to evaluate a mastering job. Now granted, if you're unhappy with the mastering on a particular song, you're going to have to be a bit more specific than "it's not better" with the mastering engineer. But for your own evaluation purposes, that's really all there is to it.

I mean, you know you were singing and had a physical reaction when you printed the mix, right? So, if you can actually listen to the mastered record and not sing, it's not right. If you listen to the master and you don't have the same physical reactions you did when you were printing, there's a problem.

When I get a great mastering job back, I try my hardest to listen to the job, but I also know that if I end up singing, I don't have to worry—it's right. Of course, for some reason I usually catch myself singing and skip back, and then, of course, I just end up singing again. I can promise there's no evaluating going on if you're singing over the track, so you might as well just accept that if the track can still make you sing, it's a great mastering job.

Retaining Your Influence

Once you find a mastering engineer that you like, you're going to want to steer your clients toward them. If your client loves what you're doing with the mixes, it would be pretty silly for them to then go to a mastering engineer you think is a hack. Yet this is exactly what will happen time and time again—mostly because your clients understand mastering less than you did before reading this chapter. Therefore, you should discuss mastering with your client early and often in the mixing process. The best time to start is at the height of your mix capital.

Really, you can get into all sorts of reasons why your client should use your mastering engineer. You can talk about how your favorite mastering engineer does nothing but master records and show your client her impressive discography. You can discuss the stellar quality of her playback. You can discuss loudness and how she typically deals with that. You can discuss anything that you think will sell your client, but your most compelling argument will also be your simplest. Tell your client that you send your mastering engineer your mixes, and she sends them back better.

You're never going to get yourself in trouble for caring about the ultimate product. Your name is going on the album, and a bad mastering job can completely desecrate your mixes, rendering them nearly unlistenable. It's critical that you keep some influence over what happens to those mixes right up until the time the CDs are pressed. The best way to accomplish that is by educating your client about the process and making them realize that it's in their interest to have you involved in the project to completion—and I do mean completion.

There are all sorts of things that can go wrong with the mixes at the manufacturing plant regardless of the budget. Embedded video content and anti-piracy encoding can change the overall sound of your mix, among other potential disasters, so if you can get a test press and compare it to the final master, you can be sure the client's mixes stay exactly as they were intended. Unfortunately, test pressings can be expensive, so it might not be an option for many projects.

Putting Up the Good Fight

I mixed an album quite a few years back where the label requested a particular mastering engineer for the job. I'd never had anything mastered by this engineer, but he was a legitimate pro with an extensive discography, so I really had no room for protest. Before I even had an opportunity to hear the reference disc for myself, I was informed that everyone was over-the-top ecstatic about the mastering job. Just the same, I requested a copy.

Given the overall level of excitement, I expected to hear nothing less than a kick-ass mastering job. What I got was the annihilation of my hard work. That may seem like hyperbole, but my once beautifully wide mixes were now nearly mono. Hard panning sounded more like soft panning, and not a single person had noticed this issue, including the mastering engineer, even after it was brought to his attention. The difference was immediate and obvious in an A/B comparison, so I called the producer to register my complaint.

If I told you the producer was pissed, I'd be understating his reaction. I mean, he was yelling at me, and he's a good friend! Hey, that's how emotional mastering can be. The band thought I was crazy. I was the only person who had a problem with the mastering job. Of course, I was also the only person who was listening to it in a proper studio, and they all needed to hear the record as I was hearing it. Why argue what can easily be demonstrated? So I invited them all down for a listening party.

It took some explaining, and not everyone in the band heard the differences right away, but within five minutes' time the problem became apparent to everyone in the room. I went from the asshole mixer who should just stay the fuck out of the mastering process to the hero who prevented near-mono mixes from going out the door. That's quite a swing.

The offending engineer mastered the album three more times—two of them after he was already fired from the job. The problem must have been in his playback and monitoring system. Not only couldn't he hear the issue in his mastering suite, but the last job he sent was run flat and it still had the imaging problem.

In the producer's defense, he was out of town, and I listened to the mastering job before he even had an opportunity to listen in his most trusted environments. The moment he did, he heard exactly what I was talking about. By the time we had our listening party, the producer and I were on the same page. It was the band that was convinced I was wrong. Boy, were they surprised.

I suppose some might argue that if the band couldn't hear the problem outside the studio, then it shouldn't matter. I would reject that argument outright. Your CD contains the artistic intent. If the stereo imaging has been reduced on the final master, then it will reproduce like that everywhere. We already know that the music is going to be reproduced in all sorts of fucked-up environments and on all sorts of less-than-ideal playback systems. There's nothing we can do about that. Our only control is in making sure that our purposeful intent gets burned permanently onto the CD. While the quality of any given consumer playback system will most certainly have a negative effect on the impact of your mixes, it will have the same relative effect on all mixes. In other words, the overall atrociousness of a consumer playback system remains constant. Therefore, you have to make absolutely certain that your great mixes not only sound exactly right, but retain their ability to manipulate the emotional impact on and physical reactions of the listener. Otherwise, what the fuck do we do?

Stems

Stems are typically eight tracks of submix that combine perfectly at unity gain to make your 2-track mix. Stems are usually requested when a song is being inserted into the body of a movie. The rerecording engineer uses the stems so he can change the mix for dialogue purposes. While at first blush this might cause you to recoil, song appearances in movies are usually relatively short in length and almost always occur simultaneously with other audio—lots of other audio. The rerecording engineers have to have some control over the mix for a whole host of reasons, and none of them are about fidelity. A typical stem would break down like this:

> Bass (mono)
>
> Lead vocal (mono)
>
> Drums and percussion (stereo)
>
> Harmony instruments (stereo)
>
> Background vocals (stereo)

The reason I bring up the issue of stems is because you will come across some mastering engineers who will request them. If they do, leave. If you're on the phone, hang up.

If you give your mastering engineer stems for the purposes of the CD, you are no longer delivering a mix. Once the mastering engineer is using stems, he's mixing *for* you. This is unacceptable. *You* are the mixer. If he thinks the mix sucks and can't be improved with a 2-track mastering job, then he should either tell you what's wrong with the mix, or finish the limited job he was hired to do. If you want to entertain mix suggestions from your mastering engineer, be my guest, but it's not really the mastering engineer's job to judge whether your mix is good or not. It's for him to prepare the master for its final delivery format.

You're also going to have clients that request stems. Unless those stems are being used specifically for a movie (just ask), deny the request (with a smile if you like). It doesn't matter what the intent; if it's not for a movie, then a request for stems is a hostile act. If your client is requesting stems because your mix isn't good enough, then go back to the mix and fix it. If you let someone else fix your mix by giving them some control over internal balances, you're never going to learn how to make a good mix on your own. Besides, stems are a lame way to adjust a mix. I mean, there's just no reason to use stems if you can recall the mix perfectly in your DAW. You've been hired to deliver a mix, and that's exactly what you should deliver—two tracks, left and right. Nothing more, nothing less.

If your client wants stems for the future possibility of a movie placement, print the stems and hold onto them. Give your client the stems in a year or two if you don't want to hold on to them longer than that. In the short term, you must protect your mix, and the only way to do that is by providing nothing more than the mix itself.

Let's review: No stems!

Mastering Your Own Work

Invariably, every mixer decides he can master his own work. Just as invariably, every mixer realizes he actually can't. I know it seems kind of ridiculous. You mixed the damn record, why can't you master it? Well, you can! It just won't be any good.

Mixing is a far more aggressive sport than mastering, or at least it should be. Mastering also requires an entirely different way of thinking, and just as it takes years to master the art of mixing, the same is true about mastering. I mean, if you've delivered great mixes, you've proven yourself to be an important and valuable asset to the project. You're now going to make sure you're also the weak link?

The tools for mastering and mixing are completely different. A mastering engineer has a limited number of tools in her chain, and she chooses them based mostly on fidelity and accuracy of reproduction. Mixers need considerably more gear, and tend to choose their gear based on how it colors sound. Remember, the playback and processing of your mix during the mastering process is burned onto the CD. If you're using average converters, you're getting average playback. That means you're doing harm to your mix. This is exactly why I suggest you examine your potential mastering engineer's gear list. Playback alone can be the difference between a great mastering job and a disappointing one.

The mastering engineer is the last line of defense where translation is concerned. So let the mastering engineer do her job after you've done yours. If she's really good, she'll enhance what you do. If she's not, keep looking.

Chapter Seven

Thinking Outside the Box

How you think about mixing is what will set you apart from your competition. We've discussed your thinking in great detail thus far, and this final chapter is no exception in that regard. If you haven't figured this out by now, mixing is a highly creative activity within some relatively strict guidelines. We don't deal with a blank sheet of paper; we deal with an existing product, and we bring that product to fruition.

Given that mixing requires equal parts artistic and technical prowess, and given that the mixer is part of a team creating art, there are few analogous occupations. In fact, there's only one that I can think of, and it was my friend Peter who put it best when he told me that the mixer is to music as the framer is to art.

I'm quite certain he wasn't talking about the guy behind the counter at your local Aaron Brothers when he said this, and I must confess, at first I didn't get the analogy. But that's only because at the time he told me this, I had never spent any real money on framing. Still, it stuck with me.

It couldn't have been much more than a year later when my first wife handed me a $750 framing bill for a $150 lithograph bought several years earlier. For the record, I don't think a $150 piece of art is expensive. I don't even think $750 for a frame is expensive in the grand scheme of things, as surely there are framing jobs that cost in the thousands of dollars, if not more. I do, however, think it's absurd for the frame to cost five times as much as the pleasant little print it surrounds. Or at least I did.

This incident happened in the mid-'90s. I was just starting to collect art at the time, and I certainly didn't mind spending money on something great. But this was ridiculous! Yeah, I liked the print. I found it pleasant. Yes, I wanted it framed, and I wanted it to look good. But $750 for a lithograph? Of course, my attitude changed completely the day she brought the print home, and it was then that I finally understood Peter's analogy.

The lithograph was of a cat lying on a wall. Purely as a print, with no framing whatsoever, I quite enjoyed the piece. Let me tell you, my enjoyment increased 20-fold once it was framed and matted. My pleasant little cat lithograph was transformed into a large and stunning piece of work. The piece was now nearly twice as large as the print itself, which in and of itself made it far more impressive. The frame and the carefully selected mat border set off the colors in the lithograph. The matting gave the image importance, and the frame gave it focus.

Between my former wife, who was active in the design, and the framer who implemented it, the artistry that is framing was revealed to me. Every time I look at that print, I'm reminded just what a good mix is supposed to do.

Like a mixer, a framer must have some technical ability. Cutting miter joints so they line up properly is not an easy task. Cutting multiple mats perfectly straight to produce color borders as slim as 1/16th of an inch not only requires the proper tools, but years of practice as well. Then there's the art of it: Selecting the frame that best complements the overall vibe of the piece it surrounds.

Selecting the thin color borders between the mats to enhance the colors in the painting, making it pop. The attention to detail, which sets up the big picture—all of this requires an eye for detail, and an appreciation for the potential impact of the work.

Mixing is similar in nature. You're already handed a work of art. Your job is to frame it—to set it off. To enhance what was done before the work was sent to you. Part of that job is technical in nature. But anyone can learn that part. It's the artistry that separates a great framing job from a technically well-executed one.

The mix is the framing of the art. And a great mix will bring out everything great about a work of art. We can't change the art. All we can do is try to frame it in the best way possible in order to bring out all the good the track has to offer.

Turning Weakness into Strength

The conventional thinking where mixing is concerned is to maximize a given track's strengths and minimize its weaknesses. Overall, I'd say this is a good plan. There are times, however, when there's a better option. Every now and then you might choose to overexpose a weakness.

There are two levels of psychology that go into this. First, the listener would never assume that the artist would give prominence to anything he considered weak, and so exposing deficiencies makes them seem purposeful. Second, if a part is particularly awful, it can serve to make everything else in the mix good in comparison.

The moment you give a part any kind of prominence in a mix is the moment you give that part importance. Once you make weakness important, you instantly make it a strong point of the production. Of course, the mute button usually works better.

This sort of paradoxical thinking can be quite useful if you pull it out at the right times, and I'm reticent to give you any examples here. Keep the concept in your back pocket, and if you're struggling with something in your mix that can't withstand the mute button, consider overexposing that weakness in your mix. You'll fool everyone. Even me.

Kismet!

When you let a little fate into your life, good things happen. Some people call them happy accidents.

Whether an accident becomes a good idea or whether it triggers one indirectly, you still get a good idea out of the deal. You have a limited amount of time to mix a track. If you try to control everything that happens on a mix at all times, you're going to miss out on plenty.

Good ideas come from all sorts of places. When mixing on an analog console, I like to leave my EQs and inserts in as I plug in the new mix. This has the dual benefit of giving me a good starting point on the constants (like drums, bass, and vocals), and a desirable randomness on the other parts. This method can put an unusual combination of processing on a part, often with surprising results, particularly if the module was previously used for a radical treatment. Of course, it doesn't usually work out well, and I typically pull out the insert and EQ the moment I hear the offensive treatment, but every now and then something magical comes from this strategy.

Mixing is partly a hit-or-miss puzzle anyway, so why fight it? Use hit-or-miss techniques to your advantage. If you have a part that you're not sure what to do with, process it in ways you wouldn't normally consider. Try out all those plug-ins you've never used before.

When you're working on your mix, mute swaths of instruments to try out different combinations of parts. You might just find a great drop, or the perfect underdub for your mix. Allow yourself some time to try out wacky ideas that randomly pop into your head. It very well could lead to something useful.

Factory Work

Like any worthwhile job, there's a certain drudgery involved in mixing. I suppose if you become a name mixer, you could hire a full-time assistant to take care of the more mundane framing tasks, but you're still going to have to go through discovery, so I'm not sure what that buys you, seeing as these two processes are best done concurrently. Unless you're already familiar with the production you're about to mix, the framing and discovery period is critical to learning and determining the arrangement. If you focus on the discovery part, you can reduce the slog involved with the more janitorial tasks involved in framing.

If you really think about it, the large preponderance of rock tracks are similar in arrangement, containing the usual bass, drums, guitars, and vocals. Surely, there are many variations on that, but if we took a poll, I can assure you that would be the most common answer. Every genre of music will have its own similarities in arrangement.

While there's no doubt you'll repeat many tasks *ad nauseum* throughout your music-making career, you should do all you can to eradicate the bad habit of using cookie-cutter defaults. As we've discussed, there are some mixers who treat every mix identically. Their goal is to have a homogenized and consistent sound on every mix, and let me tell you, the labels love that. I'm sorry, but there's no art in that. Any mixer who chooses to treat all music the same clearly views his role as more important than even the artist.

This is not an argument against taking reasonable steps toward reducing your workload. There's a big difference between decisions that are formulaic in nature and ones that are designed to help speed up the process. If you've already mixed one song out of 10, and the drums were all recorded in the same room over the course of a few days, it would be wise to import your drum processing to the next mix right from the start. I mean, why on earth would you want to go through all of those decisions again when you can merely adjust them from a relatively good starting point? I'm all for *smart* mixing.

As you become a more seasoned mixer, even seemingly unique instrumentations will fall neatly into the realm of familiarity. Parts that at one time in your career may have seemed almost exotic in nature can become nearly commonplace. Even on those occasions when you come across an instrument you've never heard before, you'll know what to do with it based purely on its function in the arrangement. For this reason, mixing can quickly become mundane if you don't do all you can to avoid patterns.

Any craft performed on a daily basis risks becoming nothing more than factory work. Unless you're in the upper tiers of the mixing pay scale, you'd probably do better to actually go work in a factory than to treat mixing in this manner. At least working in a factory gives you a full-time job with benefits, right? If you find that concept as distasteful as I do, then I would advise you to take a careful look at how you approach mixing, and do everything in your power to avoid doing the same things on every song. This may seem basic, but I promise you, it requires constant vigilance to avoid ruts in mixing.

Art vs. Commerce

Even if the song you're mixing is completely derivative in nature—and most songs are, to some degree—that doesn't mean that the production should be treated as anything less than a unique piece of art. If you frame every song the same, you're no longer serving the song, and frankly, you're not serving the artist, either. After a while, you'll only manage to make everyone sound the same, and you'll have eradicated any semblance of artistry from your life.

There is nothing in the functionality of *popular* art that can't be broken down to a formula regardless of how artistic you are, and regardless of how unique your approach is. It doesn't matter whether you're songwriting, painting, writing a book or even an article—there are certain tried-and-true structural rules, particularly where keeping the attention of your audience is concerned. Yes, you can break the rules and get away with it, but on those occasions when you broke a rule with no ill effects, you probably followed 10 other general rules in the process. From that standpoint, mixing is no different than any other creative endeavor. For instance, I could proclaim the following rule:

Never pan the lead vocal.

That's a pretty good rule where mixing is concerned—one you should adhere to in all but the rarest of cases. Placing the vocal in the center of your mix gives it great importance, particularly when it only shares that position with the kik, snare, and bass (the low end of which isn't directional anyway). You can't possibly put forth a reasonable argument that placing the vocal in the middle isn't a solid approach, given that nearly every successful song since the invention of the stereo field places the vocal in the middle (and please don't bring up the Beatles, because they didn't really know how to deal with stereo when it was new). Going against every accepted convention certainly won't increase the level of artistry. In fact, if you don't work to some degree within the bounds of accepted convention, you're just going to create an exceptional pile of crap that no one but the artist's mother will want to hear. I generally advise against this.

If your purpose is nothing more than to create art that is so unique it can only be described kindly as "ahead of its time," by all means, go out of your way to break every tangible rule in the book. Ultimately though, the artistry lies in creating something salable, which by its very nature affects as many people as possible. And don't confuse salability with selling out. Only teenagers view wide-ranging success as selling out. Unless making music is nothing more than a hobby, and unless you have no designs on ever making music professionally, part of everyone's job on a project is to make a product that can sell. I can assure you, sample-replaced drums and vocals that sound like a synthesizer are *not* driving forces in sales.

For a time, the use of fashionable techniques may help make your mix sound modern, but in the end it only dates the work. I can promise you, fashionable production techniques—like the overbearing gated reverb of the '80s or the current trend of transforming vocals into synthesizers with ultra-aggressive pitch correction—will rarely, if ever, directly result in sales. You have an entire history of sonic treatments at your disposal; don't limit yourself to using techniques that have nothing to do with the salability of a song.

Just because a song doesn't sell doesn't mean it was a creative failure. How great a world would it be if the mere creation of something awesome guaranteed its timely success? There are too many other factors beyond quality of work that prevent a song from making its way into the mainstream consciousness. Conversely, just because a song has strong sales doesn't necessarily make it a heralded piece of artistic mastery; it could just fit the mood and the times ("Don't Worry, Be Happy" comes to mind). Artistic merit can only be judged based on how a song and its production fare over time. The mastery in art designed for commerce lies in creating something seemingly new and compelling while adhering to the conventions that make it salable, preferably for the unforeseeable future.

Let me put it this way: If your client is investing his money in a recording, in most cases (short of vanity projects) you can safely assume the goal is to make money—if for no other reason than so the artist can make more recordings in the future. You're not doing anyone any favors when your decisions don't assist in that goal.

The Price of Mixers

A quality mixer—that is to say, one who is paid for his work rather than his name—will charge anywhere from $1,500 to $3,000 per mix. Depending on how fast one mixes, that can be up to five times the pay of a tracking engineer.

At the height of the lunacy we call the music business, super-mixers (who are paid based on their name and reputation rather than the actual quality of their work) could earn as much as $10,000 for a mix. The highest-paid tracking engineers were getting $1,200 per day. These days they get probably half that, and in many cases possibly a quarter. It's difficult to tell, since as of this writing I'm neither a super-mixer nor for hire as a tracking engineer. The hard numbers on this are pretty much irrelevant. They will fluctuate depending on how well the music business is doing in general. What doesn't change, and probably won't in the foreseeable future, is the ratio of how much recordists are paid compared to mixers. Mixers are paid exponentially more, particularly if we compare pay scales as they relate to actual time invested.

This brings us to the next obvious question. How much should *you* charge to mix? Well, that depends on both how good a mixer you are and how many people are aware of how good a mixer you are. It also depends on what the competition charges.

As a mixer I never, ever, *ever* compete on price. I'm operating from a position of value as a mixer. To try and compete on price would only serve to devalue me, so any time someone tells me about a cheaper mixer, I readily point this out. When someone comes to me for a mix job, it's because they like my work. Why would I ever discuss what some other mixer charges when what attracted the potential client was the quality of my work?

That's not to say my price is etched in stone. There are other incentives that can make a project worthwhile for less than the usual fee. If there's not enough money to pay me up front, then there's always profit sharing. Unfortunately, points are becoming less and less likely to pay off, given that so few records sell substantially these days.

Basically a point is one percentage point of the Manufacturer's Suggested Retail List Price (MSRLP). If a CD is listed at $15, then one point means I would get $0.15 per CD. Of course, major labels have all sorts of crafty deductions that come into play, so you're lucky if you get two-thirds of that. And now with iTunes beginning to dominate, which tends to sell more songs than albums, that often becomes 1/10th of two-thirds of $.15, which amounts to $.01 every time the hit song sells on iTunes. Don't get me wrong; if an album sells through the roof, it adds up to a nice check, and I don't ever scoff at points, but if a song sells a million copies, the payout on one point is $10,000. The standard fare is a point for the mixer regardless of fee. If more points are awarded to the mixer, it's usually because there was insufficient upfront money for the job.

The overall quality of the project is another consideration. If I think the music is great, I'm far more inclined to reduce my rate to work within a budget than I am if I think the project is mediocre. Another great album is only going to reflect well on my discography. Still, there has to be a reasonable offer there.

One of the advantages of mixing fast is that you tend to level the playing field a bit where your competitors' prices are concerned. I'll give you some examples, and keep the numbers simple. If the studio down the street charges $1,000 per day, but the engineer can only mix one song a day, a 10-song album will cost the client $10,000, as long as the mixer stays on schedule. If you charge $1,000 per mix and you can mix two songs per day, you pick up that $10,000 for just five days' work. It costs the client $10,000 either way, but they get a mixer out of the deal, and you make $2,000 per day for your work. Yeah, you charge by the mix, but you judge the value of a project by the day. If a band is going to put you through the ringer for two months to mix their album, that $10,000 doesn't look so great anymore.

You can avoid that two-month mix scenario merely by interviewing the client. You want to get an idea of what their expectations are. If they think it's going to take two months to mix, they'll probably tell you that, and you can instantly pass. If they're not sure what it takes, then you can explain the process to them, and work within those parameters. This has the added benefit of protecting you. If mixes do start to take three days for some reason, you can refer back to your two-mixes-per-day quote. It's unreasonable to spend two-and-a-half days on mix notes. If the band wants to mix their album themselves, then they should do it. They don't need you there manning the controls for $25 per hour.

Really, you can only charge what the market will bear at any given time. The best thing you can do to make yourself more valuable is to improve your mixing skills, and build up your discography. You don't have to be in Los Angeles or New York to do this. You can build yourself up to be the big fish in a small pond. Granted, you won't necessarily be working on a whole lot of major label projects, but if you can get your name out there by producing impressive mixes, people will find you, and they'll pay more, too. How much more, I can't tell you.

I don't really know anyone who got into engineering for the money. Yeah, you can make good money as a major label mixer, and even better money as a major label producer, but we got into this business mostly because we love it. We stay in it because it's what we do best. Still, you're a professional, and you have to be paid for your work, and that pay should be commensurate with the demand for your services.

Creating a Reel

Until you've amassed some work, creating a reel isn't really a big problem. Once you have several albums under your belt, there's a certain psychology to putting together a reel for a potential client.

You should almost never put anything on it that is musically similar to the artist who is courting your services. It's too risky. The last thing you want is for an artist to think you're going to make them sound like someone else. You're far better off putting together a diverse disc of tracks. This lets the clients evaluate your mixing in general, with no direct relationship to their own music. Just because you mixed a previous project that was similar in nature doesn't mean you're going to mix theirs the same way, and you most certainly want to avoid that misconception.

Sometimes I just put the most famous songs on my disc. The most famous songs on any given reel aren't necessarily the best mixes in the grand scheme of a discography. That's irrelevant. Those famous songs are often going to be the best mixes to a potential client. They're not even going to listen to the mix. They're going to get excited that you mixed a song they love, and think about the time they got laid while that song was playing. This bodes well for getting the gig.

If you have tracks on your disc that people are going to easily recognize, they should go on your reel. Even if the mixes suck, they should go on your reel. If it's a great song, and it gained any notoriety whatsoever, it's a great mix, too.

Mixing Can Take Time

I've mixed songs in which there were literally three completely unique productions available to me as the mixer, with no clear delineation as to which parts went to which production. This takes avoiding commitment to totally new heights, and leaves each and every decision purely up to the mixer. I can tell you, sorting through that many tracks is absolutely exhausting, and working out the best arrangement of tracks can easily take half a day, which is often the time required for an entire mix.

Run time will also affect how fast you can mix a song. A seven-minute song takes twice as long to mix as a four-minute one, and a 12-minute song takes a minimum of two days. I've mixed two 12-minute songs in my career, and I'd be quite happy if I never had to do that again. The biggest problem with the 12-minute song is establishing continuity. Since each section must set up the next section, the continuity from one section to the next can only be checked in succession. Sure, you start by working in sections, but if there's a continuity issue at the eight-minute mark, each time you go to check the transitional impact, it takes eight minutes just to get there. Twelve-minute songs are also a nightmare because there's really no way to mix fast.

Outsmarting the Band

It's always advisable to watch whose car the band uses when they want to reference music. There's usually a preferred listening vehicle, and the band almost always sits in the same seats. Consider this information as you place parts in your stereo field. If it's the guitar player's car (and you're in America), put his part on the left so he can hear himself nice and loud while he's driving. If the drummer sits on the passenger side, put his percussion parts on the right. This usually works quite brilliantly, although the plan does have its flaws. If you get two guitar players in the band, and they both sit on the left, one behind the other, you're fucked, and all bets are off. I suppose you can try panning both guitars to the left, but I'm thinking that concept will be met with resistance, if not a considerably stronger reaction.

Shootouts

Sometimes clients have a difficult time choosing between two mixers that they like, and request a shootout. In general, I don't have a problem doing a shootout, particularly if it's a project I'd really like to mix, and particularly if I can pick up a new client out of the deal. You have to pick and choose shootouts carefully, because there are certain pitfalls. Shootouts for major labels are rarely problematic, because the shootout is being used to determine who's best for the job. This is not necessarily so in the case of an independent group, particularly if they're looking to bargain. If you do a shootout against another recordist who charges less than you, even if the band likes your mix best, they're going to try to get you to bring your price down to that of the other mixer. When they do, say no.

If they liked his mix better, then they would already have hired him. I mean, he's cheaper *and* better, right? If they thought his mix was better, but they want the cachet of your name on their record, well, guess what? They have to pay for that. If the label is telling them to hire you anyway because they're more comfortable with you, well, that extra comfort costs money. The more likely scenario is that they liked your mix better. Now you're going to negotiate?

No! They have to *pay* for better mixes.

There are a few strategies to doing shootouts. First, never do your mix first. Too often the reason you're doing a shootout is because the band has a friend that they want to mix the album, and they need to prove to the label that their friend is better for the project. The last thing you want to do is have your mix given to their friend, automatically giving him the advantage of comparing his work to yours to be sure to beat it. This also gives the other guy the ability to make sure he delivers a louder mix, and I can promise you, the louder mix usually wins (within reason). Obviously, this means you want to either put a brickwall limiter on your mix, or hire your mastering engineer to do a quick job on the track for you.

Some mixers only deliver MP3s, or only provide a portion of the track. I think this is unnecessary, and it's difficult to evaluate an MP3 or an incomplete mix. Give them a mastered WAV file of the entire track. You want to put your best foot forward and win the gig. The likelihood that someone is trying to steal a free mix from you is low. If they love your mix, they're going to hire you for the rest of them. Protectionism doesn't serve you well here.

When involved in a shootout, be sure to listen to the rough. This will give you the most insight into how your potential clients hear things. Yes, you want to beat the crap out of the rough, but at least you know what they were thinking about before you mix. Just make sure you know their opinion of the rough. If they hate it, then clearly this wouldn't be a good strategy.

Lastly, make sure you're mixing a song you like. There's no point in doing a shootout on a song that you think sucks. Ask for a few songs to choose from, and then pick the track you think you can do the best job on.

Shootouts are a great way to get business that you might not otherwise get, and should be considered a reasonable way of building your mixing business.

A mix can be great and not have great sound.

Quality of sound doesn't exist without context. One man's great sound is another's awful one. Sometimes, the trashiest, shittiest-sounding, most obnoxious snare drum is the best, most awesome snare you'll ever record, particularly if it works beautifully for the production. Conversely, the best-sounding, most beautiful piano you've ever heard in isolation can be the worst, most vile, and most offensive sound imaginable for an aggressive rock track. So really, when we talk about things sounding great, we're talking about them sounding great in the context of the track.

Also, you cannot separate sound from performance. Sound and performance are inexorably attached; one does not exist without the other. Great takes naturally sound better than bad ones. This was the most stunning revelation I've ever made as a producer. When the band isn't playing a take well, I find myself struggling with the monitor mix. When the band hits their groove on a take, the monitor mix is in perfect focus and requires no attention whatsoever. Not once in 20-plus years of recording have I ever found a master take that didn't sound considerably better than the outtakes. This means sound is performance, and performance is sound.

There's nothing in my definition of a great mix that has to do with sound. Sound is a means to an end. It's what we process and balance in order to manipulate the listener. As long as the mix is providing the desired physical reaction and causing the listener to sing, it's doing its job. Therefore the mix will sound great to someone who appreciates the song and the performance of that song.

While a certain balance in frequency is required to make a mix sound good, sometimes that's counter to the goal. Sometimes the goal is to agitate the listener. Sometimes the goal is to create an exceptionally raw and dynamic work that takes the listener for a ride. As much as I talk about using stereo compressors to keep your mix within a certain dynamic range, there are times to abandon that course. A great mix serves the purposes of the production and the song, and that's it. If great sound is counter to those purposes, then the quest for great sound should be abandoned.

I'd give you specific examples, but I'd prefer not to inadvertently dis someone by proclaiming their mix to have bad sound, even though by doing so, I'm saying the mix has great sound. It gets a bit convoluted, I realize, but if you just listen to your record collection, I guarantee you're going to find songs that sound like shit, but that you think sound perfect just the same.

Break Time

Mixing, by its very nature, is an obsessive activity. Far be it from me to advise someone who possesses the requisite compulsiveness for mixing how often they should break—and I won't. If you break too often, you never get into a good flow with your mix. If you break too rarely, you're going to spend more time fucking up your mix than improving it, and you're going to utterly exhaust yourself. It's good to reset your brain every couple of hours, and two hours on a mix is the equivalent of five minutes in your basic mundane job where the perception of time is concerned. If you don't break, it's only a matter of time before you're afflicted with two particularly debilitating conditions—oversaturation and hypersensitivity. I discussed these in my book *The Daily Adventures of Mixerman*, and I'm quite certain I'm not going to improve upon that explanation, so here it is:

Oversaturation and Hypersensitivity

Oversaturation causes one's brain to be incapable of discerning and evaluating subtle and even not-so-subtle differences among such things as timing, tuning, expression, musicality, and balances. It's quite like a numbing agent of the brain. If you could inject the part of your brain that processes hearing with Novocain, this would be similar to the effect of oversaturation. I would imagine that people of all walks of life have experienced this to some degree. I sometimes refer to it as "the wall," and when you hit the wall, there are only two cures. Time and fatties.

Hypersensitivity is the function of one's brain being so aware and sensitive to minute changes that you are beyond any kind of "real-world" standards of listening. It is the exact opposite of oversaturation. This temporary condition can make differences that are normally nearly impossible for the human ear to detect seem like enormously drastic changes. Although this condition is generally less debilitating than oversaturation, it can cause the wasting of inordinate amounts of time, as the phenomenon will cause one to endlessly make adjustments that seem to make a big difference but, in reality, make no difference whatsoever. Once again, there are only two cures. Time and fatties.

After hours of listening intently, either one of these phenomena can occur. The best method of preventing these two temporary conditions is to take breaks. But breaks become less effective and are required more frequently as either of these disorders sets in, and at some point, only a good night's rest will rejuvenate one to the point of functionality. Unfortunately, rest and breaks do not appear time-efficient, and they are often abandoned for the far worse option of powering through.

Sometimes even a good night's rest can't prevent one from starting the day with either one of these ailments, as the cumulative effects of working long days on end take hold. And sometimes, both the hypersensitivity and oversaturation conditions can be present and occurring simultaneously. When this particular brain-fuck happens, watch out, because the phrase "dog chasing his own tail" is given a whole new level of meaning.

Mix Session Files

Occasionally a client will request the actual mix session files. Actually, these days that request seems to come slightly more than occasionally, and you need to be prepared to deal with this.

If you're using summing boxes and external compressors, the session files are relatively useless to your client. Regardless, you should deny this request under nearly all circumstances. How you arrive at your mix is proprietary information. It's what makes you valuable as a mixer, and your clients have no right to that information. They're paying you for your mixes and nothing else.

I don't even supply record companies with the recall information. That's not their information to have, and I want to be sure to prevent a recall of one of my mixes if I'm not involved in it. The only way to ensure that is to maintain control of all the proprietary information.

If you give your client the session files, you only risk them making unauthorized adjustments to your mixes, and I'm telling you they absolutely will. If the terms for mixing a project include the submission of session files, turn the project down outright. Seriously, you're only going to get burned on this, and it's not worth it.

Drugs

Aside from caffeine, nicotine, Loratadine (Claritin, for allergies), Nasonex (also for allergies), insulin, and perhaps the occasional THC, there really aren't any drugs that are going to be helpful to you as a mixer. Alcohol completely fucks up your hearing, so anything more than a drink is inadvisable. I realize it can be difficult to go to sleep after mixing all day, given that your brain is running at such a remarkably high frequency, but there's nothing worse than trying to mix with a hangover, so be careful not to go too nuts trying to relax yourself with alcohol.

It's going to be absolutely impossible to mix on hard drugs, so let's not even go there.

Really, the only drug that can actually be beneficial to mixing is marijuana, and that depends on how you react to the drug. It can be exceptionally useful for those times when you've hit "the wall" and your brain is having trouble deciphering sounds, but then rest is good for that too. If you smoke marijuana all the time when you mix, you won't be able to mix unless you're stoned. This would be highly inadvisable, as you never want to be dependent on being fucked up to do your best work.

I realize people think I'm some big weed smoker because of my first book, but I'm not. Marijuana is useful for sleep, and sometimes it's a great way to enhance your creativity and even focus, depending on how it affects you. But you'll also tend to mix with too much bass and not enough top end, so keep that in mind; and whatever you do, don't print your mixes while you're stoned. Not that I would know anything about that—I've just heard it from others. Ahem.

Food will also affect how you hear. Mixes sound totally different to me when my belly is full, although I've also taken a break, so it's not something I can prove. That said, I really don't think it's controversial to suggest that increasing your blood sugar is going to change how your brain processes sound.

Mixing Outside the Box

Before the existence of automation, everyone who was involved in a project was a part of making the mix. There were potentially 24 tracks to deal with, and the mixer needed every hand on deck. I started out mixing on an unautomated desk, and I can tell you, mixing in this manner can be a blast. I mean, it's so much more social than how we mix now.

When mixing without automation was prevalent, the mixer basically took on the role of director. First, he planned out what faders belonged at what level and where in the song. Once he had his plan, he then divvied up mix assignments to the band and producer. There were masking tape strips next to every fader. There were pen markings of many different colors to indicate fader level.

Next to each mark one would often find section indicators, like "C" for chorus, "B" for bridge, "V1," "V3," mostly because the crew could rarely remember which color marking went with which section of the song.

Before the advent of automation, the trick to mixing was for the engineer to allow her compulsive nature to shine through during the recording process—not to wait until the mix. The recording *was* the mix. Since the engineer was typically both the recordist and the mixer, she was only screwing herself if she didn't keep the tracks in good order. The inherent track limitations of analog tape decks forced arrangement decisions (although it wasn't long before producers were able to double their track count by synchronizing multiple decks).

By the time the mixer was finished framing the mix, it was time to actually start printing! Every available person was brought in to the control room, and the mixer gave each deputy mixer various responsibilities to perform. These included riding faders, turning mutes on and off, panning, and even EQ moves when necessary. With only two hands per person, and more mix moves than hands, it wasn't unusual for a mix performance to look similar to a giant multi-person game of Twister. Given the lack of space on the console, there was usually a roving mixer, and his job was to squeeze in and out of everyone else to pick up his moves. Occasionally, there were even acrobatics involved, particularly when the roving mixer had to get to the other side of five others in order to pick up an otherwise stranded mix move.

Although the goal was always to make it through the entire song as if it were a single performance, it was exceptionally rare to get through more than one section at a time, and even then it usually took many attempts to get a reasonable swath of mix right. Of course, that's why razor blades were invented (and you thought it was for cocaine). Once the mixer and the band made it through the entire song, the engineer would cut and splice the sections together, and *that* was the mix.

For those occasions when there just weren't enough people to assist, the mixer had the option of mixing down to two tracks of the 2-inch tape machine. Since the master tracks and the mix tracks would exist on the same tape, the mixer could easily punch in and out of his mix and adjust his faders between punches. I've mixed like this using a console and Radar, and it's actually a great way to work. The best part is that by the time you get to the end of the song, the mix is done. You gotta love that!

In the '80s, new analog consoles started shipping with automation and recall systems built in. The SSL E series console had a compressor, gate, filter, EQ, FX send, insert, and bussing matrix on every channel. The large-frame automated console made it so one person could single-handedly program a mix and then play the finished mix for the clients before ever printing the mix. Once the mix was approved and printed, the engineer could take an internal electronic picture, which recorded the position of every knob on the board. As long as the outboard gear was documented by hand, a mix could be recalled later for fixes. Although not perfect, recalls were generally close enough for making mix changes, particularly if the studio hired diligent assistant engineers. The big hassle was the three hours it took to turn every knob on the console in order to match the position in the picture.

As the technology changed, the art of recording also changed. The more control technology offered us, the lazier recordists and producers could be during the recording process. Mixing on a console with no automation and an entire group of deputized assistant engineers works fine with a highly focused and well-recorded set of 24 tracks. But large-frame consoles with automated mutes and faders meant the engineer didn't have to be nearly as anal retentive about the recording, and the producer didn't have to be quite as decisive in his arrangement. DAWs have only made this problem worse. The conventional wisdom is that technological advancements like the DAW have increased productivity. In actuality, technology has only managed to slow things down—especially where mixing is concerned.

The playback of a high-quality analog multitrack machine into a Neve 8068 desk is far superior to that of a digital recording on a DAW. In the aggregate, it's actually nearly twice as fast to mix a fully analog production as it is to mix a fully digital one. I don't say this as some old fart who can't let go of the old technology. I'm not really all that old, and I don't have an aversion to technology— quite the opposite, really. I say this as someone who has extensively used just about every combination of mixing technologies available throughout the history of recorded music.

Invention Is the Mother of Necessity

Not to belabor the point (okay, maybe to belabor it a little), but it's faster to mix an analog recording through a good console than it is to mix a DAW recording through the same console, which is faster still than mixing entirely in the box. The irony, of course, is that the DAW has been heralded as a time-saver when in reality it's actually increased the time it takes to record and mix. As if that's not enough, the overall time burden has shifted from the musician to the technician. No longer does a musician have to get the part right on her own. "Close enough" is good enough, and the technician can use the manipulative power of the computer to fix any flawed performance.

This isn't meant as some sort of complaint, but I think you should recognize that the technology itself is mostly responsible for the necessity of the technology—not the other way around. There are all sorts of digital multitrack files from the '60s floating around the Internet these days. These usually consist of four to eight tracks of some classic and popular songs, and all you need to do is bring up the faders, balance the tracks, and you have a great mix. The artistry was in the recording, not the mix. If you make a great recording of great musicians playing a great arrangement of a great song, you don't need a DAW.

While all technology is born out of necessity, our working habits also change to fit the technology. The more control given to the mixer, the more important the mixer becomes. Whereas the recording *had* to be the mix before the existence of automation, now the mix isn't even part of the consideration.

The first time I mixed on a Neve 8078 desk, I was certain it was better than its Neve 8068 predecessor. The 78 had an extra band of EQ, which gave me more control! Why wouldn't it be better? It wasn't until I started out my workday on a 68, and moved later that same day to a 78 that I realized that the 68 was a superior-sounding console. I finally had a basis of comparison, and it shattered my perception of these two consoles. Since the 8068 sounded better, I didn't actually *need* that extra band of EQ. This is a clear example of need following a seeming technological improvement.

All systems have inherent advantages and disadvantages. The global nature of our business is argument enough to mix on a DAW, since perfect recall is a near-necessity for unattended mix sessions. But perfect recall, a smaller overall footprint, and seemingly limitless processing doesn't change the fact that our technological advances in this business have favored convenience and affordability over quality.

278 Zen and the Art of Mixing

Develop Skill, Don't Defer

There was a point and time when the mixer was king of the hill in this business. For quite a few years it was almost as if the labels considered the mixers to be more important than even the producers. For some mixers (who will remain unnamed), that was absolutely the case. Now it's the mastering engineer whose importance has been elevated beyond all reason. We've deferred the skill sets that once were reserved for the early part of the process all the way to the last possible stage. But the further we defer, the less control each subsequent audio professional has. As a recordist, I can absolutely tie the hands of the mixer in such a way that he has no choice but to use my vision of what the mix should be. Instead, the importance of recordists has been reduced to nothing more than DAW jockeys and editors, and the mixer is often completely shut out of the mastering process.

Surely the deferment of skill has been beneficial to the mixer. It means we can command more money, since we have the skill set to compensate for those lacking before us. But it's not beneficial to the industry as a whole, because even with today's technology, the best mixes happen from the best recordings of the best performances of the best arrangements.

Also problematic is the lazy musicianship that DAWs have inspired. Why should a musician concern herself with playing in time if her timing can be fixed? Why should she worry about singing in tune when there's Melodyne? The overall quality of our entire pool of musicians has declined because the technology has made it possible to have a successful music career regardless of overall ability. Mediocre musicians means a mediocre recording every time. I don't care how great a recordist you are.

Add in the heavy-handed use of brickwall limiting by mastering engineers, and we've reduced the quality of our overall product to what any child with an Mbox can produce from his bedroom.

Most of you reading this book probably don't mix exclusively yet, and you shouldn't, either. If you work mostly with local bands, you're likely used to acting as the producer by default, and without any of the credit. Given this, you should seriously consider developing all of your skill sets, like producing, arranging, and recording, even playing an instrument. You're working with music, and the more you know and understand about music, the better you'll be at recording and mixing music. If you can shift the importance of musical impact to earlier in the game—as early as preproduction—and then follow through with that during recording, you're going to be far more successful in this business than most of your peers.

If you think that our technological advances in recording have only managed to improve over time, then you would have to also think that records have gotten better and better sounding over time. If you think that, then there's no reason to explore using older technology. If on the other hand you recognize the validity of records that predate your existence, then you should probably consider adding older technology to your arsenal. Most of us who have been doing this for a while think the older technology is far superior for making records, and until you actually mix in an analog environment and experience it, you can't really make a judgment.

It is inadvisable to reject any technology that could prove useful for your professional and creative endeavors. Even the shoddiest, most neglected piece of gear can prove brilliantly useful at least once in your record-making career. Making and mixing records is a creative profession, and as such, you should leave yourself open to using everything and anything you can to improve your work. Otherwise, you can't really claim to be all that creative.

Educate yourself on what it's like to mix on an analog console with analog processing. Try recording your mix to tape. Try cutting tape, for that matter. Record a band directly to 2-track, an exercise that forces you to both record and mix simultaneously. Pick up analog tape delays so you can hear for yourself what they sound like. Hire an analog room for an hour and record the return of an EMT 140 on a vocal in need of reverb. Rent the local church and use it as a makeshift chamber. Rent analog compressors and try using them instead of plug-ins. Give yourself *some basis of comparison* so you're not operating from a complete position of ignorance, like 90 percent of the people arguing on audio boards.

If you want to mix and record, then do it right. Don't assume that what you have is good enough. It's only good enough for now. You can treat what you do like a job, or you can treat it like an art. The difference is in how you approach it, and I can promise you, the sooner you treat your work like art, the sooner you'll be an artist at whatever you do.

Conclusion

You may have noticed by now that I've given scant few concrete examples of great mixes in this book. Seeing as we're at the end of our time together (for now), that's not going to change in these closing remarks. There are a number of reasons why I've refrained from giving specific examples—copyright issues being just one of them. There certainly is no shortage of great mixes out there, and you should listen to great mixes as often as you can. Unfortunately, evaluating great mixes doesn't tend to accelerate your abilities as a mixer, although it might help with your production chops. Which makes you wonder why it is that we can readily recognize a great mix done by someone else, but when it comes time for us to create a great mix in the early stages of the learning process, we somehow fall well short. The answer is simple: mixing isn't a paint-by-numbers activity.

Every song and production is wholly unique, and although there are obvious similarities in music production—particularly given the nature of how we hear Western music—there are also endless possibilities and a seemingly infinite number of considerations to take into account. This means you could often find yourself choosing the exception rather than the rule, which is why I introduced rules as tools right from the start.

Given that exceptions are not all that uncommon in mixing, it would be nearly impossible for any given reader, regardless of expertise, to agree with every statement made in this book. That's fine. If you prefer a technique that I advise against, then you shouldn't necessarily stop on account of my opinion. Some of our disagreements will resolve over time, as success in recording and mixing music in general is an evolutionary process. You never know—I might even change my mind in some cases, and it wouldn't be the first time that's happened. But overall, you should find the basic principles provided here to be sound and useful in accelerating your success as a mixer. If you treat this book purely as a "how to" book in which no deviation is permitted, you'll only manage to retard your own learning process. Don't do that.

The best way to improve your mixing is to actually mix. The most effective way to evaluate the principles contained within these pages is to implement them in your own mixes. This offers you an opportunity to make direct comparisons and gauge the overall effectiveness of the strategies presented here. Frankly, I've offered you so many tidbits on how to think about mixing that it would be impossible for you to absorb everything in four readings, let alone one. Some of the information won't really make sense until you have more mixes under your belt, and so it would be advisable to revisit this book every now and then. It took me many years to learn all that I've offered here, and I learned purely through experience. If you take my experience and figure out how it applies to you and the music you're mixing, then you will save yourself unnecessary heartache.

The second best way to improve your mixing is to write about it. There are plenty of places on the Internet where you can actively debate mixing principles. When you have that "a-ha" moment, share it. Merely putting your thoughts into words will give your learning experience longevity. Besides, someone might point out a solution you (and I) hadn't considered. This will cause you to experiment further, learn more, and improve your overall skill set. You can even debate with me directly if you like, but be forewarned: I can easily defend every position I've taken here, and will do so to the fullest extent of my abilities. I'm not trying to scare you off with that statement; it's a good thing. How often do you get to directly challenge the author of your new favorite book? If you're confused or disagree vehemently with me, then I *want* you to challenge me. Even with all the nonsensical noise and bravado on the Internet, multi-way communication can clear up misunderstandings and refine the learning process for everyone. Myself included.

I've given you all the rules I can think of and I've offered them to you as tools, not rules. In music, it's often those who are innovative and bold who have the best chance of achieving mega-success. Without pioneers willing to push forward and progress, without the erosion of hardened boundaries, we risk stagnation. Fortunately, that's just not a possibility, given how humans are wired.

After writing nearly 90,000 words on the subject of mixing, I'll tell you now that there really is only one hard-and-fast rule: To effect a positive reaction from as many listeners as possible. Of course, that's more a goal than a rule, and you are but one part of the equation. Still, it's a good way to think, and when all the stars align, you'll be ready to deliver the ultimate mix of a great song. As long as your decisions work toward garnering a reaction from the listener, and as long as you can learn to objectively evaluate what's happening in your mix from the listener's perspective, you will have some success where the art of mixing is concerned.

Let's face it: you can't be both aggressive and timid at the same time, and if you were to passively accept any and all rules without exception, you couldn't possibly claim to be aggressive. So, if a tool that I've provided for you here doesn't suit a particular song or production, and if you can readily defend your position in a demonstrable way to yourself (and your client), then fuck it—you're making the right decisions. You'll never get into trouble if you allow the song, the production, and the performance to dictate your mix decisions. My main objective here is to get as many young mixers as possible to think in this manner.

Every major mixer and producer that I know understands the tenets in this book. My best friend actually got annoyed when he read it, not because he thought I'd led you astray, but because he felt I'd "given away the farm." Maybe so. But there is such an abundance of misinformation written by people who have no business offering an opinion (let alone mixing a record), that I feel a certain responsibility to correct the record fully and without interruption. That's the beauty of writing a book. Of course, now the fun begins as I discuss and defend my positions on the Internet. Make no mistake: I will be challenged, sometimes by people with authority; sometimes by people pretending to have authority (when in reality they don't have any basis of comparison whatsoever); sometimes by people with an agenda to sell something.

So how do you tell the difference between seasoned pro, wannabe, and shill? How do you discern between the acoustician telling you that converters don't matter, and me, who's telling you that they do? How do you discern between those who think an interesting way of recording acoustic guitars is in stereo, and me, who's telling you that you want to avoid anything that potentially distracts the listener? How do you discern between the large corporations who put out white papers that 99.9 percent of us don't have the expertise to understand past the first page, and me, who actually implements these tools on a daily basis, and can tell you unequivocally that digital summing is broken? It can be difficult at best. I understand. And as much as I love the Internet (and I do! I do!), you must view all arguments with a certain distrust, at least until you can determine for yourself the truth of the matter.

So why should you listen to me, amid a vast sea of differing opinions? You shouldn't. You should evaluate anything and everything on your own. You should listen, and test, and re-listen, and figure out what *you* find important for your methodology. If you don't hear the difference between a mix summed analog and one summed internally, then that's not an important difference—for you. Not yet anyway. This might change three years down the line as you improve both your ears and your monitoring. Or perhaps digital summing will magically improve, and you'll never have to upgrade that portion of your mixing chain. That's fine. Technologies change. Formats change. You'll change with them, and your workflow will too. What won't change are the basic principles of arrangement, the physics of sound, and the manner in which music touches people. If you can tap into that, your success in mixing won't be denied.

As long as you can defend your positions with logical, identifiable, and demonstrable arguments, as long as you think about your positions and can justify to your clients how your decisions best serve the song, then you're in the right. Be confident in the here and now, and if you ultimately determine that your confidence was unfounded, learn from your mistakes and do better next time with even more confidence.

Now go forth and mix.

Finding Mixerman

Get general information about Mixerman, including excerpts from his first book *The Daily Adventures of Mixerman.*

Mixerman.net
Myspace.com/_mixerman_

Hang with Mixerman and friends at The Womb Forums. Discuss anything and everything that has to do with making music; join in on the collaborative events; enjoy *The Mixerman Radio Show with Slipperman and Aardvark (names listed in order of importance)*; and make friends and contacts from all over the world.

Thewombforums.com
http://www.youtube.com/TheWombForums
The Mixerman Radio Show (at the Womb)

Find out what's happening on the Internet by joining Mixerman's social network pages. As Mixerman puts it, "Never miss out on a good *merde*-fling again."

Twitter: @mixerman
Facebook Page: Mixerman

To contact Mixerman directly: mixerman@mixerman.net